C000001489

Beyond Redemption
The first ever history of sales promotion
"The sex, drugs and rock and roll of marketing"

BEYOND REDEMPTION

First Published by
Sales Promotion Publishing in 2010
70 Margaret Street, London W1W 8SS
020 7291 7741

COPYRIGHT
The rights of Colin Lloyd and Ken Spedding to be identified as the authors of this work have been asserted in accordance with the Copyright, designs and Patents Act 1988

ISBN 978-0-9564381-0-2

Printed in England by TJ International Ltd

ACKNOWLEDGEMENTS

Very many people have given us information for this book and, as far as possible, we have credited them for their contribution; if so their name will be found in the Index.

A big thank you to Heather for her editorial guidance.

To Robin and Chris and everyone at KLP who shared the journey with me.
CL

To Graham Paul, a creative genius, who got me into the business and who died much too young.
KS

CONTENTS

Introduction

In 2005, when introducing a House of Commons debate, Hugh Burkett, then Chief Executive of The Marketing Society said: "Sales promotion is the sex, drugs and rock and roll of marketing. Highly enjoyable, often effective in the short term but dangerous to the user and very difficult to control once the habit has started." He also said: "Advertising offers a life of fidelity, sobriety and classical values."

The authors of this book share most of Hugh's view of sales promotion and have been calling it that for so long that we were felt unable to change to the newly fashionable 'marketing communications' or the even newer and more fashionable 'promotional marketing'. Based on his, in our view, pretty accurate description of the industry we also wonder why the hell anyone under 40 wants to go into advertising. Maybe it's the money?

Because we share his view we decided to write this book not as learned discourse on the business but as an entertaining but useful round up of where the industry has come from, what it has achieved and a look into the future with the views of the major practitioners on the next few years. The emphasis is on a balance between information and entertainment and our role model is Bill Bryson. Probably wishful thinking, but we've tried.

Between us we have spent more than 90 years in and around sales promotion and various associated businesses and we agree on at least one thing – it has been a roller coaster of a ride. Exciting, worrying, elevating and depressing, in fact every human emotion except one. It has never ever been boring. And of course we even made a good living out of it.

With the help of numerous contributors to who we are very grateful (but not so much that we will pay them) we hope we can pass on some of this to our readers. As far as possible we have given them credit for their contributions but if we missed you out we are very sorry and will try to do better next time. We have combined research with conversations and contributions from many of the people who have made the business what it is today. We have found with our correspondents that it is much easier to get people to talk about disasters of one sort or another than about their successes. Perhaps they just don't like to boast but we are very grateful, because we think they make it a more entertaining reading. We have grouped these stories together in chapters that we have called 'Interludes'. On the same theme Chapter 13 is, as far as we can tell, the definitive coverage of the Hoover debacle.

WHY ARE WE WRITING THIS BOOK?

1. Because no one has ever written on the subject, despite the fact that it is a multi-billion pound global industry, bigger in fact than the spend on advertising, which has numerous books dedicated to it.

2. Because it employs thousands of people and impinges on the lives of almost every living person in Britain and most of the mature world who are exposed to sales promotion of one sort or another throughout their lives.

3. Because we think that the wonderful thing about our business is its cast of characters, with their anecdotes, successes and disasters and we believe it's high time that this is properly recorded while the people who built it from small foundations in the Fifties to the mature industry it is today are still alive to tell us how they did it.

4. Because the large proportion of the people working in this mature industry are under 40 and we think they should know where the business came from and how it got to where it is.

THE AUTHORS:
COLIN LLOYD

Coming from a family of three generations involved in Fleet Street publishing it was a natural choice for Colin to follow in the family tradition. At 16 his sales promotion future die was cast as he joined Argos Press working on Competitors Journal the magazine for promotion competition entrants.

He then joined the ad department of the Daily Herald newspaper (now sadly The Sun, he says) and from there went through two ad agencies, Downtons, which became part of Saatchi & Saatchi and Lonsdale's (then Greenly's) which he bought during his later KLP life. In his mid-twenties he joined Ritchie Dickson, the vanguard of Sixties below-the-line agencies.
Two years later at the ripe old age of 27 he formed what was to become Kingsland Lloyd Petersen (KLP). As founder and CEO he led KLP to become the largest promotion agency in the UK. In 1983 KLP floated on the London Stock Market and was the first below-the-line agency to go public in Europe. KLP expanded rapidly during the Thatcher Eighties to become an international business operating across the globe and he was inducted into the Marketing Agencies Worldwide Hall of Fame. In 1990 KLP was bought by RSCG of France – now Havas – with Colin as President worldwide for RSCG marketing services.

He left RSCG a couple of year's later, tried retirement and failed at it. A golf course and some lecturing later he was approached to be CEO of the Direct Marketing Association, an interesting challenge at the time. He joined in 1993 at the beginning of the 'direct' revolution. Seven years later the DMA became the largest marketing trade body in Europe, with Colin as its inaugural president and he was inducted into the DMA Roll of Honour.

During his DMA tenure he founded the International Federation of DMA's bringing 42 counties under a global umbrella and was made its first President. He chaired CAM, the industry Education Foundation for 10 years with an enduring passion, having been a CAM student in the Sixties. CAM awarded him a Fellowship.

In 2000 he left the DMA to take up non-executive roles, which he still holds and is chairman of Motivcom PLC and chairman of the Telephone Preference Service. In 2005 he became chairman of the Fundraising Standards Board, the self-regulatory body for the charity sector and was formerly President of the Institute of Sales Promotion. In 2006 the MAAW inducted him into their Roll of Honour. 2010 marks 50 years in the business for him, which he still enjoys with a passion.

KEN SPEDDING
The son of a Met Police sergeant, Ken was born in Hackney, so is a qualified Cockney. He grew up at Northwood in Metroland, went to school in, not at, Harrow (the grammar school), started training as both an architect and a RAF navigator (not at the same time) and did not qualify as either. He landed a job selling drugs in Bethnal Green for Allen & Hanbury which got him into advertising, then journalism, PR, more advertising, print sales and publishing to end up in 1970 joining the then US owned agency Marden Kane UK at Tattenham Corner as production director. He was part of a breakaway in 1977 that set up Masterguide and he left there in 1988, a year after it was sold it to Holmes & Marchant.

With old partner Graham Morse, he launched the 10 million circulation magazine The Coupon Book, Britain's first free standing insert, as a joint venture with Reed. After the end of his three-year contract, he was CEO of travel incentive company Flexibreaks. When it merged with the sales promotion division of publicly quoted company, Watermark plc, he was client services director for a few years before sliding, not very gracefully, into semi-retirement and decided to write this book. Over the years he has written numerous features for the trade press and spoken at various conferences but this is his first (and almost certainly last) attempt at full-length production. It turned out to take a lot longer than he expected. He had breakfast with Colin after the 2003 ISP Award Dinner and persuaded him to join in this venture, which will teach us to be careful who we join for breakfast.

Along the way he has collected an ISP Fellowship and spent four years as an ISP director and four more as a sort of non-executive director of the Institute. Apart from writing this book he still gets paid occasionally as a marketing consultant as he likes to keep his hand in and the money is useful. Also he is better at it than he was a golf.

CHAPTER 1

What is sales promotion?

For those readers who do not work in the sales promotion or SP industry, let's start with an explanation of what it is, or is not. Even if you do work or have worked in SP you might find that it is not quite what you think it is. It has changed and developed over the years, though on closer inspection, perhaps not as much as first appears. As it has been described as "The sex, drugs and rock and roll of marketing", perhaps we should start with a definition of Marketing. The Chartered Institute of the business (CIM) defines it as "The management process responsible for identifying, anticipating and satisfying customers requirements profitably"

Finding a definition of SP is not a simple undertaking as people in the business are rarely unanimous about what it should be called. While some are happy with the term 'sales promotion', the cool and trendy might call it 'promotional marketing' or, even 'marketing communications' which was cool and trendy the year before last.

One slightly scurrilous theory behind the last name, as adopted by the agency body, the Marketing Communication Consultants Association (MCCA) - previously the Sales Promotion Consultants Association (SPCA) - is that it moves the said agencies nearer to the goal of being advertising agencies, which may be less fun but make more money.

In recent years even the UK's main trade association, the Institute of Sales Promotion (ISP) had second thoughts, renaming their gongs the Promotional Marketing Awards until 2008, when they went back to the simple ISP Awards. However as this book was going to press, the Institute had third thoughts and voted to change the name of the organisation to the Institute of Promotional Marketing (IPM). Could this be an example of title inflation, such as Personnel to Human Resources, Transport to Logistics and Road Shows to Experiential? We will stick with the title of this book and call it all Sales Promotion.

But what does it actually mean? Opinion has varied over time.

The ISP's forerunner, the Sales Promotion Executives Association (SPEA) had a code of practice in 1971 with a very elaborate and very long one sentence definition of SP as: -

"All manner of marketing devices and techniques applied practically or strategically, in such a way as to emphasise, enhance or add to the communication of the basic marketing proposition of a brand, group of brands or a service with a view to increasing acceptability by consumers or distributors, excluding the techniques of media theme advertising, basic product display and the press relations area of public relations activity."

Another definition features in The Manual of Sales Promotion by John Williams, which has been the basic industry textbook for years; "Promotions are short term tactical marketing tools which are used to achieve specific marketing objectives during a defined time period. While promotions are a means of offering temporary added value to the customer they should form an integral part of the brand's long-term strategy. Promotions, unlike advertising, act at the point of sale."

In September 2005 the ISP came up with a new definition:
"A planned and implemented marketing activity that both enhances a product or service appeal and changes customer behaviour positively, in return for an additional benefit for purchase or participation".

However, not satisfied with this, in 2006 the latest version from the ISP said it was:
"A marketing initiative whose purpose is to drive action which has a direct and positive impact on the behaviour of the promoter's target audience."

This could be considered a rather fancy way of saying SP is anything that helps to sell the product or service but could also be considered as a possible definition of advertising. Confusing isn't it? At the same time the ISP was coming up with a new logo and a tag line that said "when promoting sales is your business" which seems to sum it all up rather neatly.

There have been lots of other attempts to come up with an acceptable definition and, incidentally, almost as many attempts to value the size of the industry, none of which has proved satisfactory. The problems are linked. If you are not sure what constitutes sales promotion, how do you decide what it is worth?

The earliest definition we have been able to find comes from the impressively titled Committee of Definitions of the American Marketing Association, which in 1950 set it out as follows:

1. In a specific sense, those sales activities that supplement both personal selling and advertising and coordinate them and help make them effective, such as displays, shows and expositions and other non-recurrent selling effort not in the ordinary routine.

2. In a general sense, sales promotion includes advertising and supplementary selling activities.

By this reckoning, sales promotion is the king pin and those pesky ad agencies which thought that they were the top dogs, with SP something nasty in the tool shed, have got it the wrong way round. Oddly, this view is not held by anyone we know who works in an advertising agency. In the 1966 edition of the American Sales Promotion Handbook the same heresy is repeated:

"There is a too-evident desire to subordinate sales promotion to advertising when the trend is the other way, to subordinate advertising to sales promotion."

The author does admit that advertising usually involves spending lots of dollars but comes to the conclusion that, whether the advertising dog wags the sales promotion tail or the other way round, prevailing practice combines the two functions.

There are also a number of pithier definitions such as the popular:
"Advertising leads the horse to water, sales promotion makes it drink." which co-author Colin Lloyd penned when he has trying to explain, as his company was going public, to city analysts what his company actually did.

The US sixties handbook comes up with something similar:
"Sales promotion moves the product towards the buyer while advertising moves the buyer towards the product."

Generally, Americans are great believers in never using one word when you can use ten, but another contributor called it "Merchandising the advertising" which is also worth thinking about.

Back in the UK, University of Lancaster academic Peter Spillard was wrestling with his own definition in his 1975 book Sales Promotion. Incidentally, you can tell he was an academic because one chapter is headed 'Where a firm is an oligopolist'. He defines SP as:

"The function in marketing of providing inducements to buy, offered for a limited period only, at the time and place the purchasing decision is made, which are supplementary to a product's normal value."

This definition was favoured by that doyen of SP in the Seventies and Eighties, Ian Fryer of Heinz, when asked in the boardroom what he did. For the benefit of those who did not like such long-winded definitions, he boiled it down to "Sales promotion means special offers".

The aforementioned Spillard also hit on a sore point for SP when he suggested that for some people:
"Sales promotion had a rather tawdry image of the bargain basement kind - a nasty, cheap, hysterical and unflattering way of obtaining extra sales." Looks like he subscribed to the "Sex drugs and rock and roll" view of the business.

Heaven forbid that he should be even half right in suggesting that this is the case. Mr Spillard also proposes that the rationale of sales promotion is unashamedly Pavlovian in that it provides the direct stimulus to produce a desired response by customers. Very academic and just the thing to drop into your next presentation along with 'oligopolist' and hope no one will ask what it means.

Another writer, the late Chris Petersen, one of the founders of KLP, devoted three pages in his 1979 book Sales Promotion in Action to the question of definition. In his usual thoughtful and carefully balanced way he played with the idea that a new definition might be helpful if it got rid of all the restrictive ones, but concluded this could be a further hindrance. Ultimately sales promotion should be an entrepreneurial function he said, and rather than trying to come up with a neat definition he put forward the elements that should be incorporated in such an effort. They were:
"A featured offer of tangible advantages not inherent in a product or service for the achievement of marketing objective".

With so many definitions fighting for attention, our feeling is that you have to make up your own mind which you prefer, or even invent your own.

Any definition would seem short lived at any rate, as over the years agencies or consultancies have tried to extend the remit of SP, driven by a desire to get their hands on income producing work. In the early days selling premiums to companies was the main field of activity and profits. Now a promotion can include SMS texting, websites, viral campaigns, roadshows, trade incentives, employee motivation, sponsorship, sampling, competitions, handling and distribution, door to door, e-mail, point of sale (POS), direct mail, sourcing, research and, if they can get their hands on some of those luscious above-the-line budgets, radio, press, outdoor and, the holiest of financial grails, TV advertising.

One senior advertising executive, when introduced to the complexities of a large promotion, albeit with a budget one quarter the size of the 'supporting' TV campaign, said: "I really don't want to know. It is ten times the work and one tenth the profit."

This probably explains why most SP consultancies would like to be advertising agencies.

So, now you know what Sales Promotion is or perhaps you're just more confused. At any rate, you might have an inkling that it is a dynamic sector that has changed dramatically over time. And this is where the story starts to get really interesting.

Although you might think that SP was invented quite recently, certainly in the 20th century, our research turned up so many interesting facts about sales promotion before that period that we have started with a chapter covering a wide time scale from the Garden of Eden to 1900.

It all started in the Bible

Sales Promotion as we know it today is a relatively youthful discipline and this book concentrates largely on the last 100 years 'below the line' as it is sometime known. However, there was plenty of interesting activity before the 20th century, some of it surprisingly effective and some of the techniques surprisingly familiar.

First, it may be useful to explain why sales promotion is referred to as 'below the line'. It does sound derogatory and as it was coined by advertising agencies, may well have been intended that way. The story goes that in their accounts, commissionable sales such as media buying were listed 'above the line' and other income, such as sales promotion that did not carry commission payments were listed below this possibly imaginary line.

However, sales promotion has been around for a lot longer than advertising agencies, or indeed either of the authors of this book, which is long enough for anybody. In fact you can go back to biblical times for the first practitioner who was a certain serpent (a good name for an SP agency perhaps) in the Garden of Eden. His special offer "Free Knowledge with Every Fruit" was very effective but the unexpected consequences would undoubtedly have got him into hot water with the ASA if it had been around at the time.

There was more SP in the Bible. The lottery crops up from time to time in the New Testament, and further back in the Book of Numbers 16: 55-56 we are told that Moses ran a census after the Israelites were awarded their land by lot. The Romans liked lotteries and slaves were a popular, if not politically correct prize, and there is evidence of more mundane promotional activity in the ruins of Pompeii when money off at the point of sale is advertised on some walls. Although not it seems outside the brothels.

A sales method that has made great use of sales promotion techniques first appeared very early in our history. This was the home shopping catalogue. In 1498 a publisher called Aldus Manutius, based in Venice, produced a book catalogue with prices. It was almost 200 years before any record of another publication of this type, this time in England in 1667. Not surprisingly, it was a gardening catalogue by William Lucas. Some 60 years later Benjamin Franklin (who became President of the United States) in Philadelphia started the Junto mail order library.

In 1833 Antonio Frattorini launched a watch club in Leeds and later founded Empire Stores, a major player in home shopping catalogues in the 20th century. In 1872 Montgomery Ward started up in the USA to be rapidly followed in 1874 by Sears Roebuck, possible the two most famous names in the business. Freemans was the first real mail order catalogue in the UK, opening for business in 1903. The first Book of the Month club was begun by Sherman and Sackheim in the USA in 1926. The whole business grew rapidly for the next 50 years or so and is only just meeting serious competition from online purchases.

Closer to home, state lotteries are recorded in England in 1569, followed by a large number of dodgy efforts which were parting the peasants from their hard-earned groats. So much so that in 1698 Parliament keen, like all politicians, to hang on to their lucrative monopoly, brought in licences. This was not particularly effective as officials responsible for state lotteries were putting their expertise to good use by running unofficial ones on the side at the same time. Camelot is unlikely to follow suit.

In the Middle Ages price promotions continued to be popular, including the 'Baker's Dozen' of 13 for the price of 12. (Baker's Dozen was the bakers way of avoiding fines for selling underweight bread) This is still around today and used by at least two direct sale wine merchants.

By the 19th century many of the promotional techniques we use now were invented. The first recorded 'roadshow' which became 'field marketing', before being upgraded to 'experiential marketing', was run in 1881 by Hudson's Soap, recreating a stagecoach run from London to York with salesmen flogging the product to consumers and trade at the numerous stops. Could work today.

IT'S IN THE BAG
One promotional technique introduced in the last few years of the 19th century was a major product mover until about 1948. This particular technique is what is now referred to as a 'container premium', until someone comes up with a cooler and more 21st century name. These days it usually takes the form of a jar or tin full of product which can be reused for storage, such as a tea caddy. In the 19th century, the container in question was the feedsack. These first appeared in the early 1800s, full of products such as corn, seeds, sugar, salt or animal feeds. They were made of heavy canvas and, most importantly, were reusable or in today's terms, could be recycled.

Towards the end of the century the mills in the northeast of the US began to use an inexpensive cotton fabric with the brand name printed on the outside. Thrifty farmer's wives soon discovered that these large cotton bags were a great source of utilitarian fabric which they used for dishcloths, napkins, nightgowns, dresses and so on. Manufacturers soon decided they could take advantage of this and started producing sacks with various prints and solid colours in order to create loyalty, as it would take three sacks to make a dress.

They became such an important part of everyday life that magazines and pattern companies published designs to take advantage of the feedsack craze. Bags even came ready for sewing with pre-printed patterns and themes such as Disney, movies, comic books or nursery rhymes. They even gave directions for using the strings from the sacks in knitting and crocheting. As recently as 1942 it was estimated that three million women and children from all income levels were wearing printed feedsack garments.

In 1941 there were still 31 textile mills manufacturing the sacks and at that time many of them featured wartime symbols. By the end of the war cheaper and more effective paper and plastic packaging became available, and by 1948 feedsacks had almost died out. However some Amish and Mennonite communities still demand and receive their goods in them. Maybe if they were relaunched as "green", they could have a new lease of life today.

In 1903 a British company had an idea which has echoes today. HP Sauce tried sending teams of uniformed salesmen around the major towns on a sampling exercise. Although they may not have had the pretty promotions girls you would see today, they had something almost as eye-catching - zebras to pull the carts. However, zebras were not easy to train and soon had to be replaced by much less exciting ponies and donkeys. It was a good try though.

The first decade of the new century sparked off the arrival of a number of products that are still around today as promotionally active brands. The same year, 1903, saw the birth of Pepsi Cola, nine years after the formula for Coca-Cola was turned into a new product with a new owner. It also saw the invention of peanut butter, which became a staple ingredient of childhood in the US. By 1907 Cornflakes, Oxford Marmalade, Perrier and Marmite could also claim larder space.

STAMP COLLECTIONS

For retailers a real ground breaker was the introduction in 1844 of the Co - operative Society's Dividend, to become known to millions as the 'Divi'. That makes loyalty programmes, or customer relationship management (CRM) as its know today, about 160 years old.

Trading stamps, both Red and Blue, had appeared in the UK in 1851 as a competitor to the Co-op's scheme but did not appear in the States until 1896, launched by Schusters of Milwaukee. Gold Bond Stamps arrived in 1930 run by Curt Carlson, a name that became synonymous with incentives, and in 1958 Green Shield hit the UK market with remarkable results. Green Shield Stamps was a dominant technique for UK retailers up until the late Seventies and merits its own chapter later in this book.

For some reason soap manufacturers have been particularly inventive in launching new and creative promotional programmes. A certain Benjamin Talbot Babbitt, of Bab-O cleaning products fame, came up with a new twist for laundry soap in 1850. He neatly wrapped his soap in branded paper as a change from the retailer cutting chunks off a long bar. Initially the product flopped, but he was not easily beaten and simply turned the wrapping paper into a coupon and offered to redeem 25 of them for a coloured lithograph print. He even had a roadshow with a Barnum Bandwagon travelling the country promoting his special offers. Soon many manufacturers were enclosing picture cards in their soap and other products, with the result that picture cards dominated promotions in the 1880s and 1890s.

You may think the craze for collecting badges is new, but in 1893 a certain Mr. H. J. Heinz, a name we will hear much more of, had an exhibition stand in Chicago. This was not very popular until he started to give away a metal badge showing a 1 ¼ inch pickle enamelled with his name. His stand literally buckled under the weight of punters and in the next few years he gave away millions of them.

Before the end of the century consumers were being tempted by coupons, special events and SLPs, or self liquidating premiums. This is a product that the brand sells to the customer at cost, thus paying for the price of the promotion. The consumer gets the advantage of bulk buying; the brand sells a few more packs.

One of the earliest identifiable occasions was a promotion by Davis Milling, which was later taken over by Quaker Oats. It had used an Aunt Jemima rag doll as a premium to promote its pancake flour since 1895. This giveaway with purchase ran successfully for 17 years on the "if it ain't broke don't fix it" premise, but in 1912 the company took what was then considered to be the daring step of offering the doll by mail in return for one coupon and 10c.

In 1914 Quaker offered an aluminium double boiler for just $1 and five coupons. In the 1930s this promotional technique which, with the American ability to come up with a more impressive name for something relatively ordinary, became known as the 'modified premium system', was given a boost by the big new medium of radio. The airwaves were dominated by a large number of 15-minute dramatic serials, which acquired the generic name of 'soap operas', although many of them were for other products.

Driven by the combination of heavyweight media exposure and a shortage of cash, depression-era housewives jumped at the chance to get useful items at low cost. Quite a number of offers redeemed more than 500,000 units and one or two actually reached one million.

THE PRICE WAS RIGHT

Price promotions were a winner too. The eponymous Jesse Boot, founder of Boots the Chemist, used advertising and promotions to expand from his Nottingham base. A typical example from the 1880s was a special offer on Epsom Salts, which were very popular at the time. The normal price was 1/2d per oz, but Boots' special and widely advertised offer was 1d per pound. It is difficult to imagine what anyone could do with a pound of Epsom Salts, but the promotion went mad.

He followed this up with promotions on soft soap and even tinned salmon. Not an item usually found at chemists, but a profit was a profit. At a time when not many homes had a tin opener, the shopkeeper had to provide a tin opening service, making Boots a major talking point at the time.

Long before pre-packaged and pre-weighed goods became the norm, retail outlets of all types were trying to promote themselves by giving away various goodies, particularly at Christmas. These would carry the name of the generous donor, as would the bags and wrappers, which often carried puzzles, interesting pictures or curious facts to entertain the purchaser. Among the gifts handed out towards the end of the 19th century were pocket mirrors, pencils, pin cases, pen wipers and even ping-pong balls.

In 1862 an independent retailer in North London, not be outdone by the big boys, was shifting tea in large quantities by offering a clock with every case purchased. Another tea merchant, Johnson Brothers of Islington, appealed to the housewives by giving away a free magazine, the Family Grocer. The inhabitants of Islington must have had political leanings even then as the publication carried the Johnson's view of the Schleswig- Holstein crisis. The Sun it wasn't.

Before the turn of the century Pears Soap was giving away jigsaws of its famous 'Bubbles' picture. Sunlight responded with press-out models, Colman's had a special edition of Little Red Riding Hood for Christmas 1896 and Bird's Custard started a popular tradition by offering recipe books from 1880 onwards. Beecham blew up a storm with free Kazoos.

Sunlight Soap was big in the premium business. Wrapper collections were all the rage and by 1894, Sunlight had given away more than 230,000 prizes ranging from bicycles to watches and books. These were worth more than £40,000 at 1894 prices, perhaps £40,000,000 today. The Victorians may have been a lot cleaner than they are generally credited for.

SEE YOU IN COURT

We owe Philip Circus, the leading exponent of law relating to promotional marketing in the UK, for details of an early promotion that ended up in court. This was Carlill v The Carbolic Smoke Ball Company and it is one of the most important cases in contract law. It is a wonderful case because it is the authority for a number of aspects of the law and of course an unusual example of a promotion in court.

The Carbolic Smoke Ball was a device that was 'guaranteed' to cure a number of conditions including asthma, bronchitis, snoring, headaches, neuralgia, whooping cough and something called throat deafness. In 1893 the company advertised a £100 reward for any person who contracted influenza after having used the Carbolic Smoke Ball in accordance with the directions, and as evidence of their good faith they said that £1,000 was deposited with the Alliance Bank in Regent Street. Maybe this is where The Reader's Digest got the idea.

After using a Carbolic Smoke Ball, one Mrs Carlill ended up getting flu and sued claiming her £100 reward. The advertiser came up with the wonderful argument that in effect nobody believed what they saw in an advertisement because in those days ads were littered with porkies and when anyone challenged them, the advertiser would say they were advertising puff. Indeed, the history of the past 100 years or so has seen the steady reduction on what advertisers can pass off as puff - although the concept of advertising puff is still with us. The court did not regard the offer as advertising puff but rather a genuine claim and a genuine promotional offer and therefore Mrs Carlill got her £100.

In the last few years of the 19th century, magazine publishers had some pretty dramatic promotional offers. There was great rivalry between Sir George Newne, who owned Tit-Bits and Strand magazine, Lord Northcliffe of the Harmsworth family and Arthur Pearson, a major publisher of the time. Sir George had what may be the first cause related marketing (another use of the initials CRM) or charity promotion, when he promised to pay £10,000 to hospitals if his readers would raise his circulation to one million. They got it up to 850,000 and he paid out in proportion, which was pretty decent of him.

In 1888 Northcliffe launched the magazine Answers with an amazing contest in which readers were asked to estimate the total value of the gold and silver in the Bank of England on December 4th 1889. If they got it right they won £1 per week for life. Although every entrant had to find five people to support their entry, a staggering 700,000 people entered. This success led to the launch of The Daily Mail.

Sir Arthur in the meantime started a magazine called, with great imagination and no small ego, Pearson's Weekly. He ran such mind blowing competitions as counting how many times a certain word appeared in several books of the Bible or supplying the missing word in poems. Some became such a gamble that the law intervened, deeming them to be illegal lotteries. A situation Player's Cigarettes Spot Cash faced some 80 years later.

DIG FOR VICTORY

Another effort with an echo in more modern times was a treasure hunt organised for Northcliffe's Weekly Despatch in 1904, following a similar scheme by rival Tit-Bits - plagiarism was rife at the time. The publisher heavily promoted it in the Daily Mail and Daily Mirror and it became an instant success. In fact it was too successful if you were unlucky enough to live somewhere that clues printed in the press suggested as the site of a buried prize token. These were exchangeable for various cash prizes and pandemonium reigned as hordes of treasure hunters armed with an assortment of tools attacked possible burial spots often in private grounds.

Targets included an attack on Pentonville Prison, successfully repulsed by ten police constables. The clue indicated that the token was hidden "where people went against their will", and a fever hospital was also under siege. And boy, did it work. Having paid out just £2,935 of a buried total of £3,790, not to mention leaving a trail of destruction around Britain, the Weekly Despatch had raised its circulation from a few thousand to almost one million.

Some 80 years later Cadbury's ran an almost identical scheme for Creme Eggs with almost identical results, other than the assault on Pentonville. It had to call a halt when numerous landowners found punters digging up their private gardens well away from any of the buried Golden Eggs.

Our transatlantic cousins may not have beaten the Brits in the invention of loyalty programmes such as stamps, but they were hot on the sales promotion trail in the 1880s. Around that time the eponymous Adolphus Busch was running a sampling operation backed up with a spectacular gift. This was a two-bladed pocket knife with a gold corkscrew - beer came in corked bottles in those days – and a small glass eye on the handle, through which the owner could see a picture of Adolphus. Wouldn't he just love Busch Gardens? And wouldn't the health and safety police love him?

By 1896 he was distributing framed lithographs of Custer's Last Stand, which seems an odd choice as it was not exactly a great victory for the General. However, it proved immensely popular and he reprinted 19 times in 10 years distributing more than 1,000,000 copies. It was a bit like Carrefour offering paintings of Agincourt or Waterloo. Busch was a very active promoter, inventing dime-sized free beer tokens and handing out watch fobs in the shape of the company's logo, playing cards and even sheet music for songs celebrating his beer. Early karaoke perhaps? He also invented mass produced point of sale material for his products.

As well as feedsacks, other container premiums were hugely popular in the 19th century. There seemed to be a competition as to who could come up with the most unusual shape, particularly in the biscuit business. Packs appeared in the unlikely shapes of classic books, toy ships, prams and forts.

The first in-pack premium seems to be the cigarette card, sighted in Canada in 1879 and destined to be a major technique well into the next century. Other manufacturers picked up the idea, including Holloway's patent medicines, which helped the owner to fund the magnificent Victorian Gothic Holloway College at Egham, plus an equally magnificent asylum just down the road at Virginia Water. Long after cards dropped out of fag packets, Brooke Bond Oxo ran tea cards very successfully for many years.

The Quaker Company was the market leader in original promotional techniques at this time. Not content with a plethora of printed freebies such as puzzles and comic books, in the 1890s it started packing china plates and bowls inside the product. Daring or what? It turned Quaker into the biggest distributor of crockery in the US, a claim echoed in the mid-Seventies by the UK's Milk Marketing Board. It offered free stainless steel cutlery via the milkman and its agency, Marden Kane, became the UK's largest importer of cutlery that year.

Quaker was also keen on SLPs, offering useful if unglamorous items such as handkerchiefs, stockings, socks and pipes at half the retail price, as long as you provided the required proof of purchase,

FIZZING WITH SUCCESS

Around the start of the new century, Asa Chandler was handwriting coupons for his product. The name of Chandler may be unfamiliar, but not the product as it was, and is, Coca-Cola. Invented in 1886 by Atlanta pharmacist John Styth Pemberton, his partner Frank Robinson came up with the name because he though the alliteration of the two Cs would work well in advertising. Chandler bought the formula for just $2,300 in 1888.

The trade mark was registered in 1893, the first bottling plant was set up in 1894 and the iconic contour bottle arrived in 1915, in order to protect the brand against a growing army of imitators. The product was introduced into the UK in 1900, followed in 1901 by Heinz Baked Beans. Persil also saw the light of day in 1909 as 'The Amazing Oxygen Wash' with another logo that has not changed much in almost 100 years.

In 1919 the Chandler family sold Coca-Cola to local banker Ernest Woodruff and a group of businessmen. By the beginning of the 21st century Britons managed to drink more than 12 billion servings of Coca-Cola a year.

Fizzy drinks go back a long way. It is claimed that the oddly named Dr. Pepper was launched one year before Asa Chandler got going, which would make it the world's oldest soft drink. It got a big push at the 1904 World's Fair Exposition, which was attended by a staggering 20 million visitors. The same event saw the first sales of burgers and hot dogs in buns and the first ice cream cones.

Procter & Gamble was getting into below-the-line activity just before 1900 with offers such as watch chain charms in return for soap wrappers, and C. W. Post had 'money off next purchase' coupons on Grape Nuts boxes. If you upped the value from the one cent of the time, you could run that today – the brand is still around.

Hovis was an enthusiastic promoter early in the 20th Century. The name Hovis was coined by a London student with the rather unfortunate name of Herbert Grime, who won a national competition set by the original bakery S. Fitton and Sons. They wanted a name for their flour which was rich in wheat germ. Mr Grime, obviously a classical scholar, came up with the winner based on the Latin phrase "hominis vis" which our well educated readers will know means "the strength of man". He won £25 for his effort.

Another classical educated scholar came up with the name Bovril. This was a combination of Bo(vine) for beef and Vril, meaning mystical strength, a popular word with late Victorians. Not many people know that.

Having got a name, they ran the Hovis Great Prize Scheme. What made it great was that every competitor could win a 'prize', based on the number of proofs of purchase (PoP) they collected. The rewards included pianos, bedroom suites, bikes, desks, sewing machines, and two fresh Hovis loaves every week for a year. The PoP was the band around a Hovis loaf or from a bag of Hovis flour, and the more bands, the better the prize. A fairly low value prize - a framed picture that "has an appearance and value that would grace any room", needed one hundred, so it seems unlikely that Hovis would have delivered many Rosewood pianos, valued at £31 10s.

So, by the start of the 20th century loyalty programmes, premiums both self liquidating and free, coupons, field marketing, point of sale and price reductions were all alive and kicking in both the UK and the US. What would the next 100 years bring?

Quaker leads the way

Clients and agency relationships never run smoothly
Incentives appear and so do scams
Promotional bans sweep Europe. We blame Napoleon
Licensing and sponsorship are introduced
The industry's first trade association takes shape, then the war

From 1907 Quaker was still hard at work outfitting the country's dining rooms with a promotion that ran for years. Each pack contained collectable coupons exchangeable for silverware - 12 got you a butter knife or tablespoon, six a teaspoon. It was an approach much copied, not least by Kellogg later in the century.

Quaker kept up their pacesetting with new technology. In 1921 it offered a kit for a radio to be built into a Quaker Oats pack, consisting of a 50-foot coil of insulated wire, two porcelain insulators, a set of headphones and a 100-foot coil of seven-strand copper wire. Where all this wire ended up is difficult to imagine, but it was a lot of kit to get for just $1 and two proofs of purchase.

Then as now, promoters and their agencies had differences of opinion. Monthly trade magazine Advertising World carried lively legal reports of who was suing whom. A 1910 case dealt with what would now be termed an intellectual property dispute. In 1907 the impressively named Action Imperial News Agency of London, had proposed in writing a "pushing scheme" to Paul Brothers, millers of Birkenhead.

Consumers had to colour in outline drawings on packs or in press advertising to win picture books and other small prizes. It may not have been a potential Grand Prix winner but the campaign was big budget for the day. So expensive that the agency, on 10 per cent commission, would have collected several thousand pounds.

Thrilled with the project, the agency went out and ordered lots of letterpress printing blocks (remember those?) and waited for the go ahead from Paul Brothers. This failed to materialise but an almost identical scheme appeared in its stead. The agency sued and Paul Brothers defended with the argument that it had seen the idea in the US some years before. The case went to a jury who found for the defendant. It seems it rarely pays to sue a client.

NO-WIN SITUATIONS

The lawyers were busy again in 1910, this time at Bow Street Magistrates Court where Messrs Douglas and Feleus were before the beak, charged with conspiracy to defraud. They ran ads offering "£2,000 in prizes – no entrance fee!" The entrants had to piece together scraps to make a picture of a famous Admiral or General. If they got the right military figure - Lord Charles Beresford in this case - they got a big prize and if no one guessed, there was a prize of at least £100.

There were 26,000 entries, so many that the promoters employed assistants to open the letters and note names and addresses. However, it transpired that all the entries were then simply dumped and no effort was made to judge entries. Furthermore, to collect your prize you had to subscribe to a magazine called Profit & Pleasure at the cost of 3s 6d. Having done so, the entrants were sent a "Valuable Bond", actually a share of the minimum prize, divided by thousands. Douglas and Feleus had generously increased this to £150, but they had collected a massive £45,000 and not sent out a penny.

Similar brass neck was shown by a Far East supermarket chain in the Eighties when it offered the chance to win a brand new Rolls-Royce. This proved extremely popular but no cars were won. When questioned, the promoter pointed to terms and conditions that barred entrants who were "connected to the promotion in any way". His rather liberal view was that anyone entering the promotion was obviously connected to it, and therefore automatically disqualified.

Another case in the courts looks like the forerunner of the scams of today where 'winners' have to spend pounds on a premium line phone to claim their prizes. In the early 20th century, the same basic idea had everyone entering a competition winning a watch but to collect it you had to buy a watch chain for 7s 6d, where the total value was, in fact, only1s 9d. It even had a member get member programme that paid 10s if you sent in the names of 10 persons who would be stupid enough to buy the chain.

Still on a legal tack, Marks & Spencer was busy suing a catalogue advertiser for non-payment. The amount owed was just £53 while the circulation was claimed to be 400,000, with 231,000 sold via wholesale houses and the rest distributed in M&S stores. The total value of the space was £2,215 but the advertiser was unhappy with the result and claimed that M&S had not circulated the full 400,000 copies. The court found for M&S and awarded costs. However, acrimonious correspondence continued in the columns of Advertising World for several months.

The Weekly Telegraph also ran into legal trouble when accused of running an illegal lottery.

The proprietors distributed numbered medallions and advertised them as worth £100. Winning numbers were published in the paper, which of course you had to buy. It saw a 20 per cent increase in circulation but unfortunately it was a lottery, so illegal. No one had thought of the 'plain paper' entry route at this time, so more recent promoters can claim to have invented one new trick in the past 100 years.

IF IT AIN'T BROKE...

Many of the legal techniques used today were popular by the Edwardian era. How about 'Cashbacks', often used to sell cars? Henry Ford made the first recorded offer in 1914, returning $50 against the purchase of a $490 Model T. This ran for 12 months but other promotions went on for much longer. It seems that clients in those days did not have the urge to do something different for the sake of change. Maybe that is a lesson for us today.

However using novel ideas and technology to liven up promotions is not that new. Around the turn of the century, biscuit maker Peek Frean pushed its Pat-a-Cake brand with a 'Pebbles on the Beach' promotion for children. Successful entrants from the preliminary round were invited to a beach and asked to find the wooden pebbles containing various value money vouchers that had been launched into the sea. To add to the excitement, they let of a loud shriek when opened.

Around 80 years later Heinz ran a similar promotion that required the final round of winners to dig for treasure on a beach. The effort almost collapsed when the arrival of the diggers was delayed, provoking a mad panic as they raced against the incoming tide.

About this time character licensing started to become big business. In two years after its 1910 launch, the Jungleland Moving Picture Book had a 2.5 million circulation. In the early 1900s the biggest strip cartoon character in the US was Buster Brown and his sister Mary Jane. There were more than 200 consumer products licensed to use the characters. For decades boys had Buster Brown haircuts and suits and girls wore Mary Jane shoes. By 1950 a shoe company was still using the characters and sponsored the then popular but now extinct Saturday morning film shows for children, killed by TV and video games of course.

For longevity the American P&G Ivory Soap carving contest takes some beating. It finished in 1961 having run for 37 years. But actually the winner in the long life stakes is the home-grown Robertson's Jam Golly, launched in 1928 and killed off, possibly influenced by political correctness, in 2001. Commemorative Gold Gollys now fetch upwards of £200 on eBay.

In the 1920s, events were taking place in Germany that have continued to affect sales promotion activity in Europe to this day. The economic crisis in Germany was such that it was felt there was a need to curb excesses in the field of premium offers. The Germans seem to quite like banning things, and introduced the Zugabeverodnung in 1932, which as most of you will know, translates as "free gift decree". This effectively banned almost all sales promotions and is only now being relaxed.

This enthusiasm for banning things later spread to other European countries, with France in 1951 and the Netherlands in 1955 adopting a similar stance. This seems to follow the Napoleonic tradition which says that you can only do what the law says you can do. The UK legal tradition is almost a mirror image and you can do pretty much what you like as long as there is no law against it. Consequently the UK has the most liberal and probably the most effective sales promotion regulations in Europe. The anomalies for European promoters are examined in a later chapter.

In the UK and US, this period saw an enormous growth in the "coupon plan" where tokens were collected and exchanged for goodies. B T Babbitt's colour lithograph in 1851 was an early example and the soap business was for a long time the greatest user of the technique. In 1910 in the US there were 70 soap firms offering premiums plus 30 tobacco companies, 25 coffee roasters, 15 condensed milk brands, 10 flour and feed mills and 10 cereal makers.

The growth of the self liquidator in the 1930s challenged coupon or voucher collection for a while, but an exception was the Raleigh cigarette brand. Launched in 1932, by 1962 it was distributing $15million worth of premiums per year with a thousand item catalogue and the average smoker redeeming 1,230 coupons per year at one coupon per pack. This represented a redemption percentage at the staggeringly high figure of 82 per cent and probably a staggeringly high death rate for the enthusiastic smokers.

EARLY MULTI-BRAND ACTIVITY
An interesting development in tokens, but one that never really caught on in the UK, was the omnibus programme. where a number of manufacturers issued coupons that could be added together. A typical example was Gift Stars, operated by the Premium Corporation of America. It launched in 1957, became a major project by 1963, but disappeared into Gold Bond stamps. Unlike contemporary multibrand schemes which are generated by an operator such as Air Miles or Nectar, these programmes were put together by manufacturers, linking up to make their offerings more widely available.

Incentives or what we now call motivation arrived around 1920. Group travel incentives were not that uncommon and the most famous was the 'The Famous 50'. This was a sales subscription contest sponsored by the Philadelphia Inquirer newspaper in the Twenties offering a week's trip for the top 50 subscription salesmen to the city hosting the World Series that year. As only US and Canadian teams play in the 'World Series', in effect this limited the range of the trip.

However, leisure travel was not a major concept at the time and the majority of people spent most of their lives in the area where they were born. A trip to the big city was as exciting to them as a trip around the world would be today. Sales force incentives were normally short breaks and not too far away as the boss did not like to have his best people away from the office. Consumers had more time and promotions such as the very popular jingle writing contests awarded the winners with trips to exotic destinations such as New York and Hollywood.

The father of incentives, or at least of all incentive houses was the Elton F MacDonald company. The eponymous founder introduced the first incentive catalogue in 1927. Customers included Buick and A C Delco and the promotions were so effective and well recognised that they were referred to generically as 'MacDonalds'. (Nothing to do with hamburgers.) The depression and World War Two put an end to this type of activity but McDonald came back in the Fifties, both in the US and the UK, with another company, Maritz. MacDonald merged with Carlson in 1981.

IN TEN WORDS OR LESS...

Tiebreakers were a popular way of deciding the growing number of competitions in the early 20th century. In 1910 Oxo offered a cash prize to the best reason for using the product, and were generous enough to allow the entrants up to 100 words, rather then the usual ten, which was all that Wright's Coal Tar Soap allowed for a slogan to win £150.

Some premiums even overtook the product. Wrigley's started life as a soap powder manufacturer and used chewing gum as a promotional item. This was so successful that they stuck to gum. A strange reversion of this saw chewing gum companies giving away baseball cards, which were so successful that Goudey and Topps dropped gum altogether in 1990 and just sold the cards. One rare card from 1909 featuring the splendidly named Honus Wagner sold for an unbelievable $600,000 in the Sixties and an even more unbelievable $2,350,000 in 2007. Topps itself was bought by ex-Disney CEO Michael Eisner for $385,000,000 the same year.

Sometimes cards were for more than a simple collection. A novel scheme by Player's Navy Cut in 1922 asked competitors to collect pictures of footballers from each pack and select the teams for a variety of cup competitions. Tobacconists supplied a leaflet and smokers inserted the photographs. They could send off for any players not collected and won a cash prize if they matched the actual team. It is a forerunner of fantasy football, cricket and rugby schemes so popular in recent years.

John Player certainly got its money's worth as it sold collection albums for one shilling or you could swap 25 cards for a 'cabinet' portrait of your favourite player, with more than 1,000 to choose from. You think football is big now? At the time ordinary league matches were attracting regular crowds of 50-60,000 spectators, most of who had to stand on unprotected terraces. The loos were not up to much either.

There were massive press circulation wars in the Twenties and Thirties as new high speed printing techniques produced mass circulation daily papers. Publishers vied to reach a two million circulation and offers abounded. A staggering 50,000 canvassers operated door to door trying to persuade the public to change their choice of newspaper or take an additional one. There were numerous mammoth contests which required very little skill, offering the popular 'pension' prize of £10 a week for life. Research showed that up to half the newspapers were in fact never read, and in 1932 a sort of truce was arranged. Incidentally, 1931 saw the launch of the Audit Bureau of Circulations in the UK.

COOKING THE BOOKS

But there was life in the promotional dog yet. In March 1933 the Daily Herald (where author Colin Lloyd worked in the late Fifties) announced that its readers would be introduced to "A stupendous attraction". Within a week it had become a "stupendous sensation", and turned out to be a sixteen-volume set of the works of Charles Dickens. Amid florid descriptions, the books were claimed to have a retail value of £4 4s but Herald readers could buy them for just 11s.

The public, suffering from 12 months of gift withdrawal symptoms, went mad. So did the opposition, in the shape of the Mail, Express and Chronicle. They initially warned consumers that the cost of the books was less than the 11s they were being asked to pay. Then all three offered their own sets of Dickens for 10s. Millions of sets of Dickens were distributed, but did little more than add a touch of class to the nation's bookshelves and enrich a number of printers. Circulations remained similar with both the Herald and the Express reaching the two million circulation target. Lord Beaverbrook later admitted that he was buying readers by the hundred thousand at the cost of 8s 3d each. Today CD and DVDs play a similar role and the promotion of newspaper remains as fiercely competitive as ever.

The early Twenties saw the arrival of what might well be the first premium agent when the Central London Agency offered to supply 'the hundred best books' at an attractive 25 shillings a set as a premium item for advertisers.

Instant wins were around as well, with the now defunct News Chronicle sending out the strangely named Lobby Luds (there was more than one of them) to seaside resorts. If you spotted them and were carrying a copy of the paper, you won a cash prize. If you were mistaken in your identification you probably won a very rude answer.

Prize contests became major national events. Would you believe that a chance to 'Name the Bubble Baby' would draw several hundred thousand entries? In 1938, Kelloggs ran another offbeat competition, which allowed the winner to open its brand new factory near Manchester. The lucky lady, a Mrs. F L Millward, described as 'a British housewife' had the honour on the 24th of May and the plaque still exists.

Into the Thirties and the depression forced manufacturers and retailers into price-cutting, playing into the hands of the big boys with deeper pockets. The need for an alternative that was less expensive and harder to copy led to a rise in loyalty schemes. If money was short and you could get something useful at no cost, you kept buying the brand because it offered coupons.

These catalogue gift schemes were not universally popular and one retailer called them "A menace to the structure of British trade" and referred to the products that were given away as "foreign made junk". Did someone mention China? Politicians got in on the act and tried to bring in a Gift Coupons Bill, which would have banned the distribution and redemption of such, while generously allowing cash discounts to continue. The public, which was quite keen on getting something for what appeared to be nothing, did not like the idea and the Bill was defeated.

These schemes were so numerous that you could almost furnish your home with free gifts. By 1931 it was claimed that more than £3million worth had been claimed. There was a healthy trade in coupons, mainly via Exchange & Mart where you could buy the vouchers you required, without purchasing any of the advertised products. So that is where eBay got the idea!

The promotions were funded by manufactures trying to get extra distribution and shelf space. With no all-powerful retail chains, it was possible to incentivise independents by offering them coupons in exchange for orders. Even a lowly product like matches was in on the act. Bryant & May had a scheme in the mid-Twenties that allowed retailers to collect coupons for gifts, up to and including a Standard motorcar. That must have been an awful lot of matches.

Sales forces numbered in their thousands and retailer branch managers or owners had a great deal of autonomy at this time. Apocryphal tales abound of supermarket managers with an extra home to store all the free gifts and samples they had collected. Popular goods collected for included pots and pans, household utensils, bicycles, mowers, jewellery and even pianos. The main job of the sales force during this price-led period was to get the retailers' minds off price and on to the latest gift scheme, new display material or an advertising campaign.

SP STARTS TO ORGANISE
By 1933 the depression was in full swing with massive unemployment and unpleasant rumblings from Europe. It also saw the launch of the Mars Bar and, towards the end of the year and almost unnoticed, apart from a few trade press paragraphs, the British Sales Promotion Association was born.

The forerunner to the Institute of Sales Promotion held its inaugural meeting in Fleet Street and six men attended: two advertising agency executives, a publisher and three promoters with proper jobs. The BSPA had a draft constitution, which was agreed and worked right up to the fifties when incorporation took place. Membership was open to senior management working with or in sales promotion. The annual subscription was a very reasonable guinea, which was a classy way of saying £1 1s. This included a sub of 7/6d for the magazine Sales Management which became the official organ of the new outfit.

The BSPA grew slowly in fits and starts with monthly meetings addressed by a speaker. Membership grew, with business tours to such educational sites as The News of the World, Scotland Yard and the odd factory. By 1937 it even had an MP, a Mr G Gledhill, as President and argued about a name change – some things never change. One suggestion was the Business Management Association and the BSPA almost became the Sales Promotion Association, which is not far from the 70's Sales Promotion Executives Association which morphed into today's ISP.

Members were an optimistic lot because in July 1939 they ran a conference in the Connaught Rooms, entitled 'Expanding sales in Britain'. It had a great range of speakers and was great value at 15s including a five-course lunch and buffet tea. You would not have enjoyed being the after lunch speaker. However events overtook them and just six months after the conference members agreed to a policy of inactivity for the duration of the Second World War.

Back to 1934, when the lawyers were busy again thanks to a new Betting and Lotteries Act. This included the much argued about definition of "a substantial degree of skill". One very keen Metropolitan Commissioner of Police, who it seemed had nothing better to do, decided that popular crossword and picture competitions with cash prizes run by most national newspapers and large circulation magazines were illegal under Section 16 of the new Act. Most dropped the picture competitions but kept the crosswords, which seemed skill based. The Commissioner disagreed and a case came to court.

The test case was taken out against Odhams, publisher of The People and Daily Herald, and related to one particular crossword. The prize was very large for the time, £2,000 to be shared by all the correct entrants. There were 196,608 entrants and out of these there were 19 fully correct, 306 with one mistake and 2,105 with two. What complicated the matter was that the mistakes were words where alternative answers fitted the design but altered the meaning. The 'correct' answer was the one the crossword designer had selected. The cop thought this did not show a substantial degree of skill, but the court disagreed. Case dismissed.

New technology was also making itself felt. International Refrigerators offered a free gramophone record in a promotion run in Good Housekeeping. Not a compilation of slightly dated pop music now so common in the Sundays, but a record supposed to be the fridge talking about its merits. Classic brand manager promotion.

There were other influences during this pre-war period. Commercial radio, although banned in the UK in favour of the very uncommercial BBC, was beamed in by Luxembourg and the shorter-lived Radio Normandy. This gave a new opportunity for promotions including the Sunday night League of Ovaltineys with a comic, badges and code book spin offs. The brand was not averse to a little poetic licence, such as:

Humpty Dumpy sat on the wall,
Humpty Dumpy had a great fall
The fall didn't hurt him because he had been
Made healthy and strong with Ovaltine.

The Ovaltineys were an early example of nostalgia marketing when they were brought back in the Seventies by KLP, which ran the first post-war Ovaltineys promotion.

In the US, radio become a dominant medium and continued to be so until the arrival of TV in the Fifties. From 1925 Betty Crocker was running the catchily titled 'Betty Crocker's Gold Medal Flour Radio Cooking School', which was a bit of a mouthful for continuity announcers. Betty would send you a box of recipes for $1 and you could get new ones four times a year in exchange for proof of purchase.

As well as letting Mrs Millward open its factory, Kelloggs ran some of the last pre-war promotions. There was a self-liquidating model aircraft with a 30-inch wingspan on a buy one, get one free basis. Finally, just before all this came to a halt in September 1939, Kelloggs had an offer of model ocean liners, including the Queen Mary and the Bremen. They were 6 ins. long and made out of waterproof cardboard. For the record, a pack of Cornflakes cost 5d when the war started and 8d in 1950.

However, another 'recent' sales promotion technique did appear again during the war. This was an example of CRM or cause related marketing. In 1942 the Austin Motor Company offered to make a donation to the RNLI of one shilling per horsepower for every lifeboat engine delivered and fitted, along with a cheque for £240 as the first such donation. The donor asked permission to publicise the scheme, obviously realising the value of good PR linked to CRM.

Someone must have had a good memory, for what is usually acknowledged as the first major charity promotion was the Birds Eye 'Launch a Lifeboat' promotion in 1969 which pioneered the 'pence per pack returned' technique used many times since.

As we shall see, from 1939 it was about 15 years before SP came alive and nearly 25 before it was really kicking.

INTERLUDES -This is the first of our 'Interludes', offering a bit of light relief from the serious or fairly serious stuff. They deal with promotional activity that, for one reason or another, did not turn out exactly as planned.

INTERLUDE ONE - IT SEEMED LIKE A GOOD IDEA AT THE TIME
- PRIZE WINNERS
Winners who didn't want the prize, some who really enjoyed the prize and some who didn't
Inappropriate prizes
A prize that helped the police with their enquiries and one that didn't.
A really original tiebreak entry

In a practical discipline like sales promotion there are plenty of "there but for the grace of God go I" moments which can serve as light relief from the serious business of the history of SP. As well as being amusing for anyone except those affected, these calamities serve as a warning to current practitioners. They are collected in a series of interludes throughout the book and include a varied collection of cock-ups and disasters, great and small. They are culled from a number of sources, many of whom wish to remain anonymous, and in some cases with good reason.

Sales promotion is a complicated business, working to tight deadlines, which means that the chance of something going wrong is very high indeed. Sales Promotion practrioners were once described as being in the prototype business with all the inherent risks. There are 'acts of God' which can be anything from a warehouse burning down to a computer crashing. One promotion for Blue Band was scuppered when a boatload of sledges was lost when the ship carrying them hit, of all things, an iceberg. There are also suppliers who failed to honour their contracts or who were substandard. However, a large number of problems arise because someone along the line has made a mistake with very large consequences.

The most famous disaster in recent times is the notorious Hoover Free Flights promotion, and this has a later chapter to itself. In the meantime, let us look at a number of other promotions that did not work out quite as planned.

GRATEFUL RECIPIENTS
First, there is the bane of every promoter's life - the prize-winner. You would think that anyone winning a nice prize in a competition would be delighted with what they had received. Big mistake!

Possibly the worst winners to deal with are those who win travel prizes. They regularly want to go to a different destination at a different time with a different number of people. One woman won a two-week holiday for two adults and two children in Florida. First of all she wanted to go to California as she had a sister there. When this was turned down she wanted to know if they could take three children. Next on her list were two rooms, one for the parents and one for the children. When it was pointed out that the prize specified a family room, she became quite agitated and wanted to know how she and her husband could have sex with the children in the room. It seemed that he performed better on holiday! Her final request was for the company to pay the taxi fare to Gatwick airport… from Bath.

Then there was the family that won a prize trip to see Father Christmas in Lapland and turned it down because they did not like the cold, and did not realise it would be in the winter. A recipient of a day's Ferrari driving turned it down because he could not get a child seat in the back. Oh yes, and there was an all expenses trip to see the FIFA World Cup entered and won by group of football haters.

One couple living in a rather downmarket Glasgow flat won a trip to Hong Kong in a competition run by a national bakery chain. They had no phone, so the local branch manager went round to deliver the good news. The lady who opened the door seemed unimpressed, asking "Where is Hong Kong?" and said that the manager should speak to "Dad" who was watching television, clad in a vest and clutching a can of strong lager at 11a.m. He proceeded to inform the manager in colourful language that he wasn't interested in going to Hong Kong as he hated travelling and hated foreign food even more. The rather bemused manager asked if this meant that they did not want the prize. "Not f---ing likely," said Dad. A runner up was on standby, but first the manager got the unhappy first prize winner to confirm his lack of interest. This was just as well, as a week later the promoter received a solicitor's letter from a son in law claiming his client had been denied his rightful reward. A copy of the signed letter killed the case stone dead.

At the other end of the scale was a prize of an overnight stay with supper at The Nags Head, a pleasant, but unremarkable pub in the Yorkshire Dales. This was to be presented to the owner of the winning nag in a novice hurdles stakes run at Wetherby race course, not too far from the pub, which was sponsoring the race. When the race ended it was clear that the prize was unlikely to be taken up. Not only that, but as the rules said it was not transferable, Her Majesty the Queen could not even pass it on to Charles and Camilla.

Of course, there are also satisfied prize winners. A 50-plus female prize winner who suffered from a heart problem was very worried about over-excitement during her trip to Hong Kong. One of her friends was a paramedic, and as the prize was for two people, and she was a widow, she wanted to take him. Of course they would need two rooms and the hotel was very accommodating. After a couple of days there was a call from the hotel. It seemed that the winner and her paramedic were on very friendly terms and would like to move to a double room. The new arrangement was followed by a stream of postcards, telling all concerned about the wonderful time she was having but without going into intimate details.

WISH YOU WEREN'T HERE

Prize winners can act in very strange ways, particularly if they are not used to overseas travel. Over indulgence in free alcohol is very often to blame. On one Watneys' sales incentive trip to the Holstein Brewery in Hamburg, the infamous delights of the city were too much for one publican who, to this day, has never been heard of again.

Then there was a husband in Rome who said he was going out for a drink and disappeared, which lead to a fruitless police-led citywide search. At 4.00 am his frantic wife found him sound asleep in the bath. Another errant husband left his hotel in Copenhagen after his wife had gone to bed. A 3 am phone call asked for someone to come to the police station to bail out the man. It seemed that after a good number of schnapps, he had gone to a sex show and decided that what it needed was some audience participation. The producer did not agree and called the police.

Some winners simply suffer from bad luck. Like the winner of a lot of money in a Silk Cut competition who died just after the judging – it was the first time she had ever won anything. Another prize winner was a lady who won a Cussons Pearl Soap competition, but was unable to attend the prize ceremony as she was in hospital with a rather unpleasant skin disease.

Some prizes turn out to be real stinkers. A promotion by Swift Meats of Connecticut in the Seventies offered large freezers plus sides of beef as prizes. Unfortunately, in one of the hottest summers on record, the logistics went astray and the large chunks of raw meat arrived many days before the freezers to keep them in – imagine the smell.

HELPING THE POLICE WITH THEIR ENQUIRIES

It is not only prize-winners who contact promoters. In less safety conscious days, a number of promotions were run offering knives, including a vast numbers of free steak knives handed out at garages when everyone got tired of free glasses. One promotions manager received a call from Stoke-on-Trent police asking if he could tell them who had been sent a particular knife. Someone had been stabbed by the aforementioned knife, and the police wanted to know the details of the recipient to ask him a few "routine questions". This was before computers were in general use and everyone was building data bases, consumers had been asked to send their names and addresses on a piece of paper. These were frugally used as the return label, so the promoter had absolutely no idea who had received any of its knives.

On another occasion the promoter was much more useful. A woman had been stabbed in Brighton, and although an eyewitness had not seen his face, they had noted that the assailant was wearing a Marlboro branded jacket. When the police called the promotions department and described the design it was obvious that it was from a particular promotion with a relatively small number of recipients. Police were given names and addresses of three who lived in the Brighton area. One of them assisted the police so much with their enquiries that he was arrested, charged and found guilty of the attack.

It is not just prize winners who can create problems when competitions are run – sometimes it is the entrants. Simon Mahoney of SMP tells of a tailor-made promotion for Andrex called 'Cash in at the Co-op'. This was worth £10,000 a month for three months and required entrants to identify foreign currencies and complete the tiebreaker: "I always cash in at the Co-op......". One correct entry received top marks for originality with the ditty "I always cash in at the Co-op because I was caught shoplifting at Tesco". Unfortunately for him, his ingenuity went unrewarded. Luckily for the promoter, the judge's decision is always final.

CHAPTER FOUR-

After the war was over

Austerity and rationing give way to a buyer's market and sales promotion rises from its wartime grave
Teething troubles for the revived trade associations
A new Queen is good for business
Commercial TV comes of age

From 1939 to 1947 there was little need for sales promotion as it was a seller's market with precious little consumer choice. Shoppers bought whatever was in the stores, which was precious little, and as much as their ration books or the black market would allow. FMCG may as well have stood for Fastest Mover Can Get. When something did get into the shops it moved off the shelves a lot quicker than it would today, so it paid to be around at the right time or you missed out.

There were understandably few new product launches during the war, although Andrex Toilet Tissue found its way into the nation's outhouses in 1942. Well, some of them anyway. Less well-heeled readers may remember their parents cutting up pages of the Radio Times, which seemed to be printed on softer paper than the newspapers. Perhaps they thought you should get a little extra for your licence fee.

When it came to loyalty, good customers might find that there was something 'under the counter' reserved for them. In this environment, choice was a luxury and you ate what you could get. It is possible to tell someone who lived through those days because they will eat most things and have a tendency to clear their plates - they probably only stopped licking them around 1947.

Austerity did not end on VJ-Day in 1945. Rationing and shortages were the norm for years afterwards, finally ending in 1953, eight years after the war. Bread was actually rationed for the first time in the post-war period - it had not been thought necessary during the war. When sweets were taken off, the nation's children emptied shops almost overnight and, much to the disgust of those with a sweet tooth, sweets went back on the ration in no time.

BSPA RESUMES LIFE
The first recorded sign of a return to SP life was in July 1947 when the British Sales Promotion Association was reborn with a membership of twelve. Its official magazine, Sales

Management was a casualty of war and was not included as part of the subscription, which was reduced to one guinea. A tentative winter programme was planned but with a total income of £12 12s there was not much scope for lavish expenditure. The less-than-riveting choice of subject for its first meeting, held at the Charing Cross Hotel in London, was 'Efficiency in Packaging'.

In 1948 there was a suggestion for the launch of what has become one of the most successful legacies of the various SP associations - education. The subjects to be covered were product design, publicity, packaging, display, printing and sales training. If you passed three of these subjects, you would be awarded a Diploma in Sales Promotion. However, at the AGM there was a strong feeling that such an initiative was taking on more than the recently revived organisation could handle and the membership, now grown to 90, told the board to concentrate on building membership and income instead. In other words, get us some money!

More than fifty years later, in 2009, the ISP had greatly expanded its membership and also its various courses, covering very different areas to those that were chosen in 1948, which spread the net a lot wider than the ISP does today. Over fifty years later there were many more aspects to education, but they concentrated on the hard core of promotional marketing in its various forms. There were now two Diplomas, one in Promotional & Interactive Marketing and another in Motivation, together with Certificates in three areas - Promotional & Interactive Marketing together with the recently discovered joys of Experiential Marketing and the even cooler Digital Promotions.

There are Intensive one day courses covering Measuring Promotional Effectiveness, Strategic Thinking, Fundamentals (sub headed Promotional Virgins Welcome), Promotional Marketing for Brand Managers and Creativity That Sells. As befits the Institute of Sales Promotion they were offering an incentive which they called (rather inaccurately) a BOGOF. This allowed members to enroll a client for half price if they booked a member of staff on one of the courses. This not really a BOGOF by a BOGOHP (Buy One, Get One Half Price). Good idea but a bit tricky to pronounce.

Another suggestion at the time was to establish a Tyneside branch. However, the driving force behind this idea had his company relocated to another part of the country, Edinburgh to be exact. The idea did not catch on in Scotland, perhaps because the subscription for full members had increased to two guineas, with associate members getting in for one guinea.

In 1950 there was an attempt to replace the loss of the official journal with a duplicated four-page Bulletin first published in December. The following year, the debate switched to declining membership, which dipped to a low point of 58, and had only risen to 68 by February 1951. With some optimism the BSPA decided that the answer to this problem was to become a larger and more inclusive professional body covering all aspects of SP. This decision means that today the Institute of Sales Promotion is a unique industry-wide body, covering all sides of the business.

By October 1951 membership was still only 73 and again, with some optimism, a subcommittee set the target of gaining 1,000 members and a London office within two years. New Labour would have been proud of the BSPA's pluck. It managed the easy bit with an office in Hill Street, Westminster by December 1952 but the membership drive stalled with only 50 new members by 1953.

THE NAME GAME
However by that year, sales promotion was beginning to have some impact and it was decided that a definition was required. The incentive for the membership to come up with a suitable definition was a £10 prize. Not surprisingly, given the historic difficulties in defining SP, this prize was eventually split between two competitors, as no one could decide which was best or which to use.

1953 also saw the launch of Daz washing powder and the Queen's Coronation. The latter produced the usual outbreak of souvenirs which sparked a good deal of promotional activity, mainly concentrated on any items that could carry a picture of the new Queen. Considerable ingenuity was used in finding and making such widgets. The following year was the similarly auspicious 21st Birthday of the BSPA, which was celebrated by a dinner dance for 100 guests at the Mayfair Hotel. This marked a rapid rise in membership, which had doubled by 1956.

It also marked the end of the BSPA in that particular guise as early 1957 saw a name change, brought about by the bureaucrats at the Board of Trade, which was responding to an application to turn the organisation into a limited company. The new name was the not particularly catchy Association of British Sales Promotion Executives.

On the wider marketing front, the launch of Independent Television in 1955 saw the first UK TV commercial, which was for Gibbs SR toothpaste, closely followed by one for Cadbury's Drinking Chocolate. A year later the Brooke Bond PG Tips chimps appeared in the first of more than 100 commercials.

Not being ones to miss out on a promotional opportunity, the newly renamed ABSPE made good use of its Silver Jubilee in 1958. It renamed the long-running Bulletin, now a mini-magazine, as Promotion and had a couple of parties. In keeping with the social scene of the times, there was a cheese and wine do in January (£26 5s loss) and a dinner dance later in the year that only lost £8 1s 4d. This was also the year in which the dominant retail promotion of the next twenty years was launched – Green Shield Stamps. This was so big that it merits a later chapter to itself.

At about this time someone 'invented' marketing, which led to more name changes. The Incorporated Sales Managers Association became, firstly, The Institute of Marketing and Sales Management and then, in 1968, The Institute of Marketing. To celebrate all this, the ABSPE theme for 1959/60 was 'Sales Promotion and the Marketing Concept'. It all coincided with the 1959 debut of the original Mini, which would go on to become a great automotive and marketing success of the next few decades.

This emphasis on marketing at this time is perhaps understandable, because in the world of advertising, 'sale' remains a four-letter word. To quote the late Alan Scaping, who for many years ruled Nestlé's promotions department with a rod of iron: "Marketing directors do not like to dwell too much on promotional response levels. If they had failed the figures might all too easily prove the manager's fallibility and show that the investment had not worked. Conversely the qualitative nature of media advertising analysis almost always makes it possible for the advertiser and his agency to claim a substantial increase in awareness as a consequence of an advertising campaign."

As we move into the Sixties and start to look at the promotional activity of that decade, we leave the ABSPE with 174 members and an elected President. In keeping with its accounts being written up in guineas, it selected a suitably upper class candidate, the Duke of Bedford to this prestigious position. However, with the more meritocratic decade upon them, big changes were ahead.

CHAPTER FIVE

The stirring Sixties

The black bag man cometh as premium salesmen make their mark
Highlanders, beauty queens, and sperm men take to the streets
Page 3 takes off
Europe starts to meddle with UK SP
Print, cardboard and broking – the early agencies
Promotions managers take control of the new discipline

This was a decade in which British retailing changed for ever as Britain moved from the austere Fifties into an era of optimism - the 'Swinging Sixties'. There was full employment, although the power of trade unions meant that British manufacturing was seriously over-manned and becoming less competitive. It was the era of Carnaby Street, the Kings Road and the first, but fortunately not the last, miniskirt, which many men consider to be the greatest invention of the 20th Century. It was also the decade when sales promotion really got moving.

Apart from the arrival of Green Shield, which reached its peak in the next decade, lots of other things were happening. The trade press claimed sales promotion was taking 21.9 per cent of the £501million spent on 'advertising' in 1963. It was serious money for the new discipline.

The decade opened with the introduction of the Arpanet by the US military. This secondary communication system became the internet. It also saw the arrival of Fairy Liquid which didn't become anything else.

In 1961 the multiple grocers' share of the market was 26.9 per cent, a figure that would double in less than 20 years. There were thousands of small independent shops each needing individual sales effort.

As the sector boomed, efforts to police it were also born. In 1960 the Advertising Association devised the British Code of Advertising Practice and resolved to bring the Advertising Standards Authority into existence. The inaugural meeting of the ASA was in September 1962 and so began the industry watchdog that has kept self regulation alive and well to this day.

The abolition in 1964 of resale price maintenance transformed retailing right across the board. Previously this had allowed manufacturers to insist on a fixed price for their products. In 1968 the Trade Description Act also came into law; however the government of the day was keen for self-regulation to work alongside it. This was in the days before the 'regulation industry' became a major force and there were fewer boxes to tick before you could do anything.

There were still no specialist SP agencies answering briefs or pitching ideas at the beginning of the decade. Promotions were either home grown or provided by advertising agencies, when they could deign to get their hands dirty. Meanwhile premiums were pitched by salesmen with bags of goodies, rudely referred to as 'black bag' salesmen.

PREMIUMS MAKE THEIR MARK

Commerce in the US was less affected by the war than in the UK, and from 1946 onwards premiums became big business. There was an organisation called National Premium Sales Executives Inc. which was the equivalent of the British Promotional Merchandise Association. In 1962 it published a useful handbook entitled Premiums in Marketing and sold it for $10 a copy. Its weighty tone is underlined by the opening chapter's title, 'The Philosophy of Merchandise Incentives'.

The NSPE seems to have had as much trouble defining 'premium merchandising' as SP folk had defining their art. After some thought they came up with: "A premium is an article of merchandise offered as an incentive to the performance of a specific service."

One of the problems in the US was that 'premium merchandise' had long meant inferior produce. This harked back to the Thirties, when the so-called radio 'soap operas' made great use of second rate junk. Conservative sales executives would turn pale at the thought of indulging in such form of promotion and those who did were rather ashamed to do so. However, all this changed at the end of World War Two when there was a tremendous expansion in the field.

A survey by Incentive Marketing magazine estimated that total incentive usage reached $1billion in 1949 and by 1969 it had reached almost $4billion. The biggest boom area, and one that became equally popular in the UK, was self liquidating offers.

When not pondering the philosophy of premium merchandising, the writer of the book had a sense of humour and came up with common reasons for using a premium:

1. "Because the competition is doing it"
2. "Because the competition is not doing it"
3. "Because you don't know what else to do"
4. "Because the advertising manager is bored"

Another entertaining comment was that in the first 30 years of the 20th century a useful slogan for premium offers was "If in doubt, use fly swatters." By the Seventies in the UK, the equivalent was "Free Tights".

Most major companies had sales promotion managers who put the programmes together with outside help if necessary. Typical of the type of company that was starting to operate in the area in the early Sixties was Parkmount in London. It claimed to have moved away from the 'take it or leave it' approach to one where it discussed client objectives before deciding which premium would solve the problem. What an original idea.

Parkmount even offered a fee-based service as a bolt-on using its links with market research, design and advertising specialists to offer a complete consultancy service. You could see which way things were moving, but for the time being the main source of income was margin on the products it supplied.

American sales promotion houses also targeted the UK. One was Bradfute & Associates, set up by F L Bradfute, Heinz's former vice president of marketing. Still mainly premium based, Bradfute worked for clients such as Procter & Gamble and Wall's. It was big in retail promotion, such as in-store bingo and an 'invisible ink' programme where consumers had to bring leaflets into the store for a chemical reveal of the prize. And you thought this sort of thing was a fairly recent innovation?

LIFE BELOW THE LINE

That nearly 30 per cent of marketing was going below the line was worrying ad agencies. Advertisers Weekly identified some ad agencies which had realised that there was life, and more importantly money, below the line. One such agency was Norman, Craig & Kummel, a US company that linked with the British Crane Advertising. In 1964 it ran promotions such as a joint Heinz Beans and Danish Bacon 'bean feast' and Osram's Lamplighters with costumed characters touring the streets. This was long before the Health and Safety Police had an iron grip on what could be done by anyone, anywhere and the late Robin Kingsland of KLP, who was involved with the Lamplighters, recalled that it was extremely dangerous. They had to carry eight feet long Lamplighter poles (as in the old days to light the street gas lamps) on bicycles from store to store. If that was not bad enough, the promotion took place in February when blizzards hit the country with bicycles crashing everywhere. The dual effect was either dangerous or hilarious depending on your sense of humour and whether or not you were riding the bike at the time.

This latter technique of personality promotions was a promotional standby. In the Thirties the Persil Imp accosted unsuspecting housewives and gave away prizes to people who stocked the product. Oddly dressed people with unusual vehicles became quite a common sight. In 1965, the year cigarette advertising was banned from TV, there were 25 variations across Britain, hopefully not all in the same street at the same time.

The basic proposition was that an ad campaign warned residents that the characters were heading their way and would reward houses that had their product. Trebor had Nell Gwynne look-alikes touring the Midlands to promote Bitter Lemon or Bitter Orange sweets. If you had a 3lb bag of McDougall's flour when a gentleman in full highland dress and a rather inappropriate baker's hat, came calling, you could claim a carpet sweeper or various kitchen items.

Not to be outdone, Vim and Lux sent out the colourfully attired 'Rainbow Men'. There were Nescafe Caballeros, Lyons coffee couples, Nivea beach girls, Johnson's dancing girls, Outspan mystery shoppers, Miss Camay, Miss Canada Dry, the Grimbergen Monk promoting a rather obscure Belgian beer, Brobat health crusaders, White Tide men, Persil girls, plus various people promoting Colgate, Stork, Blue Band and Carlton Cigarettes. With TV advertising banned, Carlton introduced the blonde Miss Carlton, represented by two beauty queens and three finalists from Miss Great Britain. They called on tobacconists giving the owner a chance to win £5 or £10 for stocking the brand.

All this provided plenty of work for resting actors and actresses and unemployed models, as well as cost-effective marketing. A budget for two 'personalities' plus a vehicle ranged from £250 to £350 per week including planning, briefing, wages and expenses and the average cost of a call was around £1.

THE PROMOTERS ARE COMING

A variation on the theme popped up in the early Nineties with what is possibly the most bizarre version of this technique. Durex wanted to attract a younger audience. As well as TV, sponsorship, posters and on-line activity, it took to the streets with hundreds of 'Sperm men'. These were dressed in bulging white outfits with five foot single horns waving on their heads and carried banners with slogans such as 'Ban Easy-On Durex' and 'Sperm against Durex'. The same programme ran in cities around the world, baffling consumers globally.

The trade magazine of the day, launched in 1961 as a quarterly called Premium Promotions, before going monthly in April 1964. The trade body, the ABSPE was big on themes, naming 1960/61 the year of 'International Marketing and Sales Promotion'. The next year it was 'Sales Promotion in a Competitive World'. Just how competitive was shown by financial problems in 1962, another 'theme' that was to recur in the ongoing history of the various associations. Despite a membership of 236, it recorded a deficit of £24 14s 3d and raised the sub to four guineas as a result. Despite this, the ABSPE was technically insolvent several times before the end of the decade.

It also changed name again in 1963, this time to the Marketing and Promotion Association or MPA, just in time for the end of resale price maintenance in 1964. The MPA ran a conference on the subject but neither this nor the daring move in 1966 of advertising for members in the personal column of The Times did much to help its fortunes. It struggled to produce the magazine, tried and failed to set up branches in Manchester and Newcastle but did succeed in setting one up in Australia. Membership was up and mostly down.

However, the death knell was sounded when in 1969 the Sales Promotion Executives Association (SPEA) was founded,. The forerunner of the Institute of Sales Promotion, this originated in the US, although the UK version was never actually affiliated. Articles of association were distributed in 1970 and the new body rapidly picked up 100 members and received a request from the failing MPA to merge, which it politely declined. It also started its awards which provide a fascinating annual snapshot of the industry.

1965 saw the launch of the British Promotional Merchandise Association (BPMA) which now has more than 700 members representing suppliers of every possible kind of merchandise, its own magazine, a website, a yearbook and various other useful services. Its origins are in the early sixties with the Premium Luncheon Club, which must have been a pretty prosperous outfit because it met in the Edwardian splendour of Regent Street's Cafe Royal. In 1964 it started the annual award for 'The Premium of the Year', the final judges of which were a panel of housewives. They chose a scheme run by Armour & Company described as: "A wide choice of exclusive self-liquidators made available to stores in selected areas." Doesn't sound like a potential Grand Prix winner.

As the decade progressed, 1966 saw the Times replace ads with news on its front page. Barclays Bank in Enfield had the first ATM in 1967 and the same year saw colour TV launched for just 11 hours each week on BBC2 which had started broadcasting in 1964. Radios One, Two and Three also arrived, followed by colour TV commercials in 1969. Birds Eye was first with an ad in the commercial break during Thunderbirds. The same year saw Rupert Murdoch buy the Daily Herald newspaper, now re-named The Sun. Co-author Colin Lloyd worked in the ad department of the Herald which was 'the trade union newspaper', and technologically forward thinking. It developed the first colour in newspapers using the 'wallpaper' method of printing. He claims he has the only file copies in the world at home. Odhams Press was part of the group and the first colour ad in any newspaper in the UK was for Woman's Own magazine, owned by Odhams. The Herald's circulation was 800,000 and it sold for £800,000, payable in instalments.

Then the infamous "Page 3 girls" arrived and helped increase the circulation to four million by 1978, overtaking the Mirror and making it the best selling UK newspaper. Consumers were spoilt for choice and the opportunities for promotional activity were expanding all the time.

THE EUROCRATS COME CALLING

The Sixties saw the UK's attitude to regulation of SP diverge from that of the rest of Europe. The then six-country European Economic Community (Belgium, France, Germany, Italy, Luxembourg and the Netherlands) commissioned a study of unfair competition law from the impressive sounding Max-Planck Institute to see if it was possible to harmonise rules across all of the members. EEC countries had a type of administrative law, including laws against unfair competition, which did not exist in either the UK or Ireland. The so-called Ulmer report finally appeared in 1967, published in French and German.

One word demonstrates the negative approach toward sales promotion shown by most of the EEC countries, compared with the UK and Ireland. It refers to rules relating to premium offers, discounts, etc. as mainly intended to prevent "excesses" in the field of competition. Ulmer's comments reflect those of the Twenties when there were complaints that free gifts were ruining the retail market. He also suggested that the consumer would be confused by promotions and should only take into account the quality, price or service of the competing products.

It highlighted different attitudes to sales promotion, which the UK considered a 'good thing', and 'inducements to buy' which less liberal countries considered akin to bribery. In the UK it was felt that there was no evidence that premiums were harmful to consumers and, provided they were legal, could stimulate healthy competition. On of the other side of the fence is the view that consumers should not be induced to buy by such evil schemes. The Brussels bureaucrats have been looking at harmonisation for over 40 years and, fortunately for us, seem no nearer to resolving it.

IT'S SHOW TIME

The industry started to have its own exhibition around this time with the Premium Promotions and Business Gifts Exhibition, which started in a Tottenham Court Road hotel, before moving upmarket in September 1964 for three days at the Piccadilly Hotel. The 64 exhibitors included Prestige, Mappins, John Waddington and Airfix, which, sadly for our boyhood memories, went into administration in the summer of 2006.

Prestige had developed a premium business from the 1959 when it spotted the business opportunity. It had sold several lorry loads of kitchen tools to Nabisco for a cereal pack SLP and consequently decided to develop this market. The sales division was selected to undertake this work and was headed by an aristocrat, Lord John Cunningham, plus Stanley Clarke, who had flown with the Dam Buster Squadron and preferred to be called by the rather less aristocratic title, Nobby. They were joined by Bob Essery in the same year. One of its biggest customers, to the tune of an impressive £250,000 in 1966, was The Spastics Society, as it was then known, which used its products to raise funds.

Prestige was a brand leader in the premiums business and was involved in the beginning of the BPMA, which actually started life as the British Premium Manufacturers Association. 'Nobby' Clark was the first chairman, having picked up the idea during a visit to Chicago in 1963, where he joined the American National Premium Sales Executives (NPSE), a body of which he was later president. At the time only one executive per company could be involved in the BPMA so Bob Essery had to wait until he had moved to Arthur Price to join. In turn he became treasurer, chairman, and finally president. During Essery's chairmanship he changed the name to the British Promotional Merchandise Association so that non-manufacturing members could join - so the BPMA became the BPMA. Essery also negotiated with the formidable Julia Morley to take the then Miss England, Miss Scotland and Miss Great Britain to the US to promote British goods at the New York Premium Fair. Shows formidable negotiating skills, plus an eye for a good junket.

A TAIL OF MANY CITIES

A fine example of what merchandise linked to advertising can do was the famous Esso tiger tails campaign. This eye-catching campaign originated in a series of UK advertisements for Esso Extra featuring a ferocious tiger. The animal was redrawn in 1959 advertising for a subsidiary of Esso's US marketing arm, complete with the slogan 'Put a Tiger in Your Tank'. This resurfaced in 1964 when the plentiful supply of petrol produced heavy price-cutting. Esso wanted to strengthen the branding for what was then a premium product and developed a US ad campaign showing a tiger disappearing into the petrol tank leaving the tail sticking out.

The actual premium was introduced almost by accident. Esso was approached by an independent textile manufacturer asking if it could offer tiger tails to service stations as a promotional gimmick. Esso agreed and an initial small supply disappeared so rapidly that subcontractors had to be brought in to help with overwhelming demand. That they were self-liquidated did the budget no harm at all.

When the wife of one of the US directors had three separate tails stolen from her car, it became obvious that they were on to a very good thing. Tails spawned a not so minor industry for tiger colouring books, dolls, key rings, glasses and much more. In the US, in less than five months, dealers gave away nearly half a million key rings and sold 3.5 million tiger tails, 2.5 million tiger colouring books, and 200,000 tiger dolls. Better still, there had been a serious increase in sales directly applicable to the advertising and merchandising programme and all without additional advertising expenditure.

At this point the Tiger went worldwide, first to Latin America and then to Europe in 1965 coinciding with the launch of an improved quality of Esso Extra petrol. The UK campaign was an instant and massive success, despite initial British caution in ordering 1.5 million tails and then halving the order. The factory churning out 50,000 tails per week could not keep up so a black market developed and tails sold at the garage for one shilling were advertised at five shillings each. Point of sale material was stolen from garages and tails were stolen from cars, on at least one occasion by a passing motorcyclist. In seven and a half months Esso UK got through:

Four million bumper stickers
2.5 million tails
1.5 million window stickers
One million helmet transfers
500,000 book matches
250,000 balloons
200,000 lapel badges
100,000 pencils
50,000 painting books
30,000 Tiger mascots.

Collection schemes were also popular, often requiring quite long and complicated trials. Bingo style cards were commonplace with the consumer completing horizontal and vertical lines by buying certain products. Up to 48 proofs of purchase were needed to get some rewards - usually a relatively small amount of cash.

McDonald's, not the hamburger chain, but a major biscuit maker of the time (remember Bandits?) was keen on premiums. Towards the end of 1962 it reported that it had run nine premiums campaigns in the past 21 months. They included highball glasses, a water set from Sweden, dessert glasses, a free 'Kitchenaide', a picnic set, a teapot and free nylons, as stockings used to be called.

PROMOTIONS WITH LEGS
As mentioned before, the thinking of the day was that you couldn't go wrong with nylons. This was the time when tights were being introduced for everyday wear, which made the miniskirt a practical item of dress - for which much thanks. If anyone was really stuck for a quick, easy and powerful offer, the answer was always "Free Tights".

A 1964 promotion that certainly gave the idea 'legs' was a by the Liverpool Daily Post sponsored by Bri-Nylon. The winner could collect a pair of Bri-Nylon Stockings every week for five years from a local store – that would have entailed 260 trips.

One very high profile promoter of the early Sixties was John Bloom, referred to as 'The King of Incentives' who revolutionised the washing machine market with a massive direct sale operation support by advertising and a whole gamut of promotions. These included holidays on the Belgium coast, a not particularly appealing destination but for an extra 10 guineas you could upgrade to the Venetian Rivera. Sounds a pretty good deal. He also ran 'BOGOFs' or 'Twofers' as the Americans call them, his own brand of 'Supa Golden' trading stamps, and a customer's buying club called RPM that offered the owners of one of his machines the opportunity to buy a range of goods at 'privileged' prices. The initials stood for Rolls Privileged Member.

Another privileged offer was a Kellogg 1960 on pack competition to win your 'Ideal Home' with Corn Flakes. The winner got £5,000 to buy the site and could choose from 30 contemporary designs. At the same time a healthy cereal, All Bran, was being pushed hard as the "natural laxative food", a product claim that appealed until 1966, after which it seems to have vanished, probably no longer considered breakfast table reading until it resurfaced, the claim that is, in 2007. Meanwhile a kids' competition to win bicycles reinforced the brand's 'do gooder' image with entrants having to spot broken road safety rules shown in on-pack illustrations. The same product was into gardening in big way. Typical consumer offers were three rose bushes for 7s 6d and forty Dutch bulbs for 8s 11d.

A Knorr Soups offer of a half retail price Prestige stainless steel casserole in 1964 underlined the power of SLPs. Knorr wanted to order 5,000 units from Prestige. However the manufacturer said that if the order was increased to 7,000 it would cover the risk up to 20,000 pots. Week one produced orders for 128 casseroles, but after 10 weeks they stood at 20,105, and finally reached 36,796, which made Prestige delirious.

A CAR IN THE PACK OR ON THE CAN
Then, as now, cars were popular prizes and promoters were very generous in the number given away. In 1961 Kellogg offered 15 Ford Anglias boasting such luxuries as a radio and a heater. This scheme was trumped by Heinz in the same year with the first of its popular 'Win a Car-a-Day' competitions, running for, surprise, surprise, 57 days and offering the very trendy Mini-Minor.

This promotion was so successful that it ran again in the following year, reinvigorated with free soup for all entrants and the headline 'You Can't Lose'. Heinz kept with car giveaways over the years, adding various bells and whistles, such as the 1966 scheme with 57 Wolsey convertibles complete with picnic hamper, electric kettle and ladies 'freshen up compartment' kitted out by Max Factor. Kellogg had a Corn Flakes promotion offering 40 Ford Cortinas and other promotions of the period offered Kenwood Chef mixers, Magicoal electric fires and caravans, which were the aspirational items of the time.

By 1990 Heinz had upped the ante to 100 Metros, on the same "car-a-day principle". They included a 'H57' personalised number plate, the first time that the DVLA had allowed anyone to select their own registration number. All of these were negotiated by Heinz's Ian Fryer, who dealt with car companies and the DVLA. Heinz often got a better discount than the main dealers and all in all Fryer thinks Heinz bought almost 1,000 cars during his time.

PRIZES GALORE
Naturally holidays featured regularly. Heinz took all the advertising space in one issue of the Daily Sketch to tell the public about the 57 (of course) holidays that could be won with beans. The public had to list the desirable attributes of a holiday in order of merit and win that perennial favourite, the 'holiday of a lifetime'. This was a popular technique at the time, usually with 10 items to rank and a tiebreaker. This technique resurfaced in 2005 with up to 17 items to be put in the correct order and no prize winner if no one got all 17 correct. Easily insurable as the odds are astronomical, this is a cost effective method of operating on a very small budget but of doubtful morality.

The many competitions had really good prize structures even by modern standards. Here are just a few of the goodies that were handed out. Kellogg had changed suppliers and now had 32 Vauxhall Vivas with a first prize of a 'his and hers' pair. Heinz was on the treasure trove trail, allowing 100 prize-winners and friends to spend the bank holiday on a beach digging for the chance to win an E-Type Jaguar, a speedboat and two BOAC Round the World tickets. We don't think the actual prizes were buried, possibly only the tickets. Oxo gave away 50 Hillman Imps and at the other end of the motoring scale, Findus put up bunch of cars with an Aston Marin DBS as first prize.

When not in a frenzy of competition organising, promoters could attend the first floating conference. In 1964 the Mace Marketing Organisation chartered the SS Avalon, a 7,000-ton steamer from, of all people, British Railways. It was about one third the size of a modern cross-channel ferry and could accommodate 350 delegates in dubious comfort, but was so oversubscribed that it was repeated later the same year.

These conferences restarted in the nineties on the Canberra, gradually going upmarket to newer and larger vessels. The idea was simple but effective. First, invite as many senior marketing executives as you could persuade to spend two or three days on a free cruise up and down the Channel. Next, find a few good speakers and finally sell places to the multitude of eager sales people who could then track down their quarry in a confined space, with no escape. Actually this was not quite true for one senior executive who obtained enormous credibility when lifted off by helicopter.

BRAND CHARACTERS

There cannot be many people who could not recognise Spillers Fred the Flourgrader in his black suit and bowler hat; the promotion ephemera now fetching good money in antique markets. It may come as a surprise to learn that he was invented by an American agency Geers Gross in 1964 as a quintessentially English character. The designer, Tony Cattano was also responsible for the Tetley Tea Folk and the Country Life Buttermen.

This was the year of the Beatles and they were everywhere. One week in 1964 Kellogg had a fan club badge in Rice Krispies, Rank's Showtime magazine SLP-ed a black, long-sleeved sweater for 19s 11d including Beatle badges, and Rank was running local promotions offering 50 reserved seats at your neighbourhood fleapit to see A Hard Days Night. Despite only being promoted by leaflets in retail outlets, they received a staggering five million entries.

INSTANT WIN ARRIVES WITH A BANG

The extremely popular "instant win" promotions first made an appearance on a large-scale in the UK towards the end of the Sixties with a petrol forecourt promotion called Shell "Make Money", (the co-authors choice for best promotion ever). Brought to the UK by US consultancy Glendenning, it was based on the popularity of sweepstakes in the US. This really took off when it became possible to operate a legal lottery.

The layman's definition of a lottery required two aspects: the prize had to be distributed on the basis of chance, and there had to be a contribution to the prize fund which included making a purchase. Take either of these away and it was not a lottery and therefore legal. What made this programme work was the introduction of an alternative method of taking part, without necessarily buying the product. The 'plain paper' method, identified by the immortal words 'No purchase necessary' allowed the consumer to take part in an instant win promotion by sending their name and address to the handling house, who would enter them into the promotion or, in the case of petrol promotion, for simply asking for an entry.

By contemporary standards the Shell promotion was pretty basic. When you went to a garage and bought petrol you were given an envelope containing half a mock banknote with various values up to £25,000. In order to win and 'Make Money' you had to obtain both matching halves. The promotion took the country by storm and did wonders for Shell sales.

Consumers were rather less sophisticated in those days and had not worked out that the prizes were controlled by limiting the numbers of one half of the notes. This led to newspaper advertisements offering to share the cash prize to anyone who could come up with the other rare half of the note. To stay on the right side of the law, it was possible to walk into the garage and ask for a Make Money envelope without buying any petrol. Despite this, a large number of motorists apparently drove from garage to garage buying a gallon at each.

Shell did put a number of quite legal restrictions on who could and could not obtain the notes and how winners should make their claims. Each half note carried a claim form to be filled in with name and address and vehicle registration number. The staff was instructed to dispense game pieces only to the driver of motor vehicles, including motorcycles or of course anyone who had the nerve to ask without buying fuel. When, 18 years later, Shell revived Make Money it seems that the public had not learnt much about instant win promotions as once again they were advertising in the press for missing halves of high-value notes.

In the 21st century this would just be another promotion, the only notable aspect would be the fact that it operated with bits of paper, not bits in a computer. However, at the time it took the country by storm. It got massive media coverage, was a talking point wherever people met and best of all for Shell, it did wonders for its sales, giving a massive increase in market share. The opposition hated it. A number of experienced SP professionals, including the authors of this book, consider it the most important promotion in recorded history.

THE LEGAL BIT
Unlike Players' rivals at a later date, the other petrol companies did not attempt to persuade the government to take legal action against Shell but it is likely that if someone had taken action on the 1966 version, they could have been found guilty of 'competitive striving' as the promotion really did not have a major skill aspect. Lord Parker, the then Lord Chief Justice, convicted Whitbread for a similar element in 1970. He reasoned that the category of competitions involving insufficient skill includes those with no element of skill at all. Thankfully the Law Lords in 1972 overturned this in their 'Spot Cash' judgement with the view that a promotion requiring no skill was not a competition.

1966 also saw an important legal decision when a Bradfute promotion for KitKat ended up in the Divisional Court. This introduced the doctrine of 'severability' which became known as the 'Bradfute razor'. This slices a promotion into separate components, each of which must be independently lawful, so that any lawful first stage cannot legalise an unlawful second stage or visa versa.

The point at which dissection takes place is where the gaining of the prize becomes apparent.

There was the additional qualification that prizes need not be cash or merchandise but could be something intangible, such as a right or eligibility to move on to another stage. In the KitKat Bingo promotion the pack label was either lucky or unlucky and the discovery depended on the purchase of the pack, so it was clearly a lottery. The winning label provided the right to attempt a relatively simple skill test that constituted the separate and lawful second stage. In other words, as stage one was a lottery it did not matter how legal stage two was. Another point made at the time was that such a skill test is not a tiebreaker. Failure at this stage does not make the prize available to other competitors. So we are back to that good old faithful the 'plain paper' entry.

The massive popularity of instant win has spawned a myriad ways of telling people that they have not won. In a way, 'instant win' is a misnomer. It should be 'instant loss'. However, accuracy loses out to shelf appeal. The advantage of this type of promotion is that it is very unlikely that the full prize fund will ever be distributed, although some companies recirculated prizes or donated them to charity. One American publication suggested that redemption could be as low as 10 per cent of the quoted prize fund.

THE BIRTH OF AGENCIES

Towards the end of this decade, sales promotion consultancies began to emerge. The big American companies had established a foothold in the UK and proved that you could make money from promotions in ways other than flogging widgets. Clients were now demanding rather more input, and even prepared to pay an occasional fee. Spurred on by the development of Green Shield and other stamps, a spirit of enterprise developed. Stamps and coupons were being printed by the millions and around the fringe of these operations were point of sale and print houses, in particular, the infamous print brokers. These sharp-suited middlemen managed to make a good living by putting highly competitive printers together with very demanding customers and at a very nice mark-up. Why they could do this better than the printer's own sales force is difficult to understand but some of them got quite rich doing it.

A classic example of this period was a promotion by Heinz that required the distribution to 40,000 retailers of a large dump bin and sales presenter. Its army of salesmen had to fight for a gondola end in every supermarket. Producing them was a very profitable process. The cardboard engineer was as revered as the creative director is today. Their origami skills would turn a sheet of cardboard into a highly complex advertisement that stood up to the ultimate test of being bashed by a supermarket trolley travelling at warp speed.

In this battleground, clients were always demanding more. They suddenly wanted their POS producers to design as well as manufacture, so POS houses moved from the grubbier suburbs of London and Home Counties to smart new offices in Mayfair and Holborn. At the time co-author Colin Lloyd had the good fortune to be working for one such company, Ritchie Dixon. In the late Sixties it was a pioneering agency and broker, which took cardboard and print execution to new heights. Clients loved the fact that they could buy from specialists rather than go through ad agencies that treated POS with disdain. This era saw ad agencies traditional vice-like grip on the client's budgets begin to loosen.

There were also enormous changes in British retailing. At the time there were more than 50,000 grocery retailers and about the same number of garage forecourts. The grocery brands of the day had massive logistical problems and marketing challenges in servicing them. Many of the shops were quite small but still expected to see the sales people regularly. There was a lot of 'dealer loaders' which were thinly disguised bribes to managers for stocking and display. A tailor-made promotion might offer a TV set as a prize and one would be supplied to each shop to display. At the end of promotion the salesman would 'forget' to collect it and it ended up in the manager's house. Graham Griffiths remembers driving around Essex to check on the display of a prize draw for a Lilo Dinghy and making sure that there was one as a spare.

RETAIL RELATIONS
The proliferation of outlets meant that brands were in charge of the destiny of their products. Multinationals such as Heinz, Cadbury, Kellogg, P&G and Beechams called the shots and had the relationship with consumers. The sales director was the brand general, and marshalled his troops to squeeze more shelf space, get more listings and win the gondola wars. Although the marketing department held the marketing budgets, it recognised that the sales force needed an extra weapon to win the battles.

Sales directors also had something else that marketing didn't - a seat on the board. It would therefore not do your career any harm to direct funds to something called sales promotion. Not wanting to lose their day jobs to salesmen, marketers only passed over some of the budgets, calling it something like 'promotional sales allowance'. Suddenly, higher ranking people in the sales department could play with marketing concepts and even brand ideas.

However, the idea of allowing a bright young graduate brand manager with a couple of years' experience loose on some of the country's most important brands was just a step too far. Keeping control of all this energy without suppressing it was a great challenge. Management came up with the idea of having someone in the middle to cope with sales demands, marketing initiatives, retail consolidation and financial prudence. They needed a tough experienced character to keep the juniors on the straight and narrow.

This newly invented post needed someone who knew everything about the company, the trade, consumers and promotional law. Up stepped the promotions manager who saluted his boss smartly and got stuck into trying to sort out the problems. Mike Slipper of Van den Bergh summed up his job description as: "Stopping brand managers making fools of themselves."

These heroic professionals formed the bedrock of modern promotional practice. Sadly, consolidation and corporate efficiencies have virtually made them extinct, which is a real loss. A roll call would include such names as Ian Fryer, Heinz; Chris Kerridge and Mike Slipper, Van den Bergh; Jeremy Sandys-Winsch and David Walker, Kellogg; Alan Scaping, Nestle; Jim Porteous, Rowntree; Roy Piercy, The Post Office; Tony Barnes, Kodak; Bill King, Gallaher; Brenda Simonetti, Quaker; David Dargen, P&G; Brian Mitchell, Kimberly-Clark; Ken Vaughan, Kraft; Jack Trigg, Tetley; John Fuller, Cadburys; Diane Rowe, Unilever Bestfoods, and the recently retired director general of the ISP, Edwin Mutton (Kimberly-Clark) although he claims to be too young to be included. The ISP once had a powerful Promoters' Committee staffed by these people and you will find a number of them cropping up in later chapters. They have tales to tell and have told them (or at least some of them) to us.

Not every promoting company had a promotions manager, and it was often left to brand management to promote sales. Naturally, they felt most comfortable working with existing suppliers. Also, in those less regulated days, most printers had a generous entertainment budget. However there were few companies that really had the right combination of entrepreneurialism, creativity, knowledge of the trade and expertise in cardboard and print that brands required. Remember, this was at the dawn of commercial television and radio, and there was no internet, PCs, mobiles, e-mail, or other pieces of technology without which it would not be possible to survive today. Magic markers, cow gum and Letraset ruled the day, and if you wanted some typesetting you sent the typescript off and got it back in a day or two, followed by a large bill.

In other words, the stage was set for the emergence of the sales promotion agency with a strange heritage, partly from across the Atlantic and partly home-grown, but at the same time the US was about to export the biggest promotional technique of the 20th century into the British market.

CHAPTER SIX

Green Shield Stamps

Dick Tompkins' holiday good fortune spawns an empire
Success breeds imitation but Green Shield remains top of the pile
The breakthrough into the multiples finally comes
Killed by its own success
Reinvented as a successful high street retailer

In 1956, an Englishman on holiday in New York stood on a corner watching the traffic to three garages. Within ten years, based on what he saw, he had built a British business that dominated the promotional market place. But he was not selling petrol.

He noticed that two of the garages had almost no customers, while the third had a queue of cars. Being nosey by nature, he investigated and found that the successful garage was giving away trading stamps. His nose led him to launch Green Shield Stamps, THE major retail promotional technique of the Sixties and Seventies, before it closed, apart from a few vestigial flickers, in 1979. At its peak Green Shield gave away goods worth almost £100 million a year at 1978 prices.

The nosey Englishman was G R F Tompkins, better known to some as 'Dick' Tompkins, to the media as Tompkins and to most of his staff as either Mr Tompkins or 'Governor'. He had picked up on a massive phenomenon, and the only surprise was that no one from the UK had spotted it before he did.

STAMPS OF ALL COLOURS

The stamp boom in America started in the early 1950s, although, as noted earlier, they were first used towards the end of the 19th century, with Sperry & Hutchinson (S&H) offering them to retailers in 1896. Department stores were the hub of the business for nearly 60 years, until supermarkets woke up to the technique.

In the 1954 just 13 per cent of the nation's supermarkets were issuing stamps but six years later, 72 per cent were using them. In that year it was reported that 84 per cent of American families were saving some form of stamp. The annual turnover of redeemed goods was more than $700million at the time. 250 different companies were selling stamps, and there were 2,000 redemption centres.

Before this fateful holiday Tompkins and his wife ran a business tipping race horses, but having seen the power of S&H's green stamps, he decided that it could work in the UK. It was probably the best bet he ever made. Before returning to the UK, Dick found out as much as he could about the S&H business and put the information to good use, including adopting their green colour. This forced S&H to become Pink Stamps when they launched Britain, in opposition to Green Shield.

In 1958 Tompkins recruited a staff of 12, including a small sales team, one of whom was Ted Adams. Ted stayed for almost 20 years, becoming an associate sales director handling the major accounts. Most of this chapter is based on his experiences and we are very grateful for the large amount of information he made available to us.

Green Shield ordered a few thousand full colour catalogues and the embryo sales team went out and canvassed the independent retailers around its office in the Holloway Road area of London. The outfit was based over a redundant Lyons teashop which was the location of the first redemption shop. Later shops were given a facelift by renaming them Gift Houses. Much, much later, following the closure of Green Shield, these well-located retail outlets became Argos. Currently owned by Home Retail Group (formerly GUS), it has nearly 600 stores and sales of more than £3billion a year.

Green Shield developed a concept of the 'family of accounts' with the grocer as the key member. Grocers had the footfall and when they signed the sales team would set about signing up local greengrocers, bakers, hardware stores and any other trade that did not compete with those already signed up.

THE SECRET OF SUCCESS – FRANCHISING!
Each had a local exclusive franchise, limited to the smallest possible area that the salesman could persuade the retailer to accept. This could be as little as a quarter of a mile around the shop. This aspect helped make Green Shield into an operation that was far more universal and therefore much bigger than any loyalty scheme run today, or likely to operate in future.

This concept never changed, so that every Tesco store, Esso garage, or outlet of a major retail group that offered stamps was an individual franchise, not a company contract. Therefore Green Shield could be collected at more than one garage or retail chain, as long as they were outside the agreed exclusive area. Soon the garage became the key member of the family, particularly where Green Shield could not get a grocery account.

The company progressed on two parallel streams. Firstly, it worked hard to promote key grocery accounts. Salesmen would drive their cars, covered with Green Shield stickers and with loudspeakers on the roof, round the area of a new grocery signing. This was backed up by a mobile redemption shop that had its own sound system. It was basic, it was crude, but it was effective.

Salesmen would also give away full pages of the book, promoted as being worth 15 shillings. This would be of doubtful legality today. On one occasion a farmer called Green Shield House asking for £5,000 in exchange for stamps. It turned out that the distribution company for the Kent area had dumped them in a drain on his farm. It was a good try but he did not get the money.

BUILDING BUSINESS

Crude or not, the system worked. Most of the shops enjoyed immediate success far in advance of the break-even point of around 15 per cent sales increase. Some even doubled their turnover. This began to impact on the sales at local multiples such as Tesco, Charles Phillips and Globe Stores, particularly in London, and the chain stores began to sit up and take notice.

By 1960 Green Shield had lots of competition but none of it serious. The Times reported that, according to the Consumers' Association, there were 30 trading stamp companies in the UK with from 100 to 7,000 member stores. Guess who had 7,000. Success also led to the Trading Stamp Act, aimed at reducing the power of stamps. For years it meant promoters had to print a tiny cash value on coupons or stamps in case they came within the scope of the act.

DOWN WITH STAMPS!

A breakthrough occurred when the small south London chain of Globe Stores started to sign up a number of its outlets. Owners Monty Bloom and John Lerman talked about the success of stamps and Green Shield got into another chain, Charles Phillips. Meanwhile, Sainsbury and the Allied Suppliers of the Distributive Alliance were basically anti-stamps, because, like all the retailers, they hated spending their own money. However, even they started to notice what was happening and a stamp war broke out. Sainsbury plastered windows with posters announcing 'DON'T SAVE STAMPS!' Green Shield printed even more in the same style and colours that said 'SAVE STAMPS!'

Stamps continued to be divisive. The Consumers' Association and just about every trade body disapproved of trading stamps, while consumers loved them. One night in the Savoy Hotel the Distributive Alliance held a meeting with all members in attendance, including the late Michel Kay of Pricerite, and voted not to take stamps.

What Mr Kay knew, but somehow forgot to mention, was that at 4am the next day, while the other Alliance members were sleeping off their excellent meal, Green Shield Stamps was fully mobilised. Almost every member of staff had an individual target to get the PoS into one of the Pricerite stores in London. Every Pricerite outlet in London was hit. At 6a.m. all the stores were opened by their managers and by 9am the first shoppers were greeted by a store covered by Green Shield Stamp material. Mr Kay, a relative and bosom friend of Jack Cohen (founder of Tesco), was breaking the Alliance's agreement.

What Mr Cohen said when he found out what was happening is not recorded, but as his background in grocery retailing went back to 1911 with his first shop in a part of London that was certainly not a leafy suburb, he probably had some suitable adjectives to hand. Incidental, as he turned over £4 with a profit of £1 on his first day of business, you can see the basis of Tesco's enthusiasm for a good margin.

The petrol retailing trade was going through a similar turmoil. At the time more than half of garages were independent and Green Shield found them an easy sell because salesmen could point to garages doubling sales, based on just one stamp for every 2.5p spent - around five stamps a gallon. It was hard for Esso and Shell to ignore.

By now Tompkins had moved the company to a modern office block in suburban Edgware named, with startling originality, Green Shield House. The company was growing like Topsy with a huge franchise department to stay on top of the mountains of paperwork this entailed, plus the arguments about how far an exclusive franchise could be extended. The Green Shield view was that if you could not see another garage, it was outside of your franchise. Garages took a very different view. They suggested that if you could drive to the competitor's outlet in less than 30 minutes it should not get stamps. Negotiations were often very long winded. An equally busy section in the franchise department was frantically trying to sort out the various grocers, desperate to get on the bandwagon. It was a major bandwagon and a salesman's dream in every way. But even better times were to come.

TESCO JOIN UP
Around 1964 one very persistent salesman finally got to see Tesco's Jack Cohen and, possibly to get rid of him, was given its three worst stores - closely followed by a £1,000 bonus from Dick Tompkins.

Green Shield made sure its stamps worked. The stores got the full treatment: a small rainforest's worth of leaflets, ranks of promotion girls, be-stickered cars, PA systems, special bonus stamp offers and everything else the sales team could think of. The three stores were extremely successful and Green Shield had cracked Tesco. From then until they were withdrawn in 1977, every store took the stamps and they were rolled out as rapidly as Green

Shield could provide the launch activity. For those 14 years Green Shield Stamps and Tesco were as inseparable as a teenager and his mobile.

By now Green Shield was a massive concern with 5,000 employees and 50 gift houses. In one year it distributed five per cent of all toys and 10 per cent of the pots and pans sold in the UK. One year four people collected enough stamps to redeem a Ford Cortina. One company director bought three cars, including a Jag, from a garage giving stamps - he got 160,000, enough to fill 160 books. One department dealt solely with charities which were redeeming minibuses.

CONTINUOUS GROWTH

Despite locking into Tesco, Green Shield could still find more grocers thanks to the finely-honed franchise system. In 1974-75 International Stores had a bad year and Green Shield rode to its rescue. Following a presentation to the board, the sales team was given the 29 worst stores to be fitted into the various Tesco franchises. They were refurnished in a week, had a massive launch and business boomed. This led to long and complicated negotiations, trying to complete a jigsaw of franchises between those held by Tesco and other retailers.

Oddly enough, Green Shield benefited from an early example of product placement that backfired on the originator, S&H. A very popular and long running TV series imported from the USA called "I Love Lucy" often carried references to stamps but could not mention the brand, calling them 'green' stamps. This was the colour of S&H stamps in America. When broadcast in the UK, green meant Green Shield, not S&H. Gold Bond Stamps, another US competitor entered the UK market via Fine Fare but were never a major influence.

Green Shield also developed its catalogue for use as a sales incentive and motivation tool with point's schemes and rewards for anything from attendance to retirement. Stuart MacMillan Pratt, who rose to general manager of this offshoot, Performance Awards, provides an example of its original thinking. One section incentivised industrial workers and was asked to encourage cotton mill workers to use all the thread on the reels as 10 per cent was often wasted. The solution was simplicity itself. Just wrap 500 stamps around the reel before filling it with thread.

Stuart had a ringside seat during this peak period. One event sticks firmly in his memory. Green Shield had a vast new warehouse near Daventry covering the area of six football pitches. It had a state of the art automated system of trucks and fork lifts picking and moving the goods to the enormous loading bay, with not a driver in sight. These worked well until one day the automatic doors did not work as advertised and were demolished by the driverless truck. Even with this kit the place needed 750 staff to run it and the loading bay held 16 articulated lorries.

He also describes the arrival of the first load of one year's catalogues, which were printed in Italy. The order was perhaps the largest, single print job in Europe and the top brass were lined up to welcome it. The Italian driver swung into the yard with typical flair and came to a dramatic halt. Everyone followed him to the door at the rear, which he preceded to fling wide open to reveal a totally empty trailer. He had picked up the wrong unit and with no mobile phones, no one had told him. Green Shield melted a phone line to the Italian printer which briskly chartered a cargo 747 to make delivery a few days later.

THE SLOW DECLINE

So, apart from a natural wear out factor and a search for novelty, what killed such a successful programme? This story contains the first hint of the beginning of the end for stamps because they had become so prolific. They were probably as big as almost every other promotional technique (apart from price promotions) in use at the time, maybe even bigger. Everybody, just everybody, collected Green Shield Stamps.

Colin Marshall, later to head BA but then running Avis, had just signed up with a launch to 1,250 staff in the Mayfair Theatre. Green Shield, using its labyrinth of interlocking franchises, had forced competing retailers, particularly petrol companies, to get into a bidding war with more and more multiple stamp offers. It was a price war in reverse but had the same effect in that it was totally counter productive in the long run.

Initially, motorists loved the escalating offers with double, treble, quadruple, and ten times stamps available. People were spending hours licking and sticking page after page of stamps, which led to the introduction of the 'Big 40' stamp, worth £1 and the equivalent of one page. It was easier to collect and also reduced production costs.

The frenzy of forecourt activity seriously devalued the stamps that Tesco and other retailers were issuing. Quite simply you got more stamps for the same money spent on petrol. Stamps were becoming less effective as a motivator. Although they worked to a point, to get growth additional bonus activity was required. An example of this was the annual double stamp weeks in Tesco, held once a year and funded by the stamp company. Traditionally, sales increased by 25 per cent, but it was declining year on year. For the last three or four years of Green Shield this pattern occurred everywhere and the writing was on the wall.

At Tesco, Jack Cohen's health was moving him towards retirement and Leslie Porter was running the company with Ian MacLaurin (since ennobled) dealing with trading stamps. Stamps had now been around for 18 years and the public was getting bored with them and retailers were seeing diminishing returns.

Tesco had milked stamps for all they were worth over the years, but there was no sentiment when, as readily as they had taken them up, they decided to drop them. Tesco's explanation has always been that its customers wanted real value, not some gimmick (despite having fully exploited 'gimmicky' stamps for years). Its answer to the new paradigm was deep discounts on thousands of brands, paid for by its obliging suppliers.

This took the form of the famous 'Checkout' promotion, which was a radical change in the company's policy. At a time when real incomes were depressed by government wage freezes and currency weakness increasing the cost of imports, food prices were a national issue. It was a situation that Tesco exploited with great skill.

The announcement that Tesco was dropping stamps and reducing prices impressed the public no end. Because stamps had been available on all items, the feeling was that all prices would be reduced, turning Tesco into a consumer champion and providing masses of positive media coverage. In the last six months of 1977 Tesco spent £2.1million on advertising Checkout. This was its first major step on the way to its target of being the dominating retailer in the UK, a store where you could buy every product and service you need in life. It has never looked back.

By coming out of stamps at just the right time, Tesco stole a march on its competitors who were following like sheep into the stamp wars. The effect for Green Shield was catastrophic. It had lost its biggest client and the move broke the spell that it had over other retailers. Other client defections followed at the same time as consumer stamina for stamps was declining, running down the clock on Green Shield.

THE STAMPS LEGACY
Notwithstanding this, the money was made and Dick Tompkins became the first UK promotions millionaire with a few more to come in later years. The fledgling consultancies looked around and thought, "Hey lads, there is real money to be made in this game," and went at it with renewed enthusiasm.

So why were trading stamps so successful? They had novelty; they were easy to collect from many sources; redemption was also simple from an outlet near you, and there was a huge choice of products you could redeem against.

It is interesting to compare them with today's Tesco Clubcard, Nectar and other loyalty schemes. The most obvious difference is that consumers could often go to competing retailers and still get the same reward, something no one would get away with today. Green Shield generally offered better value in that the stamps were worth a discount of 2.5 per cent compared with many current loyalty offers of around one per cent. In addition, Green Shield had a dominant position in the market with no serious opposition.

However, from the promoter's point of view they could do almost none of the useful things that electronic cards can do and which are one of the main reasons for running such data-led schemes. Stamps told them nothing about their customers, who they were, what they bought, not even where they shopped. There was no database, no chance to communicate with them, and no direct connection at all.

With Tesco gone, Green Shield did not immediately curl up and die. Richard Tompkins for one remained bullish, stating: "There is no evidence that the power of Green Shield will not work effectively in the marketplace in the Eighties, Nineties and beyond". It may have been whistling in the wind but at the time he had some reason to be optimistic. The sales force went out to sign up any grocer which had not been able to join because of a nearby Tesco. For instance, around 50 International Stores were signed up. However, it barely compared to the loss of Tesco.

The demise of such a large and successful operation is in many ways sad but do not feel too much sympathy for the Tompkins family. They had wisely stashed away cash to cover the possible cost of redeeming all, or at least most, of the stamps they had issued and of course being paid for. In fact they had to do this - the famous Redemption Bond. When a reasonable period had expired and their accountants told them that the liabilities left in this area were minimal, they were free to pocket this nice little nest egg, which was reliably reported to be in the region of £21 million. Some egg but, we think you will agree, well earned, particularly when compared to some of the handouts to the top brass of much less successful, in fact often unsuccessful, companies in the present climate.

In the end, Green Shield slid slowly beneath the surface and Argos, the biggest and best high street catalogue redemption company emerged like a modern Phoenix from the ashes. The infrastructure, from buying through warehousing, via delivery to the high street retail outlets, gave it everything it needed for success. Although stamps did not tell the issuing company much about the customers, it told a fledgling retailer plenty. Argos knew exactly what the consumers wanted; Green Shield had been providing it for years. It changed the name, changed the décor and changed the currency – out went books of stamps, in came cash.

INTERLUDE TWO - IT SEEMED LIKE A GOOD IDEA AT THE TIME

Over redemption
Too much of a good thing
The case of the mystery cami-knickers
Game cards that proved too easy to crack
Travel promotions that left consumers at home
The benefits of getting some insurance

You might think that a successful promotion would be one that really chimed with consumers causing them to take part in their droves. Wrong!

The thought of massive over redemption is enough to make the average brand manager wake up screaming in the middle of the night. This normally only occurs when there is either an open-ended requirement for the reward (such as Hoover) or the response is seriously underestimated.

WHO DID THE MATHS?

Underestimating the popularity of a promotion is perhaps the most common cock-up. Even companies with a great deal of experience in operating promotions can miscalculate. McDonald's ran a 'two for one' hamburger promotion that was certainly successful, when an estimated two million redemptions actually got four million.

When Van den Bergh ran a promotion offering free phone calls with Flora pack lids, it predicted 500,000 respondents. It ended up with 1,750,000 respondents and a phone bill for almost £3million. At its peak there were nine Post Office lorries queuing up to deliver applications, each absolutely stuffed with Flora Pack lids. The other problem was what to do with around 10 million Flora lids, not all of which had been washed! On the other hand market share went up substantially.

Another phone linked promotion that blew the budget was in 1994 when Mercury One-to-One had the bright idea of offering their subscribers a free phone call anywhere in the world on Christmas Day. The subscribers loved it so much that phone lines were jammed, Mercury received thousands of complaints and had to pay out compensation.

Over redemption can also affect suppliers. In 1980 John Player decided to self-liquidate a cigarette lighter for £1, a massive saving. They expected a few thousand redemptions but received 2,250,000, which was bad news for everyone. The manufacturer, Ronson, was already struggling and this promotion drove this famous brand into liquidation. In addition, brand manager Stuart Nicholson found that he had upset retail tobacconists and that market share immediately returned to pre-promotional levels anyway.

Occasionally a promoting company gets an unexpected surprise at what redeems and how. In the Eighties, agency Masterguide produced an in-flight magazine called Sky Shop for British Caledonian airlines. It offered the usual branded knick-knacks, but to add a little glamour it was decided to include Janet Reger black lace cami-knickers. The photograph supplied and featured as a double page spread was suitably glamorous, but at a cost of around £90 the airline did not expect to sell many. In the first six months only one pair was sold, but one day the handling house received an order for three pairs from the same passenger. The gentleman was on his way back to South America and it seems that they were some kind of thank you gift. The interesting point was that they were to be sent to three different addresses around London.

NO ACCOUNTING FOR TASTE
Of course, under redemption can be a problem as well and brand managers have a knack of moving smartly on when their optimism for the popularity of a particular widget proves unfounded. One handling house had to dispose of 245,000 art prints left over from the order of 250,000 that the brand manager thought he would need. Another promotion for three months free private medical insurance was so unappealing that each redemption received cost £1,000 for four proofs of purchase worth 25p each. In the 70's a promotion for free ladies wigs unredeemed with a lot of stock left over. Never one to not turn a crisis into an opportunity, the industrious agency solved the problem by persuading three more brands to run free wigs promotions. The final stock was last seen being loaded on a ship bound for Israel.

In more recent times Avon Cosmetics had to rebuild its relationship with customers when a mobile phone promotion went pear-shaped. Anyone spending £15 or more on skincare products received a voucher for an Orange phone. Demand exceeded supply by 500 per cent and Avon tried to make amends with a 50 per cent discount on the new range. However it negated its good work by adding the words "subject to availability" to the offer. Given what had just happened, this was not exactly reassuring.

There have been lots of occasions where the number of prizes claimed was rather more than the promoter bargained for. Some were legitimate errors but in others security has failed. At the beginning of the Eighties, after legal lotteries were introduced into the UK, scratchcards became very popular. Some creative souls tried to find ways of making them have the necessary element of skill and so avoid the 'no purchase necessary' requirement. So were born the 'probability games'.

These differed from conventional scratchcards in that every card was a potential winner, whereas the conventional method produced a controlled number of winning cards. The probability game had a number of scratch off panels and if you selected the correct ones you were a winner. Within this arrangement there were two variations. If you simply selected your panels by chance there was no skill and no purchase could be required, If your selection required the use of an acceptable degree of skill a purchase could be required in order to obtain the card.

One interesting technique that was used by several major brands involved a photograph of some objects arranged on a surface and then photographed at a steep angle. Alongside this would be the vertical view of the same surface with a number of latex panels. The object of the exercise was to study the angled photograph and decide which of the latex panels concealed the objects laid out on the surface and shown on the perspective illustration. In addition, it was necessary to have a large number of different layouts because if you failed to accurately choose the correct panels you could scratch off the rest and find out which ones would have been the winners. This was considered skilful and required proof of purchase.

SCRATCH AND LOSE OUT

Typhoo Tea used a variation featuring teacups which ran into serious problems. It is said that some bright City traders discovered that there were around four thousand different cards and calculated that the cost of buying a large number of packs would be less than the potential return as each pack could win between £5 and £20. Even worse, it appeared to be legal and Typhoo had not limited how many prizes a household could win. The trick was to buy a large number of packs, scratch off all the latex and see where the targets were. Then when they found a matching card they knew which patches to remove. Cunning! We have heard it suggested they got a good ROI plus a lifetime's supply of tea.

One skilful version of the probability game that ran into trouble due to serious cheating was for a major petrol company. The cards had the usual latex panels, under which were letters in a random pattern. If you selected the correct letters to spell a particular word you won. Once again there were a large number of different layouts, all looking the same. Unfortunately the cards were all packed in the same sequence and forecourt staff at one garage cottoned on to this and scratched a complete set, so they knew exactly how to win with every card. They might have got away with it if they had not been too greedy.

One other promotion called Asda Cash that caught a cold, literally, was run by KLP. After extensive research, Asda and KLP chose a specialist printer in Heidelberg Germany to print special ink scratch cards which were produced in their millions. Unfortunately huge batches of the cards were printed on what weather forecasters claimed was the coldest recorded night on record in southern Germany. The print did not set properly and thousands of happy Asda customers could identify a winning card. Understandably, Asda was pretty cross with KLP, fired them and sued. KLP in turn sued the printer. KLP, as a fledgling public company had to announce to the stock market the loss of a major client. The shares dropped £5million overnight. In the end, the final settlement was relatively small after two years of lawyers – a lesson for quick settlement. Research from the stores showed some of the biggest sales uplifts that Asda had ever seen. It's an ill (cold) wind.

Clever and original ideas are great as long as nobody managed to screw up the logistics. When you combine a production error with some ambiguous copy a large dark hole can open under your feet. Goodyear had an idea based on a jigsaw of the Goodyear leopard. One piece was blanked out and printed separately. Customers were each given a piece of the jigsaw, and the holders of the limited missing pieces won a prize. However, not only were more blanks distributed than intended, but also copy stated: "If you have one of the missing pieces that fits the jigsaw you have won" and of course all the blank pieces fitted the jigsaw. There were rather more winners than anyone had bargained for.

Even the mighty Esso can get it seriously wrong. In 1985 it launched 'Noughts and Crosses', a game which was supposed to produce a £100,000 top prize winner. A printing error produced some 20 valid claims in the first few days. Esso withdrew the game after eight days, but the press speculated that it had cost them £4.5million. Interestingly, who remembers it now? Esso knew it had a problem and took fast action which kept bad PR to a minimum.

WHOSE IDEA IS IT ANYWAY?
In 1987 the promotion came back to haunt Esso when it was sued by J&H International for running 'Noughts and Crosses' and another promotion 'Find the Tiger' through Terry McCarthy's Product Plus company. The problem was that when he pitched the ideas to Esso in 1981 and 1983, McCarthy was working for J&H, which claimed the ideas and demanded £500,000 in lost revenue for each game. The cases were finally settled out of court in 1991 for a sum believed to be around £100,000.

J&H was not the only company that consulted their learned friends. In 1999 John Donovan, MD of Don Marketing, took Shell to court claiming that in 1990 he had responded to a verbal brief for a card-based multi-brand loyalty scheme for which Shell had paid a 'first refusal' fee. In 1992 it reconfirmed its interest. However, when Shell launched its Smart multi-brand scheme in July 1995, Don Marketing was not involved. With the law working at its usual snail's pace, the case finally reached court nine years later and it seems that Shell also settled out of court.

One vital little job that can screw things up if it is not done correctly is the random seeding of prizes throughout the complete production run so that no one knows where the winners are. Nestle Rowntree came unstuck with a Lion Bar promotion where 12 bars were worth a trip for two to New York. One family that bought eight bars were delighted to find they yielded eight trips to New York. The same company's Yorkie bar had a Great Days Out promotion that saw 50 winning bars dispensed by one vending machine, providing a really great day for the students of a local sixth form college.

One area with a particularly high risk factor is travel promotions, which remain hugely popular – sometimes too popular. In June 2004 the MKM Group, which specialised in travel and leisure promotions, joined the Stock Exchange's Alternative Investment Market (AIM). Three months later it announced that turnover was up by 19 per cent year on year. This was great news, but suddenly things went downhill, helped by an unwelcome appearance on BBC's Watchdog in October and a rap from the ASA. Problem promotions included free flights offers for BT Broadband and Gallo wines, where a huge demand created a backlog. Then a Daily Express offer of a seven-day cruise for £10 ran into trouble. It was not helped by the Caribbean hurricanes, while the Asian tsunami clobbered the company's attempt to launch a new worldwide flight voucher.

WERE WE INSURED?

At the end of the day, it sometimes pays to have invested upfront on some safety measures. FKB founder Chris Killingbeck had good reason to be grateful for a fixed fee insurance policy covering a promotion by the agency for KP called 'Magic Money'. Consumers had to mail in paper coins which were turned into the real thing, and it proved to be extremely magical going £83,000 over budget.

Similarly, Becky Munday, MD of risk management company Mando, was greatly relieved to have insured a 2004 Walkers Crisps pedometer promotion. Mando estimated a take up of 300,000 but was spectacularly wrong and ended up supplying two million. Happy client, happy Mando, unhappy insurance company.

CHAPTER SEVEN

Into the Seventies

Sales promotion comes of age
Tough times for promoters as the new decade kicks off
A new breed of SP agencies emerges
The lights go out on promotions
Your goldfish is in the post
Promoting SP – the campaign that never was
Beanz build houses – how Heinz reinvented the charity promotion
The ISP gets professional and education takes centre stage

After the excitement of the Sixties the next decade went downhill quite quickly, as did the length of skirts. Retail price inflation went above 10 per cent in 1971, dropped to around six per cent in 1972 but by 1974 was an eye-watering 25 per cent with interest rates following suit. By the end of the decade, inflation was still 22 per cent with unemployment having risen steadily throughout the 10 years. And we think that 2008 was tough!

Despite this, the sales promotion industry grew extremely quickly and launched a number of agencies and real characters. These gentlemen (women didn't make their mark until the late Seventies) would lead their various companies into the well-paid uplands of the next decade. However, for now the economy made starting a new business a daunting task.

THE COMING OF THE AGENCIES

As we said in the previous chapter, the end of the 1960s saw the birth of the sales promotion agency. Although in many cases they were referred to as consultancies, because they did not in fact act as an agent for the client in the way that an advertising agent did, we will use the agency description which is now generally accepted. In this chapter we will try and trace the growth of the more high profile members of this strange new creature as told to us by the people who were actually there at the time.

It really all started around 1968, about a year before KLP and Marden Kane, when Brian Francis (later to become the F in FKB) and Geoff Marshall got together under the wing of and funded by an advertising agency, Masius, Wynne-Williams. They set up shop as a handling house in Cox Lane, Chessington and John Farrell described them as a wild and wonderful company. Like many in new companies they did not always get the promise and the product absolutely in line when talking to potential clients. The basic promise was the "We can do anything." The product was "When we get the job we'll work out how to do it".

One early and memorable job was sold to RHM who wanted someone to handle the Bisto gravy boat offer. Great stuff, if you can get it, which they did, and we suspect that they felt they were just getting on the gravy train! Sorry, couldn't resist that. However, they also had a number of problems. Firstly, they had never handled a job of this size. Secondly, the drive to their warehouse was unfinished, and thirdly, the promotion was due in a very few weeks. They organised the tarmac on the drive and just managed to get it done the day before the first load of gravy boats was due to turn up on their doorstep. It also suddenly occurred to them that pallet loads of several hundred gravy boats could not be manhandled, but it needed a forklift truck.

This was a piece of kit that they did not have, but being resourceful types they nipped smartly down to the nearest hire shop and hired a forklift truck. Something else they did not have was the ability to drive one of these things, but Brian Francis took a quick driving lesson and thought he could probably cope. Somehow they got to truck back to the warehouse and the next day the lorry arrived with their first big job. The newly qualified forklift driver whizzed down the drive, managed to insert the forks under the pallet and pressed the lift button. With the drive just laid and still soft, instead of the forks and pallet going up, the truck with the thousands of Bisto gravy boats went down -- 9 inches into the soft tarmac. In the end they hired a very large forklift, plus a qualified driver, to lift the hired forklift out of the tarmac and return it, relatively undamaged, to the hire shop.

Things did improve a little after that and in 1970 the K of FKB, Chris Killlinbeck, joined the original partners, plus Mike Johnson, in Chessington. By 1979 the company was no longer a handling house, but had metamorphisised into an agency and left the shed on the industrial estate. They had moved on to a dashing suite of offices over a tailor's shop next to Bentalls in Kingston, and soon after the arrival of Chris they were soon to depart to Soho and reach a period of rapid growth. John Farrell did not join until 1980, when it had grown into a fully fledged agency and moved to Sherwood Street in London. He went on to lead International Marketing and Promotions (IMP) one of the biggest UK agencies, to of the exotic heights of running ARC, a major group, and even farther up the scale by being exported to the US where he was made President and CEO of S.A.M.S. Worldwide. The marketing services section of the French owned Publicis Groupe and involves up to 100 marketing services companies around the world. John has recently stepped down from this role which just shows how promotions can get you promoted.

At this point co-author Colin Lloyd sold his first promotion for the newly launched Cadburys Smash instant mashed potato, the perfect product for the modern busy housewives of the era. Boase Massimi Pollitt (BMP) had created the famous Martian commercial with tin alien creatures. The Brand Manager was Bob Bayley, who crops up in several later chapters. The promotion had a big budget and the brief was full of marketing speak which Colin felt was a bit beyond him. He consulted his Tetley Tea client, Robin Kingsland the Marketing Director, and that was the beginning of KLP.

Their first idea was Free Eyelure False Eyelashes, which were the big fashion item at the end of the swinging sixties. However there was some doubt about the mass appeal of false eyelashes so for safety's sake they added the safest promotion of the day, which guaranteed a high response, Free Tights. After some discussion the client thought they the offer had gone too far the other way and a third trendy item was added, disposable ladies paper knickers - under the alluring brand name of Chukka Pants which was newly launched by the London Rubber Company famous for its Durex brand. We have no idea how these proposals were researched, or at least neither of the people concerned are prepared to allow the facts to appear in print.

The product came is sachets of three and in white, pink and blue. The proposal document was revised and the Cadburys Smash Free Triple Offer of False Eyelashes, Tights and Chukka Pants accepted ecstatically by the client.

The offer was a huge success but there was one unexpected and tricky redemption from the Mother Superior of a Convent in Bedfordshire. She said that the sisters and she very much liked Cadburys Smash and had collected God knows (they may have meant this literally) how many pack ends to redeem for the Free Offer. Not the eyelashes or tights for our heavenly sisters. They wanted 40 strips of sachets of the Chukka Pants but kindly requested that they be in large and black.

In 1982 Brian Francis, the F in FKB, was the prime mover in starting that company. Sadly he died suddenly in 2003 and with his shoulder length hair and taste in exotic motors was one of the most charismatic characters in a business with more than its fair share of colourful characters. The 70's and 80's were a time when anyone with enthusiasm and entrepreneurial flair, quick wits and some original ideas could really make things happen. You did not need a degree. It is much harder today. Brian was joined by Chris Killingbeck, who had left IMP in 1974 to join a small ad agency called Shackle and Hamner, operating under the name Stowcastle Promotions based in Paddington Street, as their token sales promotion guy. It became rather more than a token job when he was joined by Peter LeConte and Nick Gale, names which no doubt we will come across again in this odyssey. He was lured back to IMP with a directorship, £13,000 a year and an Alfa Romeo. Almost as important was the promise to relocate in London. This was the point where John Farrell came on board, together with Robert James and Chris Satterthwaite. Two years later, FKB was formed.

To give you some idea of exactly what we mean by an odyssey, here is a brief résumé of Chris's activities from joining and starting FKB. Having expanded mightily and gone public in the 80s (which incidentally made the three founders quite wealthy, at least on paper) they, like the other publicly quoted SP agencies, other than KLP, got into serious financial problems. They were acquired by Carlson in 1990 and Chris stayed on for four years. At which point he started an agency called KCJB with Keith Johnston, Chris Cloughly and Nick Baggott. This became Manifesto and is now Chemistry. At the time of writing Nick Baggott is the only survivor of those founders still working there.

Chris Killingbeck then went freelance for a couple of years before starting Gasoline which is a joint-venture with Chime whose CEO is Chris Satterthwaite. Remember him? His partners include at least one other ex-FKB executive. We have to ask, where do they get these names from? We suppose it makes a change from strings of initials or endless names a la Ad. Agencies.

On the subject of initials, here is a list selected from the winning agencies in the 1987 ISP Awards: FKB, RRN, CPM, KLP, CBH, SPA, and CBA. Memorable aren't they. The craze for weird names came in the last few years. Here is a selection from 2006: 23red, bd-nwk, Swordfish, Toucan, Jellybean, iD, The Big Kick Company, Angel, iris, Grasshopper, Elvis, Tequila, Silverpop, Imano, Initials and Logistix They might not make much sense but at least you can remember them.

1971 was not a particularly good year for promotional activity, down 14 per cent from 1970. Half of the reduction came in price reductions. Competitions were down 20 per cent, coupons had dropped a massive 64 per cent, although the ever popular SLP was holding up. However, hard times suited SP.

It was still possible to promote cigarettes and a promotion by Rothmans for its Hallmark brand showed an interesting view on who they thought their customers were. The free gift collection offered a choice of one of three books on Football, Charles Dickens or Hallmarks. Maybe the obviously well read brand manager got a little carried away.

It was a good year for some people. The winner of the, as yet un-Chartered, Institute of Marketing annual award for 1971 was American Felix Mansheer, the chairman of Hoover. It was an auspicious year for Colin Hall and Keith Bantick who founded Promotional Campaigns, which went on to be a very successful agency.

DIFFERENT TIMES

It's easy to forget just how different life was almost forty years ago. The original idea of selling groceries at petrol stations was only hinted at by Marketing magazine in 1970. The big news in the petrol market was the introduction of self-service pumps, although Shell had just 50 on its 7,000-plus sites, most of them handing out up to ten times Green Shield Stamps.

Sales force incentives were being developed in a wider range of industries but for the moment tended to be trophies rather than holidays in the Bahamas. Lever Brothers' Salesman of the Year award started in the Sixties and the winner got a tie, gold cufflinks, a celebratory dinner and a small cheque. Apparently another disincentive was that it was always won by the same person. He must have amassed a nice selection of cufflinks and ties.

In 1970 Kellogg broke new ground with an impressive consortium promotion, claimed to be the largest ever run in Britain. They said it was "The most exciting thing the company has ever organised." In the previous year it ran 48 promotions, 12 more than any other company, so this was quite a claim. The offer, which was carried on Corn Flakes, involved 13 other brands providing a cash back for each product bought, on four or more different brands. Each had a value from 3p to 6p and if you bought the lot you earned a princely 42p.

SP was beginning to throw up some real characters such as Bob Bayley, a classic example of 'gamekeeper turned poacher' having been persuaded to leave Unigate for Marden Kane, despite a job offer at Mars. At 28 he had already worked in Unilever, Cadbury and Alberto Culver marketing departments, including a stint on Cadbury's Smash during its heyday when it had an advertising budget of £750,000. "It was a time when brand managers could do anything", he says.

The Mars job was worth £5,000 a year, an increase on his £3,500 at Unigate. On the strength of it he bought a second-hand TR6, despite being known as Cadbury's 'King Smash' having written off three cars in one year. How did he get insurance? However Marden Kane trumped Mars with the offer of a shiny new TR6, a move to attractive offices at Tattenham Corner overlooking the Derby course instead of the Slough Industrial Estate, and an opportunity to get involved in an aspect of marketing that appealed to him and seemed to be going places.

Bob was the account director who somehow persuaded 13 different marketing managers to agree to the activity. He managed the same trick with Persil a few years later, winning a major ISP award. That time he corralled 10 different manufacturers with a total cash refund of £3 and managed to persuade them to each offer a matching standard cash back of 30p whatever the product. Bob later cropped up at Option One via The Sales Machine.

If the carrier brand has sufficient clout it is much easier to pull this activity together. Retailers are in that position and in 1975 the Co-op used its two million daily home milk deliveries to put together a 20-brand consortium which, if you bought the lot, would reward you with one whole pound sterling. It ran another even more complicated multibrand promotion in-store for a free Easter egg, with a retail value of 50p. To get it, customers had to buy 12 brands of packaged food, cut out a portion of the label from each, and stick it on a collector card which could be exchanged for the egg. It was funded by the manufacturers, who must have been subject to some severe arm twisting.

THE NEW BREED

The Sales Promotion Executives Association had been founded in 1969 and started its SPEA Awards in 1970. The trophy was an elongated figure holding a spear - a visual pun on the name of the organisation. Glendenning collected two Golds for promotions on Total and BPC, the infamous British Printing Corporation, later to be seriously mistreated by Robert Maxwell. Other winners included McCann-Erickson, Crawford Advertising, Pearl & Dean, and David Williams & Partners.

Also winning was the oddly named The Mouse That Roared founded by Eric Clarke. An agency that Beechams' promotions manager Roger Johnson refused to deal with because "No way will I pass an invoice with that name on it to my accounts department." He later moved agency-side to Masterguide.

In 1971 Rank Screen Services was among the winners, as well as JWT, Harris International, Lintas and McCann-Erickson again. Almost half of the awards had been entered by the promoters. 1972 must have been the worst set of promotions ever entered as 14 of the 27 available were listed 'No Award'.

During this period, more and more money went below the line as advertising agencies ceded promotions for more attractive areas of brand building, strategy, and TV. The estimated spend on SP at the turn of the decade was between £400-500 million with a large proportion on POS, which was relatively unregulated by retailers at the time. Cardboard and self-liquidating merchandise were big business, so despite their derogatory view of SP, most ad agencies had a commitment below the line, usually through a subsidiary. JWT organised a meeting of all European executives with a sales promotion brief. It even had a head of merchandising, Jerry Coveny who later became managing director of Lansdowne Marketing.

FC&B had launched Underline, and Horniblow Cox Freeman had set up Sales Promotion & Merchandising. Brian Francis of FKB and Geoff Marshall learnt their trade in the premium buying department of Masius Wynn-Williams and Y&R also had such a department. Ex-Heinz marketer Tom O'Leary was of the view that self liquidators were a useful training ground for young marketing executives. "Nothing much can be lost, and nothing much will be gained," was a remarkably cynical view of someone who became chairman of SPEA.

A Marketing Society survey of promotional activity at the end of Sixties showed that SLPs were still popular with more than 3,000 running a year, second only to price reductions. The average value was about £1 and they helped obtain display in store, which led to good sales. Redemptions were a secondary issue. One offer that produced just 150 replies, succeeded in selling 200,000 packs. On the other hand a Typhoo Tea sun lounger offer shifted 250,000 units and launched the item as a must-have accessory for the garden.

A GEM OF A PROMOTION
There were some quite remarkable offers including an American company which offered an emerald, valued at £1,200 for just £800. It sold a lot of product but nobody redeemed the cut-price jewel. In one month 300 self liquidators were counted in one retail outlet. Heinz offered a range of savings on 57 different products, including Mini Minors, and sold more than 3,000 Colston dishwashers.

Despite this success, SLPs and other merchandise were not without their critics. A writer in Marketing claimed that the average office of a merchandise supplier was "Tawdry and run down, and littered with bits and pieces of merchandise". According to the scribe: "The merchandise companies occupy cheap warehouse space either somewhere beyond the North Circular Road or under railway arches in West London."

Presumably he was not referring to the very profitable divisions of ad agencies, whose offices were anything but tawdry. However, this negativity also raised questions about the long-term effect of promotions on brand image and raised a century-old spectre of the damage self liquidators were doing to the retail trade. Kodak and Polaroid were only just beginning to allow promoters to feature their products and the first to appear was the Kodak Instamatic on a Kellogg pack and on some Heinz products. The importance of acceptable partners was beginning to emerge.

Retailers were being swamped by promotions of this type. One supermarket chain was offered 700, out of which it would feature 40. The big supermarkets were not thrilled to bits about advertising promotions. David Morrell, speaking for Tesco, said that it was "a waste of money". Strangely, at the same time his company was using TV to support a free kite promotion, which sounds like a communication breakdown somewhere. Morrell also felt that below the line expenditure would be put to better use if retailers were taken into the manufacturer's confidence at an early stage, although not vice versa. But if manufacturers were pushing their promotions so forcibly that Tesco managers were overstocking, the culprits faced delisting, he added ominously.

Rugby international and now multimillionaire, Tony O'Reilly, who at that stage was still running Heinz in the UK, said that promotions were effective for short-term sales gains but in the long-term brands needed to keep up their media advertising. Occasionally promotions were advertised on TV, including one for Ovaltine which, with amazing generosity, offered a key ring. Beechams took the opposite approach, saying it preferred to advertise its products, not promotional items – in this case 25,000 cutlery sets.

Meanwhile advertising agencies were calling for a proper balance between above and below the line. It's hard to believe now, but some said that it could be more profitable if weighted towards merchandising, which must have led some of their staff to ponder setting up on their own.

The ever-popular pester power promotions were highly visible. In 1971 there were major programmes from Shell, Reckitt & Colman, Cadbury Schweppes and Bata Shoes. Shell's World Wildlife and Bata's Big Game campaigns picked up gongs at the 1972 SPEA awards. Chivers was running Shells of the World and the other Shell followed on with Great Britons, which gave away the cards at Shell stations and sold the album for 30p. This was very popular with history masters and the 'free cards but pay for the album' technique was very popular with promoters.

SP BUILDS BRANDS

On February 15, 1971 decimal currency was introduced in the UK. Out went the old, and in came the new penny, as well as a good deal of sneaky price inflation. For younger readers, "Old Money" was 240 pennies, 20 shillings (12 pence = 1 shilling) to the Pound. A typical price might be £1 17s 6p which could also be shown as 27/6p. Aren't you glad you grew up with decimals?

At around this time Quaker Oats, an enthusiastic user of SP, found that its Puffed Wheat brand had gone into a long-term sales decline under pressure from new products, most of which added sugar and were aimed at children. The brand could not really afford heavyweight media advertising so decided on the SP route. Initially it tried to modernise and in 1971 linked with a kids' space adventure. This did not do too well so Quaker decided to return to its roots after its agency, The Sales Machine, suggested using the 17th-century Puritan or Quaker logo. This emphasised that the brand was simple, wholesome, natural and lacking in sugar and was 20 years ahead of its time in stressing what the brand didn't have as opposed to what it did.

The first 'Mr Quaker' was a Toby Jug, which was offered at half price and widely distributed as a gift to the retail food trade by the Quaker sales force. It was the beginning of a long-term programme of Mr Quaker products which included a sugar shaker, eggcups, salt and pepper pots, a money box, and even the oddly-named Mr Quaker Happy Waker alarm clock which hopefully was not misspelled. This approach took the brand through to 1978, and turned a 15 per cent annual decline into an increase of the same amount. Mr Quaker is an excellent example of what well-targeted and considered SP can do for a brand.

In terms of longevity however it would be hard to beat Brooke Bond's PG Tips and its stream of picture cards, which started in 1952 when tea came off rationing. It all began with a 20-card British bird series. By 1978 it was still going strong, having covered 30 different subjects including trees, flags, aviation, cars, space travel, prehistoric animals, explorers, inventors, costumes, ships, famous people and soccer tips. For many years PG sold the collecting albums (they cost 8p in 1975) with a peak year of 1968 when it shifted 2.4 million copies for the 'History of the Motorcar'. They even had their own highly specialised printer in Reading churning out the cards.

However, within 10 years sales had dropped to 750,000 and Brooke Bond started giving the albums away on a 'buy one take one' basis (a BOTO, not to be confused with a BOGOF). But did tea cards work from a promotional point of view? Well, in 1973 the Brooke Bond brands held more than 40 per cent of the tea market and 70 per cent of PG Tips buyers bought only that brand in a six-month period. These loyal buyers accounted for 34 per cent of all purchases. The figures for the major competitor were 11 per cent and 25 per cent respectively.

Not all promotions relied on such long-running themes. Sometimes an opportunity arose that served as a promotional hook. In 1972 Watney Mann introduced litre-sized bottles of various brands, including Guinness, for the take-home market. They had no advertising budget, but a nod to metrication and the EEC served it well in the form of a self-liquidator for a litre glass. It was the biggest ever glass provided in any promotion and, backed by POS and trade promotion, got enormous publicity. In total 4,000 outlets participated and sales forecasts were exceeded by 30 per cent on a minute budget.

Also new was the first 4-bit '404' microprocessor, produced by Intel in 1971, with the first video game, 'Pong' beeping along in 1972. In the same year Cosmopolitan was telling women they had a right to lots of orgasms, plus useful hints on how to get them. At the same time Blue Ribbon Sports became Nike and introduced its 'Swoosh' logo. The next year commercial radio arrived and the UK's first McDonald's opened in Woolwich.

TAXES UP, SALES DOWN

The introduction of VAT in 1973 did nothing to increase consumer spending. The SPEA set up a working party and organised a seminar on VAT and promotions, which unfortunately confused more than it enlightened. Prizes up to £10 did not carry VAT but over that figure they did. If you employed a demonstrator the cost had some but not all VAT elements. Most of the services supplied by an agency would carry VAT but not all if quoted separately. More than 30 years later VAT is still as confusing as ever. On the other hand the government did bring in the Fair Trading Bill, which was intended to improve the consumer's lot.

Travel incentives were the big growth area. British Airways even had an incentive advisory service and Thomas Cook was marketing its travel vouchers at prices from £2-10. At the time you could have a week's package in Ibiza for £60. Thomas Cook proudly reported that one client had bought £100,000 of vouchers, which would translate to more than 800 such holidays for two people. With sales forces numbered in the hundreds, this purchase does not sound so ridiculous.

The serious money in producing merchandise in the first half of the Seventies came from the petrol forecourt. World Cup Coins by Esso increased its market share by 19 per cent. However the premature departure of the England team rather reduced the overall impact. 'Man in Flight' coins by Shell followed along with various other themes. There were busts of footballers and figurines celebrating heroes of one sort or another. And then there were always glasses, glasses and more glasses.

However it was Marathon Oil in the US that took glass promotions to a new level. It offered free Apollo Moon Mission glasses with a minimum of 10 gallons of 'gas' and ran the promotion for Apollo 11, 12 and 13 with up to 98 per cent of service stations taking part. In the first six weeks promotion it claimed to have given away enough glasses to reach the Apollo 11 in earth orbit, with 20-30 per cent sales increases. Apollo 12 saw sales go up another five per cent.

When Apollo 13's potential disaster was leading every TV news channel, Marathon simply switched to 'A Safe Return' as the theme. The near disaster proved a triumph for the oil company. Sales increased a further five per cent and it gave away the same number of glasses as the first two promotions combined. Finally, Marathon gave away 520 miles worth of tumblers, which is around 6,000,000 glasses. It even self-liquidated 4,000 sets of eight tumblers for anyone who had not managed to collect enough. They were probably abroad or in prison at the time!

For a change from glasses, there were steak knives, which in those days were not a fashion accessory for school kids. Then came a whole range of 3-D cards, followed by 'change' cards. They both used a lenticular lens which was a patent held by Japanese printer, Toppan. These changed the picture as it was moved, sometimes producing the effect of something travelling across the card. The sole UK agent was a Unilever subsidiary called Austin Packaging, and as the average order was 40 million cards, this turned out to be an unexpectedly profitable sideline. So profitable in fact that it was normal practice for anyone who could come up with a good excuse to have an expenses paid trip to Japan where they might squeeze in a visit to the factory.

One particular job required the client, plus representatives from Austin and the promotions agency, to travel to Tokyo to 'pass the proofs'. On arrival they were met by a very polite Japanese printer. With a good deal of bowing, he stressed the company's deep regret that the proofs were not quite ready, handed them tickets to Honolulu with a booking for a hotel on Waikiki Beach, and said they would be called when the proofs were ready. We don't think the team was waiting for the phone call with any eagerness. Somehow, all this cost was lost in the overall bill.

THIS ONE WILL REALLY FLY

There was something of a feeding frenzy among the SP agencies, desperate to get their hands on these great chunks of merchandise. Such was the potential of the forecourt promotions that it paid Marden Kane to fly a petrol company executive to a glass factory in France in a private plane. The agency MD, Graham Morse, remembers that the trip almost came to an unfortunate end when the lady pilot was unable to find the factory and had everyone on board helping her look for it.

The agency put together around eight alternative forecourt promotions that they hoped they might sell to somebody. In those pre-PowerPoint days, presentations were made on large boards with montages of photographs, magic marker lettering and so on. They were referred to as Visual Aids or VAs for short. To save time and expense each had a detachable company logo, which was simply switched to match the company at whom the pitch was aimed. It was a good idea to get this right, otherwise the effect might be lost on the prospective client. This sort of thing did happen.

Simon Mahoney of SMP recalls travelling to Paxo with a beautifully written flip chart presentation. Having made the long journey to delightful downtown Uxbridge, he set it up and got the client's full attention before turning over the cover sheet to reveal a very nice proposal for Galloway's Cough Syrup. He was stuffed!

Many of the promotional ideas we take for granted now started in the Seventies. 'Free film' became extremely popular and Ian Fryer of Heinz claims the first promotional use. The Film Corporation of America ran a programme where proof of purchase could be exchanged for a film, which could be sent for paid processing and the prints returned with another free film. Initially the company flew the exposed films to the US to print as no high-speed processing plants were available in the UK.

Bounty packs for new mothers were also new and a competitor and MultiLink launched in

1971. There was also a pack for engaged couples called The Home Advisory Service. As well as mass marketing there was the occasional upmarket effort, such as one related by Edward Fulbrook, at the time marketing director of LinkDirect. In 1973 he was organising a promotion for Luis Gordon's rather posh Graham's Port brand. It offered the prize of a portrait in oils by a relatively unknown painter called Michael Noakes, plus sketches for the runners up. Since then his sitters have included HM the Queen. It's not often a promotional prize increases in value, so let's hope the winner liked it enough to still have it.

These were the days before promoters had either a PC on their desk or political correctness on their backs. The fax was probably a typing error for "the facts", and most overseas communication was done on a Telex. Mobile phones were science-fiction, and you could get an experienced account director for £5,000 a year and a top of the range Ford Capri. Experience meant time in the marketing department or having sold promotions to various clients. But in fact, very few of the leading lights in the agency business came from a marketing background, the majority having worked in sales and a few in advertising before deciding that sales promotion offered the possibility of setting up their own business. It was cheaper than launching an ad agency and many SP agencies started as one-man bands.

SP BESIDE THE SEASIDE
The year 1971 saw an Incentive Marketing Exhibition which apparently only dealt with premium merchandise. It had moved around London hotels under various names before establishing itself in Brighton by 1973 with 73 exhibitors, including two SP agencies, the Henry Goldsmith Organisation and Rawlinson's Advertising. The show was backed by the magazine Incentive Marketing and Sales Promotion and one of the high spots that year was the introduction by Snowball Sports of a really original idea which they said was, "The novel and potentially very successful idea of a T-shirt with a message printed on the front." They were right! Pity then didn't patent it. This was also the year in which the BPMA launched its periodical with the very creative title of BPMA News.

SP's Mr Exhibition is Ian Allchild, whose usually bearded, but sometimes clean-shaven face has been a fixture at just about every show since he joined as sales manager for both the exhibition and the magazine in 1975. One aspect of the show in Brighton, which has long since disappeared, was the Sunday family day, which allowed both visitors and exhibitors to bring their wives and children to Brighton for the day. This also meant that the visitors were wandering around the show casually dressed.

Exhibitors are of course quite keen to hand out various goodies to potential customers, but it was hard to tell who was who. Women in particular had a tendency to rummage around stands looking for items they liked. On one particular occasion an exhibitor was getting extremely cross with a lady until she said casually: "Oh, I think it's my husband you need to speak to. He is the marketing manager for the Milk Marketing Board." To which the stallholder broke into his most ingratiating smile and said: "Please help your self Madam."

Another feature of those more laid-back days was the habit of buyers to spend one or two days and therefore nights in Brighton, which led to a fairly hectic social life. There were lots of dinners, parties and some serious and late-night drinking, together with well-founded rumours of late-night swimming in hotel pools, often without the benefit of swimsuits. Brighton also lived up to its reputation for extramarital activity with many tales of bedroom swapping or rooms booked as a single somehow turning into a double during the show.

Ian Allchild often found himself lending an alibi for people pursuing activities which they were anxious not to publicise. If the numbers who claimed to have a meeting with 'the organiser' were true, then his office would have been huge. No doubt such helpfulness served him in good stead when exhibitors were considering rebooking. 'Brighton' as it was usually called, continued until 1983 when Ian launched the renamed Incentive '84 and moved to the Barbican, a site that the present descendant of the show returned to in 2006.

THE LIGHTS GO OUT

The low point of the decade was the energy crisis in 1974, when the miners' strike reduced Britain to a three-day working week. If you are younger than say, 30, you may find it hard to imagine most of the lights going out for most of the working week, but they did. The good times of the Sixties had come to a very sudden end. John Hooper remembers it only too well. His biggest client was Esso and it cut every promotion. In the long run the three-day week did give an opportunity for sales promotion to prove its worth, although this was not initially apparent.

With the supply of goods and raw materials becoming problematical, the ability of sales promotion to provide quick, short term solutions was appreciated by many companies. It also allowed Marden Kane UK to negotiate a very attractive buyout from its American parent. As the then chairman, the late Graham Paul said: "When you are negotiating to buy a company off its American owner, working in a British lawyer's office lit by candlelight, you tend to get away with a lower offer. It certainly did not make our prospects look particularly bright."

Marden Kane promptly celebrated their new found independence by running a 'Spot the Ball' competition for Courage's Colt 45 brand. By a stroke of irony, the product was an American import and the entry form used photographs of American football, basketball and baseball. Spot the Ball had just been declared legal in a major court case and this was the first commercial application. It obviously caught the consumer's imagination as it received 1,000,400 entries.

In the years that followed there were many versions of Spot the Ball used by brands and many of the national newspapers used revenue-earning Spot the Ball newspaper competitions. Over time the item to be spotted had many manifestations - including Spot the Beach Ball, a popular variation because the photograph include a number bikini clad beauties instead of hairy footballers. There was Spot the Sheep Dog and Spot the Sun but perhaps the most bizarre was part of the KLP launch of Fosters Lager in 1986. To embrace Fosters antipodean heritage a Spot the Boomerang competition was launched. In order to comply with the law an expert was needed to identify the position on a picture where, in their opinion, the boomerang would be. The expert chosen was the UK's leading anthropological aboriginal professor at Hornimans Museum in South London. When, after the initial approach, she had gathered herself from falling about laughing she was convinced that it was a hoax. However, a contribution to the museum repair fund convinced her otherwise and she duly placed a cross on the photograph.

1974 also saw the launch of what is almost certainly the UK's most successful use of promotional techniques to support brand image. The Andrex puppy started out in 1974 as a charity promotion by KLP. The best estimate to date is that in one form or another over 3milion puppies have been bestowed on grateful consumers. This original promotion and its successors are thought by some people to be better then Shell's Make Money. KLP kept the business for a number of years before it moved to Bluechip, and then SMP. The puppy is one of the most recognisable promotional images in Britain, rivalled only by the Dulux dog and the PG Tips monkeys. Perhaps novelty, originality and constant change is not necessarily the best way to promote a brand. It is also worth remembering the public love of animals which leads to another little story of the time.

A relatively small-scale promotion in 1974 attracted a good deal of unexpected and unwelcome attention for Chivers jellies. A series of promotions were based on collecting real things, and as coins, shells, rocks and fossils 'had legs' it was decided that live goldfish would be the next iteration. The agency, KLP went to considerable trouble to make sure that the goldfish would arrive in good condition. In return for the appropriate proof of purchase, 250,000 goldfish were mailed out in small plastic bags, with oxygen pumped in under pressure. They also provided a leaflet on the proper care of goldfish and went to considerable trouble to make sure that the recipients were at home when the fish was delivered. A few did not make it. Unfortunately animal rights, or perhaps fish rights, enthusiasts decided to kick up a fuss and succeeded in getting media coverage. At least they did not attack the handling house and release the goldfish into a nearby stream, where they might have made a tasty snack for the minks released by some other enthusiastic activist.

Up to this time trains had not figured in many promotions, although train tickets later became a hot promotional item for both Kellogg and Lever Brothers. However in 1972 Kimberly-Clark wanted to run a promotion for Kleenex aimed at moving away from price cuts and special trade terms. It planned to run a consumer competition, and what took place demonstrates the way manufacturers and retailers related to each other in those days of big sales forces and less centralised buying.

Kimberly-Clark wanted to persuade the trade that the promotion was a big deal. Its agency, The Sales Machine, came up with the Kleenex Bullion Train, which was a British Rail security carriage painted gold and branded as an Aladdin's cave of consumer prizes, plus a huge stack of dummy gold bullion bars. This experiential event was not designed for the consumer but for the trade who boarded at various railway stations throughout Britain. When they had seen the prizes, buyers moved into the restaurant car where drinks were served by the Kleenex Bullion girls wearing, you've guessed it, gold miniskirts.

Having been softened up buyers were then expected to place, on the spot, an above average order based on the expected increase in sales. Buyers also agreed to display the products in an agreed format to qualify for a draw to win a real gold bar. A total of 1,373 store managers took part. The train had to travel around Britain and Kleenex entertained 138 different trade buyers. How many buyers would be needed to deliver those stores today? And how many stores would display the product as requested, just for a chance to win an individual prize and without a large cash incentive? The results were impressive with initial sales 19 per cent up on Kleenex for Men, toilet tissue sales up 17 per cent, and kitchen towels 20 per cent more.

TOP OF THE LEAGUE

As now, football was the major spectator sport, but the players were not earning multi million pound salaries. John Hooper, in his new found situation at Scott International, had a useful contact with Bobby Moore who suggested the players most likely to be picked for the 1974 World Cup squad. They were then approached individually and offered a series of payments for their exclusive appearance in promotions run by John and his team. This was £1,000 to sign up, another £1,000 if the team qualified for the finals and a massive £5,000 in the event of them winning. They probably would not even sign an autograph for that sort of money these days. It was so attractive that they signed up 29 of the 30-man squad. It worked so well that John Hooper went to Germany and did the same thing with the West German squad. Only two things went wrong with this scheme. Firstly, England failed to qualify which meant £29,000 was wasted and secondly Germany won, but just about every promotional technique you have ever heard of was illegal in Germany. Good try though.

About this time John Hooper and Barry Clark decided that life at Scott International, comfortable though it was, was not sustainable. They decided to do their own thing and reckoned that they needed £15,000. They linked up with a design group called Quorum, one of whose partners was Steve King, later of Senior King. Although the initial deal was far from generous, the operation was so successful that they bought out most of the other partners in a year or so. Mr King had the good sense to stay with them and walked away with £350,000 or so when Clarke Hooper Ltd was floated on the London Stock Market in the Eighties.

Along with Kellogg, Heinz was one of the most prolific promoters and its copy was truly 'puntastic'. Apart from the ability to get 57 into almost anything, other promotions of the period boasted 'Souper Tasting Soups' and 'Win a Heinz Souper Trip'. When the M6 was being built it came up with 'Heinz Spaghetti Junction' together with 'When It Shines It Pours .....' for salad cream. Football fans could enjoy 'A Fan-tastic' World Cup competition, and elsewhere they boasted 'What Pretty Pickles', 'An Offer the Family Could Hardly Refuse' for spaghetti and 'Harvest a Holiday' for tomato ketchup.

By the mid Seventies, SP agencies and consultancies were increasingly churning out such bubbly copy, and helping to expand the perception and importance of SP as a modern marketing practice. Initially the majority of revenue came from the supply of premiums, prizes and print, but the concept of charging fees was taking off. Retained fees were still a rarity, with agencies such as Glendenning and The Sales Machine leading the way. Still, many clients were reluctant to pay fees as they found even the concept of SP difficult to justify.

In the middle of this process was the sales promotions manager who spent a lot of his time defending his position against brand managers. Agencies had a love-hate relationship with them. They could block ideas they did not like but did not have the authority to spend budgets on those of which they approved. However, if these gatekeepers liked an idea, it had a chance, but no chance at all if they didn't. Today the interjection of the procurement manager tends to have a similar effect.

THE HISTORY MAKERS

Brian Francis

Barry Clarke OBE

John Hooper CBE

Jeremy Sandys-Winsch

Brian Marshall

Tim Arnold

Colin Hall

Keith Bantick

Graham Morse

Ken Spedding

Robin Kingsland - Colin Lloyd - Chris Petersen

CHAPTER EIGHT

The rest of the Seventies

Making sales promotion respectable
Rude wallpaper
The original Doctor Who scores
Brussels stirs up trouble
The Year of the Child
There are all sorts of pitches.

By the late Seventies, this craving for respectability was spreading like an epidemic. It was at this time that Christian Petersen of KLP and ex-founder of The Sales Machine started demonstrating his eccentricity. Having spent one summer quantifying promotion expenditure in the UK, he announced to the world that in the mid Seventies, £10billion was spent by UK industry on discretionary promotions. What he did not flag up was that 95 per cent were in the form of price promotions, which the agency world had little control over. The £10billion claim sent reverberations around the industry and most of the agencies loved the idea that they were such big hitters.

Another 'eureka' moment from Chris led to the claim that there was no agency in the UK bigger than KLP at the time. Chris decided that sales promotion needed to promote itself in a planned and systematic way and as the industry's self-appointed 'brand leader' his company had a duty to do something about it. The answer was to mount a generic promotion campaign promoting promotional marketing to the marketing fraternity. It was bold, correct for the time and of course doomed to failure.

Never one to let logic and barriers get in the way of a good idea, Chris, felt-tipped pen in hand and layout pad to the ready, started work on the campaign to change promotional marketing forever. Out of the KLP machine came a series of concepts designed to loosen client pursestrings and make promotional practitioners feel like they worked in advertising agencies. KLP then had the task of selling these concepts to the competitor agencies that by now hated them over the No.1 claim. The greatest challenge was to get them to contribute to the cost of the campaign; an alien experience for agencies if ever there was one.

THE MAGNIFICENT SEVEN

As Chris could be a bit antisocial, Robin Kingsland had to get the competitors together. However, budgets and Robin were not good bedfellows and he decided that a classy black tie event at The Savoy was called for. Understandably, there was not one single refusal to a free dinner at The Savoy. However KLP liked to think that it was the first time that the heads of the major agencies had ever been in the same room together, let alone to discuss the industry. It was another recipe for disaster, of course.

Once they had got though the splendid fare, introductions were made and Chris set out to create a fevered passion around the campaign to change the face of promotional marketing. It was a case of light the blue touch paper and retire immediately. Never in the history of marketing had so few had so many opinions about strategy, tactics, creativity and copywriting. In half an hour of heated opinion, the master plan was in tatters. Perhaps the coup de grace was when Robin had the audacity to ask the assembled guests to part pay for the campaign. When they got their breath back the laughter could be heard as far as Mayfair.

Over the ensuing years, they and many others have become good friends, but at the time there were some seriously bruised egos. However, the aftermath brought a phenomenon that lasted for the next 25 years. The Savoy experiment brought together a goodly selection of the industry for the first time. Before everyone's dinner was ruined by the campaign idea, the conversation was convivial, amusing and there was a great deal of healthy dialogue.

At the end of the evening, Brian Francis, then of IMP, had the idea that there should be another dinner organised by another agency. And so the agency leaders dining club was inaugurated. It lasted for another decade and the fabric of the promotion industry was laid in those evenings. John Hooper euphemistically called the group 'The Magnificent Seven' and thus a legend was born. Or it would have been if anyone outside of the group knew it existed. In the latter years it became the birthplace for the Sales Promotion Consultants Association (SPCA), latterly the Marketing Communications Consultants Association.

SP SPREADS ITS WINGS

Another interesting development during the mid-70s was the spread of promotional activity outside the traditional FMCG market. P&G and Unilever-trained marketers were moving into publishing, furniture, banks, housing, engineering, travel, sport and service industries. They introduced the techniques they had learnt, and began to use SP and its practitioners. Banks at this time were seriously uncompetitive, all offering the same rates, fixed centrally, and opening seemingly at their own convenience. They began to employ marketing people, although it was said that banks had marketing departments in the same way as bathrooms had bidets. They all had one, but nobody really knew what it was for.

Even the highly-conservative book publishers were getting into the act, led by the less conservative Hamlyn's, who splashed out £80,000 on a 'Win a Hamper' scheme. In groundbreaking style it ran a major door-to-door coupon drop carrying a couple of lucky numbers that consumers checked in local bookshops. It was pretty basic stuff but at the time was considered very radical for a publisher.

There were one or two oddball promotions around this time. The most far out was in 1976 for Parozone bleach, by Jeyes. It was not exactly a high profile product, so something had to be done to justify a little more display. The idea from The Sales Machine, which surprisingly the client bought, was 'Parozone Lively Loo Wallpaper'. Jeyes did not expect to supply many rolls of specially-designed wallpaper covered in cartoons by the well-known cartoonist Larry. Produced by Sanderson, this sold at a self-liquidating price to postal applicants. The POS even obtained some gondola end displays, and the cartoons, being mildly rude, were picked up by the media for lots of free publicity, and Jeyes sold a lot of bleach.

FIVE RING PROMOTIONS
1976 was an Olympic year. The IOC had not, at this time, threatened to execute with extreme prejudice anyone running vaguely Olympic-related activity, so there were lots of Olympic promotions. One advantage they had over European or World Cup Football was that there were certain to be some British athletes taking part and even winning medals. A typical effort was Shell's Olympic promotion which had gone international across Europe. It had an album with clear plastic pages on which sticky cut-out athletes could be positioned doing their thing. You could have lots of fun with the gymnasts of both sexes.

Rothmans took a simpler approach by providing a 'bung' of £30,000 to the British Olympic Committee, subject to smokers dropping proof of purchase in collection boxes at tobacconists across the country. Connecting smoking to the Olympics - try that today!

Some of the promotions being run in one month in 1976 could be echoed today. Typhoo Tea had linked up with Doctor Who and there were a lot of sports-orientated promotions. Cadbury's Olympic Book and several other promotions with an Olympic theme were still going strong. Football, ladies golf, fishing and tennis all had promotional links, and Shredded Wheat was backing World Sport Superstars, which covered cricket, ice-skating, soccer, athletics, boxing and show jumping.

Of course, there were also lots of competitions. In that month, you could win 50 stereo record players, 200 portable cube radios, 300 watches, £30,000 cash from various brands, free whisky for life (a prize that probably shortened the winners life, so reducing the cost to the promoter!), £20 a day from a radio station, 2,000 Swing Balls, camera kits and binoculars, a holiday in Trinidad, four days at a world fishing championship, a British Leyland Mini, a £2,000 holiday, a caravan, 25 Hoover washing machines, and a child's bicycle.

Card collections were also the flavour of the month, including Shredded Wheat's world sports programme, Doctor Who, football with the then England manager Don Revie, martial arts and nature cards. And of course the free tights from four different companies. On another level, the prize of a flight to the US on Concorde was a hardy perennial for years. Overall, there were 125 separate promotions in just one month, which is a pretty good indication of just how active sales promotion was.

By 1977 the march of the big grocery retailers was well underway, although by 21st century standards it was still very fragmented. There were 182 large general food retailers with 8,000 outlets and a turnover of £4.6 billion. Conventional grocers numbered 57,000 managing a turnover of £3.25billion. Buying had become much more centralised and the sales forces had been greatly reduced.

In the Sixties Tim Arnold was one of 600 Birds Eye salesmen calling on corner shops and the relatively new Tesco. By the mid-Seventies this would be reduced by 90 per cent and nowadays it is probably down to one per cent of that number. It was still possible to run major national promotions and there were some very large budgets around. For instance, Pedigree Petfoods ran a competition across all its brands with a budget that included £500,000 worth of prizes.

CHARITY BEGINS IN-STORE

It was around this time that charity promotions, which later were upgraded to cause related promotions (CRP), became highly visible. The Sixties 'Launch a Lifeboat' programme for Birds Eye almost certainly introduced the idea and numerous promotions on these lines have followed. The biggest and possibly one of the best was run in 1976 by Heinz. The original brief was for something to counteract the rising power of the retailers. Ian Fryer wanted a promotion that was so powerful that the retailers would just have to accept it.

The budget was £300,000 with half allocated to media support and the promotion was to run in September and October. Heinz went for the charity idea, so the first task was to find a suitable charity. At the time quite a few of the higher profile charities turned the idea down as being beneath their dignity. We suspect that they lived to regret that decision. In the end, the smaller National Children's Homes was only too pleased to get involved. At that time £100,000 would build a new home, so they were very attracted by the idea of using then high profile TV personality Ed "Stewpot" Stewart to front a campaign to generate the money at 1p per label.

The promotion was a massive success with 20 million labels returned. If the contribution had not been capped at £100,000 it would have cost Heinz twice that amount. Along with the promotion, a number of tailor-made schemes were run to purchase the extras for the home. One of the research questions related to fitting out the homes and in particular paying for a TV set or two. Consumers were quite in favour of this as long as it was black and white. It would seem that they felt that colour was too good for orphans.

This was just the first of a series of blockbuster charity promotions run by Heinz. In 1977 it ran an almost identical promotion. Oddly, very few of the respondents who could recall the promotion could recall the name of the charity, just that it was to build a children's home. The 1p per label approach was popular and it was even suggested that the £100,000 target be increased to £150,000, a finding that Heinz took on board. As the research showed little, if any, recall of the advertising, Heinz did away with the media support and made better use of the money below the line. Good news for Clarke Hooper and Co. The promotion proved another success and the label contribution went up to 27 million.

THE EUROPEAN FRONT

There are some things that never seem to change. In 1976 the press told us that the bureaucrats in Brussels were burning the midnight oil to speed up the slow progress towards harmonisation of the laws regulating promotions in the nine countries that then made up the EEC. They all used SP techniques but each had its own laws of unfair competition, which were the ones that seem to apply to sales promotion. Generally speaking these laws, originally intended to protect the retailer, are complex and much more restrictive than in the UK. It was felt that not only did the retailer need protecting but so did the consumer.

The UK had a higher opinion of their consumers and much less restrictive laws. If the planned harmonisation was to be based on the other European laws, the legal constraints placed would seriously and adversely affect British manufacturers and consumers. As far as the UK was concerned, fundamental and radical changes would have to be made in order to enforce these laws of unfair competition and a harmony of freedoms would not be easy to create, induce and control. Fortunately, as we have said, more than 30 years later we are no nearer being burdened by the dictate of Brussels, in this area at least.

The year 1977 saw a great surge of patriotism as the nation celebrated the Queen's Silver Jubilee. Premium manufacturers could sell almost anything as long as it had either a silver finish, a photograph of the Queen or preferably both. The whole thing gave a very useful lift to the spirit of the hard-pressed Brits in what was otherwise not a great decade.

Lyons Tetley wanted to get into the act with Typhoo Tea and briefed Clarke Hooper to come up with something suitable. With a certain degree of low cunning it came up with an EPMS silver-plated teaspoon. These appeared to be remarkably good value mainly because most people, probably including the SP manager Jack Trigg, read it as EPNS which translates as electroplated nickel silver. EPMS on the other hand actually means electroplated mild steel which is considerably cheaper. Another useful trick on the same lines is to ask for a self addressed envelope or SAE because a large majority of people will send you a stamped addressed which will make a considerable saving on postage costs. Cunning lot these sales promotion people.

FIXED FEES ARRIVE

Something else that happened in 1977, with a lower profile but with long-lasting effect, was the launch of the first fixed fee company, Mando, then an American owned photo-processing company. It offered free film and such like for on-pack programmes for a fixed fee and took the risk at a time when over redemption insurance didn't exist. In 1980 Mando included any consumer proposition and in due course photography was dropped. Fotorama was a breakaway from Mando and in 2006 became part of Motivcom, which is a successful public company, previously called P&MM.

Around this time another massive promotion, still fondly remembered by a few old people such as the authors, was run by Lever Bros. It had seen the success of Kellogg's free child rail ticket promotions run on a one-to-one basis with an adult ticket purchase. Lever went one better and persuaded BR do a BOGOF for adult tickets. The promotion was carried on Persil with a good deal of media and POS support, but proof of purchase from Shield soap and Comfort was acceptable. Lever Bros was keen on multibrand promotions of this type with the big Persil pack as the carrier, and anyone who worked on them will remember the 'logo wars' between the competing brand managers measuring the number of square millimetres each brand got.

It is said that when Unilever allocated graduate trainees to group companies, the most competitive were sent to Lever Bros, with the most cunning and manipulative selling margarine. In 1975-76 the first of the big 2 for 1 promotions grossed £1.4million and had a net revenue of £330,000 for British Rail. When in 1984-85 Persil ran the third version it actually placed the travel voucher inside the large pack. It also included European destinations and produced revenue of £9 million.

Planning it took two and a half years so it was most unlikely that the same brand manager would have seen it through, as the turnover at the Kingston office was famously rapid and often included a stint as promotions manager. On occasions a promotion would be briefed by one manager, run by a second and the results would end up on the desk of a third. There was little continuity and often, in fact usually, the agency knew more about the brand than the brand manager.

The Free Rail Tickets scheme was supported to the tune of £500,000 and was remarkably successful. British Rail received almost five million applications and if you asked someone what they might be doing at the weekend, it is quite likely that they would say that they were 'Going on a Persil'. Years later something similar was run for Boots but by then the railways were privatised and fragmented and it was impossible to put together such a wide ranging offer. How the agency got round this you will see in a later chapter.

Later in this decade, 1979 was designated The Year of the Child by UNICEF and a number of charity linked promotions were run. One unusual and possibly unique initiative was that UNICEF and Oxfam combined under the banner of 'Together for Children'. This was coordinated by Masterguide with other agencies running promotions under licence. Radio One was a great supporter and the year culminated in a sell-out pop concert at Wembley Arena. The finale was Cat Stevens, as he was then known, singing Morning has Broken with a choir of multiracial children. Not a dry eye in the house. There were lots of other one-offs such as an attempt to launch the world's largest balloon race and the non-stop walking record. Even the National Railway Museum at York got in on the act with the largest ever sale of railway relics.

COLLECTOR CONTROVERSY

In the past few years, collection schemes that turned proof of purchase into items for schools have been very popular. Like many current promotional techniques, this is not a recent invention. Heinz ran a classic version called The Schools Foundation from the late Seventies into the Eighties. Using the cumbersome tag line of 'Help Your School Get the Things It Needs' and fronted by footballer Kevin Keegan, complete with serious hair, dark at the time. Schools could obtain a wide selection of items including musical instruments and chess sets apart from the more obvious sporting gear.

Like a more recent scheme by Cadbury, it faced a PR problem. First of all the opposition Labour Party had a go with leader Michael Foot attacking the scheme in parliament as an example of what was happening due to underfunding. He suggested that in no time the public would be collecting packet tops to buy tanks for the army – this might do well today. The media then got in on the act, pointing out that the top item - a minibus - required several million packs to be returned. The idea was for groups to get together in order to achieve this but the BBC's popular news programme Nationwide presented it as a total rip-off.

Heinz was not used to this sort of criticism and it panicked, resulting in the company promising a minibus for each TV Region. These 'Nationwide Heinz' minibuses would be handed out to deserving causes and the programme team loved the idea. A film was ready for broadcast, at which point Clarke Hooper booked space in Radio Times supporting the effort, only to be told that Nationwide had to agree to the advertisement. John Hooper politely told them to get stuffed and insisted that the publication print the ad. It did, but Nationwide never ran the programme, which tells you something about TV companies in general and the BBC in particular. Despite all of these problems this promotion broke all previous records in that 30 million labels were contributed which was worth £300,000.

People have various reasons for taking jobs and towards the end of the Seventies John Williams became a salesman for Lyons Ice Cream for no better reason than the company gave him a car, a Vauxhall Viva. He was responsible for leisure sites in the southeast of England and spent a great deal of time at the pictures, watching The Godfather 15 times. His other great ambition was to be the person who told other people what to do. A pretty popular ambition, particularly for politicians. However, having been promoted to area sales manager, he found that the decisions were taken by marketing.

So he moved into marketing with Lyons Maid and became involved in promotions, in particular character merchandising, where he claims to have the negotiated the cheapest Star Wars licence in the world. He soon realised that the people who came up with all the ideas and had the most fun were the agencies, so that became his next target. A head-hunter put him in touch with Tim Arnold, who gave him a job at his agency TAA on the strength of an interview over lunch. This was in the days when lunch meant a visit to a restaurant, three courses and probably at least one bottle of wine.

Mark Beasley, later to join John at Marketing Perspectives, clearly remembers his first exposure to such client entertaining. It was around 1981 and he was a relatively new account executive at Masterguide. He tells it like this: "We were having Lunch (it definitely required a capital letter) at the famous and famously expensive Waterside Inn in Bray, hosted by my account director, Ken Spedding. The object was to say goodbye and thank you for the profitable business (and more business at your new company, Manor Bakeries, please) to marketing manager John Archer of British Bakeries, and hello to his replacement, Ian Buchan who went on to be general manager at Kraft Foods.

Ian and I were both new to this sort of thing - he as a management trainee with RHM, me as the man who had been selling Dewhurst Vouchers. Ken claimed that his choice of restaurant was that it was the only decent pub near British Bakeries' HQ in Slough. The fact that he lived down the road in Maidenhead was not, he said, a factor. I think the defining moment was the liqueur trolley clinking towards us, fronted by a 45-year-old Armagnac as it got dark around 4.00 pm. It gave me a whole new meaning to Lunch". But we digress.

John Williams remembers receiving a brief for Smirnoff during his days at TAA. The brief arrived in the post, something that rarely happened, and enraged Mr Arnold. He was convinced that the client had mass mailed a number of agencies the same letter and thought it a waste of time. A phone call to the client determined that it had in fact been sent to only four agencies. A meeting was arranged at the client's London offices for two o'clock and both Tim and John were supposed to be there. John arrived early, waited until just after two and, in the absence of his boss, conducted the meeting and got on very well with the client. As he was about to leave, the chairman of the agency, Tim, finally turned up.

The client politely explained that he had covered everything with John and expected his visitors to depart. However Tim wanted to ask one question. Why was there only one paragraph in the brief that appeared in capital letters? It said: "WE WILL NOT PAY A PRESENTATION FEE." John, attempted to do the oil on troubled waters bit, hastily explaining that the brand wanted to work with companies that were hungry for its business. Chairman Arnold was not much impressed and remarked: "I'm not hungry, I have just had a very good lunch." See what we mean about lunches in those days? Despite this colourful incident TAA won the pitch.

On another occasion the agency was asked to make a credentials presentation to British Caledonian. It did not want the standard presentation and expected to the shown some ideas. TAA put together about 15 different idea boards and drove down to the airline's vast glass offices in Crawley. Tim started his pitch but it didn't go well. First idea: "Don't like it." Second idea: "Tried that, didn't work." Third idea: "Waste of time" and so on. Faced with total negativity, Tim gave up and said: "Look, I can see we're not getting your promotions business but can we pitch for the window cleaning contract?"

DECADE OF DISCOUNTING

It might be fair to say that the 70's were the decade of discounting, although in September 1979 Marketing said: "Studies of consumer attitude to promotions show that housewives are increasingly sceptical, suspicious and downright bored by many of the offers in-store." Probably triggered by Tesco's famous Checkout campaign, Sainsbury ran Discount '78 and Discount '79 and the now defunct Fine Fair had a Top Fifty. There undoubtedly was a serious price war in the late Seventies and, as well as the on and off major promotions run by Tesco and Co, there were also the aggressive discounters such as Kwik Save and at that time Asda, Morrisons and Halliards.

Asda had been pioneering superstore-type trading for more than 14 years and claimed to be the clear leader in this field. In 1968 there were only seven stores classified as superstores. Five years later there were 67 and by 1978 there were 195. It is interesting to see how the aggressive discounters increased their share of the grocery trade from 1970 to 1979.

	1970/71	1973/74	1976/77	1979
	%	%	%	%
Asda	1.5	2.5	4.7	6.9
Kwik Save	0.3	0.6	1.4	4.0

Similar developments were also taking place in areas with the growth of out-of-town retail warehouses, such as Comet and others in furniture, carpets and DIY companies.

The ISP was also growing and by the end of the decade offered 16 distinct services to member.

1. A Code of Practice.
2. A Guide to VAT.
3. An embryonic educational programme.
4. A biography of practitioners to which potential clients can refer.
5. Contact with governing and professional bodies across Europe.
6. A legal advice service.
7. PR on behalf of the industry.
8. A quarterly news sheet and monthly bulletins.
9. An independent judge's service for competitions.
10. The ISP Awards.
11. Regular meetings in London and the provinces.
12. Twice yearly lunches with guest speakers.
13. Work towards forming a European Federation.
14. Specialist committees such as the Consultants Committee and a Trade Liaison Committee.
15. A permanent secretariat.
16. A set of standard competition rules.

Many of these are still going strong. Some of them, such as the Consultants Committee, have spun off as separate organisations, and others, such as standard competition rules, seemed to have disappeared. (But in 2009 reappeared in a different and more visible guise as the ISP "Seal of Approval", which is described in detail in a later chapter.)

The ISP education programme was considered 'embryonic' at this stage, unlike the polished operation it is today. Alan Toop of the Sales Machine believed that sales promotion was very much in need of serious education. Although specialist sales promotion consultants had raised the standards of promotional work, little had been done to train succeeding promotional managers. As these have now almost disappeared, he has been proved right.

But have they gone because they were not needed or because there were no suitably qualified replacements? Existing promotional businesses were small and self-made and a way should be found to produce the trained SP specialist of the future, he said. As it turned out, some of these small, self-made companies would soon self-make their owners several million pounds.

GROWING ANTIPATHY

With the growth of promotional techniques consumers were becoming more aware of what was going on, and a survey that ran from 1975 to 1979 showed a polarisation of attitudes to SP. It found more people supporting promotional methods, but also more who were antagonistic and wanted to see some methods banned. The promotions slated for the axe were trading stamps, competitions, self liquidators, free gifts, cigarette coupons and, would you believe it, money off. Own label products, cut-price advertising, retailer's coupons, manufacturer's coupons, and voucher/stamp offers were viewed less negatively. By today's standards it was a rather odd list.

Things were looking up and by 1976 Marketing was saying that there had been an astonishing 60 per cent increase in promotional activity during the first six months of the year compared with 1975. It had wide implications for marketers and consumers alike. First, current marketing conditions were reflected in the figures, so promotions had to be regarded as an integral part of the marketing mix. Second, the buying habits of the housewife had changed. No longer did she always insist on widely advertised, nationally known, branded products. Sales of convenience foods were falling because of inflation. The housewife was rightly suspicious of recommended retail prices and did not expect to pay them, especially for consumer durables. She shopped wisely, looked for reduced price offers and loved coupons. For the first time, traditional grocery marketing techniques were being applied to alcoholic drinks since this was part of the weekly shop.

But was this upbeat view of the sales promotion industry accurate? Here is Ian Fryer of Heinz speaking at a conference entitled 'Getting the Best from Sales Promotion' in November 1979. In his presentation, 'Where the Buck Stops' he said: "Today, sales promotion which adds value without tinkering with price is a more important tool that at any time since rationing ended in 1951."

Echoing our comments on the economy at the beginning of the Seventies, he was pretty glum about the grocery trade. In the previous 10 years it had been characterised by plummeting manufacturing margins; the growing concentration of retailer power; a massive decline in the number of outlets, and mounting unemployment. It was not a cheering prospect for the nervous principals of fledgling agencies and worried brand managers attending the conference. As it turned out he was possibly a little too pessimistic.

INTERLUDE THREE - IT SEEMED LIKE A GOOD IDEA AT THE TIME

Premiums and plans that went astray

From drumming bunnies to nodding dinosaurs

The perils of personalisation

Cream rises

Flying petfood

Possibly the most dangerous words in business are "I assumed". As one production director put it on a large poster in his office: "ASSUMPTION IS THE MOTHER OF ALL COCKUPS".

Co-author Ken Spedding had cause to ponder how true this is when his agency, Masterguide was handling the Duracell account. It was decided to offer the famous drumming bunnies from the TV advertising as a free mail-in and it was extremely successful. Masterguide sourced the bunnies by contacting the advertising agency and finding where the toys came from. It seemed an easy and sensible approach, so when the next commercial, featuring a walking, nodding dinosaur appeared it was decided to offer the new star. Still photographs were available, plans were laid to launch the new scheme, and a considerable amount of money had been spent. All they had to do was contact the ad agency and check on the source of the dinosaurs, which would surely be readily available.

Wrong! The dinosaur that appeared on TV was the result of clever animation trickery. However, the promotion was so far down the line that Masterguide's premium buyer was on the first plane to Hong Kong. No dinosaur could be found, but with considerable ingenuity the buyer identified a walking, nodding, tail-wagging dog and persuaded the manufacturer to adapt it. This required the walking mechanism to be reversed and a new cover fitted in the Duracell black and orange colours. Success was snatched from the jaws of defeat as the dinosaur moved, batteries walked out of the stores and the client nodded at the sales figures.

RIGHT FIRST TIME?

A large number of promotions involve widgets of one sort or another. These days most are imported from the Far East, so there are lots of opportunities for things to go wrong. Not that UK manufacture is without attendant headaches, not least the serious holes in the profit margin, if in fact there is a margin left. Co-author Colin Lloyd has spent a considerable amount of brainpower trying to decide why sales promotion is more fractious than most other businesses. One of the problems is the speed at which agencies have to work. Not for them the luxury of a year-long development process, prototype testing, retesting, market research and campaign planning before launch. Just about every promotion is a prototype and generally speaking will not appear again, or if it does, only in a cunningly disguised form. Anyone in R&D will tell you that getting a prototype right first time is, to say the least, bloody difficult.

Colin has found himself deeply embedded in the excrement on several occasions. One incident in particular had nothing to do with the Far East, rather the Far West, of Britain that is. The location was Buckfast in Devon. Not a major industrial centre, but home to an ex-promotions manager of petrol company National Benzole who wanted to continue practising his promotional skills. Having spent a decade supplying motorists with free glasses, he decided that glasses were passé and that pottery was the next big thing. Supporting local industry was his big idea, although local industry did not include any of the giants of the pottery field who were all in Stoke-on-Trent. Mass production was not really on, so his USP was personalisation.

Somehow or other, he also believed that he knew the breakdown of the names of people who would be redeeming any personalised promotion. This would enable him to have the correct number of Toms, Dicks, Harrys, plus Janets and Johns that would be needed. KLP loved the idea and Colin decided he should check out the production capacity before committing to a promotion for any of its mighty brands. That the factory was set in an idyllic and historic West Country town had no bearing on his decision to do this personally, rather than send a minion. After all, his premium buyer really enjoyed economy class flights to Hong Kong.

On arrival, he received a rapid education in rural industrial enterprise. When he finally found the appropriate field, he discovered a large kiln with a distinctly mediaeval look, surrounded by slightly more modern corrugated iron lean-to sheds. One strong westerly gale would have deposited them several fields away. This did not inspire a great deal of confidence, but he decided to give the concept a go and persuaded Horlicks to run a free personalised mug offer. The promotion ran and redemptions were well ahead of expectations. There were occasional muck ups, when little Sally got a little Sammy's mug, but no one claims that promotional execution is perfect.

So, onwards and upwards. The next candidate for the three Ps (Personalised Premium Pottery) was to be the unfortunate Gales Honey, a brand that reminded many people of tea at granny's on a Sunday afternoon. Based on this, the brief required a reinforcing of family values and value for money, for what was the brand leader at the time. KLP came up with the Free Personalised Pottery Piggybank with promotional material showing pictures of endearing little porkers carrying children's names - the client fell in love with it and the Buckfast Pottery got the contract. How could it go wrong?

They soon found out. Within days, consumer complaint letters were pouring in. The pig did not look a bit like the one that little Sally saw on the leaflet. When a few consumers returned their pigs, KLP immediately discovered the problem. The returned article looked nothing like any animal anyone had ever seen. The pottery had accelerated, or perhaps decelerated, Darwin's evolution by billions of years in six weeks, so it was back to Devon to see what had gone wrong. At this point, the team discovered that Colin had never actually seen any of the workers, and having asked a few questions they found that the manufacturing process involved various body parts being made separately and being put together by outworkers before firing.

This was okay in theory, but unfortunately the outworkers in this case were the residents of a local mental asylum. It seemed that they were somewhat confused about a number of things including which was the head and where to put the cute little curly tail, not to mention the other body parts. No one ever discovered why the good pottery workers of Devon did not notice such animal re-engineering. Perhaps it was the pressure of the volume. The client decided to send proper piggybanks to all correspondents, but to this day Colin feels that the deformed pigs were the ones that the kids preferred for their pocket money. They are probably selling them on eBay for large sums of money at this very moment.

IN THEIR CUPS

Another pottery offer that flirted with disaster was run by Bob Bayley during his Marden Kane days. He had picked up some business from his old employer Unigate, promoting cream. A nice free cream jug seemed ideal and an initial estimate of 100,000 was made. A number of designs were considered with one from a small West Country pottery deemed most appropriate. Marden Kane's chairman, Graham Paul liked this one least, but it was generally accepted within the agency that his sophisticated taste was almost diametrically opposite to that of the average consumer. An initial order for 50,000 jugs was sent to the pottery and as the promotion loomed, the buyer called the pottery and asked how things were getting on. The call was met with hysterical laughter. It seemed that the pottery thought that any order for 50,000 jugs had to be an elaborate hoax and not only had none been made, but it could only produce 1,000 a week at best. This news had almost every executive in the agency visiting various potteries and in the end 120,000 jugs were despatched with the vast majority arriving within the stipulated 28 days.

Problems also arose in the Far East and Roger Johnson, at that time with Masterguide, remembers a promotion for one of the Van den Bergh's margarine brands that it was trying to give a more natural image. The answer was to offer a free wooden butter dish. Well, actually a free margarine dish, but the important thing was that it was made from a natural material, wood. A supplier was identified in Portugal, samples supplied and approved. The promotion launched and applications were received, together with the first batch of a few hundred dishes. Applications continued to arrive at a very pleasing rate, but unfortunately the dishes did not. In those days international communication was usually by Telex, but more and more frantic Telex messages were ignored by the supplier.

Finally, he was reached by telephone and asked what had happened. His reply was that he had been offered a few pence more for each dish by a large British retailer so he was supplying them instead. "What about our contract?" he was asked. At this point, his command of English suddenly deserted him but finally it came down to the Portuguese equivalent of "So sue me!" This did not appear to be a profitable course, so alternative suppliers were finally discovered, delay letters sent, the client placated as much as possible, and the insurance policy checked. It turned out that professional indemnity covers you if you make a mistake but having checked all the paperwork the insurance company concluded that the agency had not erred and was not therefore covered. If it had been the agency's fault, not the suppliers, there would have been insurance cover. What sort of message this sends out, we're not entirely sure.

KEEP YOUR HEAD DOWN
Although sales promotion is always working to tight deadlines and rarely has time to double check the various aspects of what may be quite a complicated promotion, there are times when testing something has really paid off. One example, observed by Ken Spedding, involved a promotion for Pedigree Pet Foods in the early Seventies. At this time he was production director of the agency, Marden Kane, and his responsibility was making sure that the technical aspects worked smoothly.

The client did not want to do on-pack money off coupons and the brief was to devise a multibrand money off coupon covering the whole range, using door-to-door distribution but one that would be difficult to misredeem, at least on the first occasion. In other words, the customer had to make at least one purchase before they could use the coupon. The answer turned out to be a sheet of lick and stick stamps, each printed with half the money off value, against the purchase of one of the brands. The rest of the coupon was printed on the pack and to obtain the discount it was necessary to stick on the stamp which converted the label into a coupon. Are you still with us?

Despite the complications of printing large sheets of sticky paper in damp weather, the door-to-door aspect of the promotion seemed to have been put together in a satisfactory manner. Now for the labels. The first snag was that the label varnish meant the stamps did not stick. A solution to this was to leave a gap in the varnish where the coupon was to adhere. There was great rejoicing all round in Epsom as Marden Kane had committed to print eight million of the sticky sheets. Fortunately, someone at Pedigree's Melton Mowbray HQ thought it worthwhile to print a few thousand of the special labels to make sure that it all worked. Everyone concerned was invited to the factory to see the test run, and to celebrate over a decent dinner afterwards.

The labels were packed face down beneath the runway of one of the fastest production lines in Europe. As they approached the labels the cans pick up a strip of gum. This in turn, picked up the label, which wrapped itself around a can before disappearing into the packing line. The button was pressed, a stream of cans hurtled down the runway where, to everyone's surprise and horror, they took off and were flying over the production line. Someone hit the emergency stop button and a post-mortem was held. The problem was due to the slight reduction in thickness where there was no varnish. Although infinitesimal on one label, when you had thousands, a small dent appeared, just large enough to flip the can. The agency did not fancy paying for eight million redundant printed sheets and Pedigree did not fancy having to equip its staff with safety helmets or some large nets or both. It turned out that the solution was simply to leave the varnish off a larger area, which subsequently proved to work perfectly. The moral of this is, if you can test it, test it.

CHAPTER NINE

Legal fun and games, promotions on a plate

Are lotteries illegal? Yes, no, maybe…
Coming soon to a cinema near you – glasses, bowls and cutlery
A US/UK partnership that took off
Supermarkets benefit from full plates, but it's still not enough

A cigarette promotion nearly put some bosses into jail but launched thousands of instant wins, millions of scratchcards and many tons of plates, cups, knives, pots and pans. In the mid-Seventies, the big SP story was John Players 'Spot Cash' which threatened several senior executives of the company with jail. This was not due to cooking the books to the tune of billions of dollars as seen in recent accounting scandals, but because of an 'illegal' promotion. In the Dark Ages, which this era now seems to be, you could promote cigarettes without being jailed or ostracised by all and sundry. What, it turned out, you could not do was put scratchcards inside the cigarette packets which the smokers dutifully scratched and either won (or most often did not win) a cash prize. To make it legal, it was thought that a small number of cards could be made available free at point of purchase. Big mistake!

The scheme took off in a cloud of smoke which got up the noses of the competition, mainly because it produced a staggering sales increase. Green with envy, the same competitors persuaded the public prosecutor to take the wicked executives to court for running something illegal, possibly a lottery or some such. The court found Players guilty because it judged that there were not enough free cards and they were not readily available. However, the judge did point out to the other cigarette companies that the courts had better things to do than spend so much valuable time settling a minor commercial row between companies.

THE CASE FOR THE APPEAL

Players appealed and Justice Denning allowed it. The relieved promotions industry went out and got drunk and, as soon as it was sober, started planning lots of lovely and very lucrative lottery style promotions – everyone had noticed that remarkable sales increase. For a while all went well but the case finally ground its very expensive way through the legal system and about five years after the launch, went to The House of Lords. In 1980 five Law Lords considered the case of Imperial Tobacco v Her Majesty's Attorney General.

After due deliberation they reversed the Appeal Court's decision and lotteries were out again. Their opinion was that the cards could not accurately be said to be 'free', but the decision was pretty close and the Attorney General did not get his costs paid by Imperial, which was an indication of just how close. The same Law Lords also commented on an attempt by the public prosecutor to attempt to prosecute a local tobacconist for selling 'Spot Cash' cigarettes. Not mincing words they called this misguided effort "maladroit" which, by their standards, was pretty damming. They felt the law in question (the 1976 Lotteries and Amusements Act) was unsatisfactory. Most people in the business were not too pleased about this decision, as they had run lots of nice and effective lotteries when they were legal.

A dissenting voice was the late Alan Scaping, SP manager of Nestlé and chairman elect of the ISP. With the full majesty of his position, the ever-quotable promoter said: "It is very good that lotteries like 'Spot Cash' are now illegal. They prey upon the natural credulity and greed of the young. We just do not need this highly dubious technique." It would look good on a tablet of stone, don't you think? Surprisingly, David Trench, legal advisor to that consumer champion "Which?" did not think it was unfair. However SP was not so easily defeated and in came the 'plain paper' entry route, which has since launched a thousand instant wins – something that has changed, hopefully for the better, with the new Betting and Gaming Act.

Calling them 'instant win' when most lose is somewhat misleading, but instant loss does not have the same ring to it. In the US, promoters have to publish the odds on such schemes, which they call sweepstakes. Perhaps Camelot should follow suit – well maybe not as '44,000,000:1' at the top of a ticket might dampen sales.

COLLECT THEM ALL

Our transatlantic cousins had built up a lot of experience in various games and it seems that they were probably legal in the UK. They were mostly variations on bingo and aimed to get shoppers coming back to collect more numbers each week. It was a basic loyalty programme with, critically, no requirement to purchase products or make a certain spend. The majority of them featured scratch off panels, an area in which the US printers were very experienced. They also had something called "continuity programmes". These are a simple and very effective loyalty scheme for retailers.

It has no cards, no computers, no mailing costs, no bits of paper, no sticky stamps, just a pile of such things as crockery, cutlery, pots and pans or any useful household items that can be collected a piece at a time. The retailer buys a big stock of the chosen product and offers a different part for sale each week at about cost, or even less if it feels altruistic. Food retailers were not as desperate as the US cinema owners who dreamed up this idea and gave the items away, but they still offered massive savings on decent quality goods.

In other words, it is a classic self liquidator come loyalty scheme operated in store. Instead of buying a pack of the promoted brand and sending in proof of purchase, the shopper qualifies for the low cost by spending a certain amount in the store. It is instant gratification. Having started, shoppers hopefully come back on a weekly basis. In order to both shift the stock purchased and give the offer a value, stores would also make the items available for conventional purchase at a discount to the normal retail price but still providing a profit for the store. This helped to fund the whole programme.

A typical example is one run by a group of Co-operative stores in 1986 for 'Gourmet Cutlery Kitchen Knives'. There were eight different items, and for every £5 spent, you could buy the 'Knife of the Week' for £1.99. This also entitled you to a free steak knife with each purchase. If you were not spending enough, you could buy the same knives for £2.99 and throughout the promotion there were a number of other matching items, such as a knife block, on sale at retail prices. The block would have cost you £7.99 and the steak knife £1.19, which was not cheap by the standards of the day. The scheme was simple, easily understood, and very effective, but long since overtaken by whizzy electronics. Selling cut-price weapons to the local ASBO candidates is not likely to be popular with a wider audience.

Although these became very big in supermarkets, they did not start there. Their foundation was, of all things, the cinema. In the US at the end of the Second World War there were half a dozen TV stations, which was six more than in the UK. By 1951 there were 100 and the number of TV sets had risen from 7,000 to 13 million. It was the era of great TV networks like NBC, ABC and CBS that still dominate today. They brought the likes of Ed Sullivan and Jackie Gleeson's live audience shows to the US public, which was spellbound. Until then entertainment had been the cinema, which was a family affair with attendances averaging as many as three to four visits a week. The cinema industry was booming.

However, live TV stopped it in its tracks. Cinema attendances dropped like a stone and have never really recovered. The owners were desperate and something had to be done to bring the punters back. The solution was continuity collector promotions. Dish and silverware nights sprang up at cinemas across the States. Cinema goers were given free items of crockery or glassware which they could collect in sets, followed by sets of silverware. Never in the history of promotions has so much household inventory been given to so many. At one point the whole of the glassware output of Czechoslovakia was used for these promotions.

BORN IN THE USA

Ted Adams, in a new job after the demise of Green Shield Stamps, had spotted another US trend and wanted to emulate his old boss by launching it. He went to Key Markets and explained all about continuity promotions with samples of hand-decorated Japanese stoneware. The prospective client was very doubtful of the product at the prices quoted, thinking them too good to be true. It demanded a complete case of every item and put them into its canteen for a month so that its industrial strength plate-washing machine and industrial strength dinner ladies could give them a thorough test.

It also had doubted that the crockery was 'hand painted' although technically it was. The basic plate was printed with an outline design, then very deft little Japanese ladies attached a brush to the end of each finger and dabbed a patch of colour on the appropriate section of the design – then off to the kiln. When Key Market's finance director was taken to see the operation in Japan, he got up in the middle of lunch and announced that he was going back for another look as he was convinced that the 'hand painting' was staged for his benefit - typical accountant.

The top Key Market staff were taken to the US HQ of Wallace, Ted's partner, given the red carpet treatment and promptly signed for Britain's very first supermarket continuity promotion. Three stores were selected for a trial and the marketing director could not believe his eyes when he saw the vast quantities of stoneware that was to be shipped to them. He was certain that they would never move it all. He was certainly wrong.

They moved that amount and more. The offer was a stoneware dinner plate with a retail value of around £5, for 33p with every £5 spent or £1.90 if bought alone. It took five weeks to offer all the items, and at the end they started again, sometimes running for three complete cycles – 15 weeks. At the same time, the other items to make up dinner and tea services were on sale for around half the retail price.

The 33p level was subsidised by Key Markets and Wallace charged the same price for all of the order so the other items made the promoter a profit, such was the buying power of Wallace. Over a large number of programmes in many stores, the net cost to the retailer was less than 0.5 per cent. To give some idea of how big these simple little promotions became, at one time Wallace had 400 40-foot containers on the docks in Japan awaiting shipment to various destinations. When Key Markets rolled out to all its stores it needed around 100 containers to get the crockery here.

For a while, continuity promotions were flavour of the year. So why did they die? Ted Adams has a one-word answer, "Greed!" Trading stamps had cost the retailer 2.5 per cent and here was a scheme that cost one fifth of that. Continuity promotions only needed a four to six per cent sales increase to break even, much less than stamps. Incidentally the dinner plate week was always the most successful. But despite this, selling at a loss, however small, was anathema to supermarkets. Not to mention the even more unpopular fact that they, not their suppliers had to pay for everything. The promotions were converting secondary shoppers to primary shoppers and getting the stores a bigger share of their spend. It was good, but not good enough, for the supermarkets, who wanted the extra footfall and to have a profit on their plates. The result was less and less customer involvement and a gradual fade out after about 10 years of activity.

BACK TO PRICING POLICY

Once again, the retailers reinvented price as a promotional tool but with great ingenuity came up with EDLP which stands for "Every Day Low Prices". A great advance from "Pile them high and sell them cheap" you will agree. EDLP has now also gone to the great supermarket in the sky and the retailers are straining the creative juices of their ad agencies to come up with a different way of saying that they are cheaper than the competition. They also went on to reinvent loyalty schemes with more sophisticated versions using plastic cards and rewards such as Air Miles, Nectar, Buy and Fly and of course handfuls of cleverly targeted coupons.

And, for anybody who hoped to forecast how the next decade in SP would play out, there were plenty of surprises in store.

THE HISTORY MAKERS

Ian Allchild

Andrew Marsden

Sue Short

Nick Wells

Alan Scapping

Ian Fryer

Phillip Circus

Brenda Simonetti

John Chambers

John Williams

Jeff McElnea

Mike DaSilva

CHAPTER TEN

The Eighties, Part 1

Let the good times roll!
Marketers aren't working – the dole queue lengthens
Promotions buoyed by the recession
The first sales promotion league tables reveal the major players
The rise of research and the decline of creativity

The new decade started with unemployment reaching two million and heading for three million by the end of 1982, which did not bode well for the growing number of SP consultancies or their clients. GDP was down 1.6 pr cent while government spending was up by 1.1 per cent and inflation rampant. Money was wildly expensive with the base rate reaching an all-time high of the mid-teens in 1980. In the same year John Lennon was shot in New York and JR was shot in Dallas. Steve McQueen, Alfred Hitchcock and Peter Sellers died the same year. The Iraq-Iran war started and the now three years old oil crisis also reached its peak. Altogether things did not look good, so surely they could only get better. After all it was the year that the yellow Post-it Note and the Sony Walkman were launched.

Despite the doom and gloom, SP had an air of confidence. In 1981 the first SP league tables appeared. There were 30 consultancies in the ISP at that time and by 2006 four of them were still in existence, although several others had changed their names or merged. In 1980 research company Mintel carried out a survey and asked the agencies what they thought of each other. The not unexpected answer was "not much". Mintel's general impression was of a "youthful and lively industry, linked closely to packaged goods manufacturers". It thought that the Eighties would not be as buoyant for SP as the previous decade and considered that most of these "youthful and lively companies would mature into a resilient and useful arm of the marketing effort that will be needed to survive the Eighties". How nice of them to say so.

Other developments that would have long-term effects were bar coding and laser scanners. Freddy Laker got his licence to start Skytrain, the forerunner of today's low cost operations, which really upset BA. They managed to put him out of business – he took them to court and won some compensation. Credit cards were on their unstoppable way, but much fewer in numbers. Barclaycard had launched in 1966 followed by Access in 1972 and they dominated the market. American Express and Diners Club were the big names in charge cards. In retailing, Tesco made a much unexpected announcement when it admitted that despite increasing sales by a massive 26 per cent profits, and therefore its margins, had fallen by

£5.5million. It also announced a cull among its hotchpotch of 529 stores to favour 400 superstores.

The ISP Awards of the Year were sponsored by the Post Office and it was only the second year to require entrants to include both objectives and results as part of the entry, and to award a good number of marks for results. This led to a variation on Winston Churchill's famous quote: "There are lies, damned lies, statistics and ISP Award results." A personal favourite of one of the authors was "The Agency kept the business". The Awards were dished out at a Gala Evening at the Park Lane Intercontinental and cost £20.73 per head inclusive of VAT.

Marketing magazine went weekly at this time and a diary piece remarked that the ISP Awards was very civilised compared to the advertising industry's version. For those of us old enough to remember the awards of this period, this would indicate that the ad folk must have required the Special Patrol Group of the Met Police to keep them under control. The ISP became so tired of having any civilised entertainment drowned by alcohol-fuelled uproar that it hired a Guards Regimental Band to play at one dinner, on the grounds that it would be almost as noisy as the guests. The general opinion was that the result was a draw.

The awards saw 200 entries in 1980, well up on the previous 151. The Grand Prix was won by CDP/Aspect for Gallaher's Clan Pipe Tobacco. The partial cash back offer does not look that exciting. The 25g pack sold retail for 79p out of which the tax man got a generous 46p. Robinson's Gollys, now discredited by political correctness, won Gold with "Great Golly" offers. It shifted 116,000 badges, 82,000 jean patches, 34,000 spoons and 43,000 other items, a grand total of 275,000 applications. Some years later political correctness put an end to this long running promotion.

This was a time when the bigger names in the business, the so-called Magnificent Seven, were regularly wining and dining at such upmarket waterholes as the Savoy and the Dorchester. At the same time that the 'Seven' were putting the world to rights, the younger worker bees were also getting together at parties where it seems that just about everyone worked for one promotions agency or another. According to Graham Griffiths, he often saw the future chairman of a US advertising agency, then in charge of below the line for a vast international group and still in his mid-20s, arrive in a new Porsche and, rumour had it, use it to try to pull female art directors.

The future leader of a large integrated icon of the 90s was, for some unknown reason, fond of throwing his shoes out of the top floor window, while another gentleman, who became a major nurturer of talent, was a permanent fixture in the kitchen at these parties, and we all know what went on in the kitchens. It wasn't a discussion of the menu.

PROMOTING INTO THE EIGHTIES

Tesco, having dumped Green Shield stamps was still totally price orientated with Checkout in 1980. It also had a predictable range of competitions, mail-ins and money off practically everything. At this time Kellogg was running a promotion called 'Collect British Stamps' on 30 million Corn Flakes packs and had invented a character called The Stamp Bug. The Post Office, naturally, provided useful support, which was very cost effective. The Post Office was also flogging a 1979 collector's pack of special issue British stamps for £4, which was really quite a lot of money in 1980. It was very neat, getting people buying things they would not use to post letters. Pure profit. It recruited 30,000 new members for the Stamp Bug Club and made it known that it was looking for other third parties for promotions.

Even a small cash prize would have been very welcome at this time, particularly if you had a mortgage - the bank base rate was an eye watering and very painful 14 per cent. However banks and building societies were beginning to compete, but not on the rates offered as today. A cosy arrangement allowed the chairman of the building societies to meet once a month over a pleasant and free lunch and then set the rate for the next month.

The various financial institutions were spending heavily on advertising to build up an image. The Midland Bank, as it was at the time, came up with the 'Listening Bank' slogan, although many of its customers found that having listened, it said "No!" There was also a bit of real sales promotion going on. The Abbey Building Society set up a Junior Savers club introducing 25p savings stamps, to some extent competing with National Savings. The Leeds was also aiming at the youth market with the exciting idea of giving schools posters detailing the fascinating history of building societies. Pretty cool (!) don't you think? It was still a few years before the banks began to compete with each other.

But despite all this, the promotional clouds were beginning to have a silver lining. In April 1980 Campaign magazine noticed that there was something called sales promotion. For this occasion it recruited Alan Toop, Graham Paul and Keith Bantick to provide an overview of the industry. They were pretty bullish. Since the bonanza of the Silver Jubilee in 1977, the cold winds of recession had blown through retailers with price competition the dominant theme. However at the beginning of the new decade sales promotion had suddenly become flavour of the month. And not just in grocery stores. There appeared to be a simple reason why. Desperation! The general view was "If we do not survive in the short term we will not be here to enjoy the long-term". Marketing budgets were being slashed, and most of the savings were going into short-term promotions.

This view was supported by some encouraging statistics. Compared to 1979, there was an overall two per cent increase in promotional activity with a 10 per cent increase in premium promotions. There was an eight per cent increase in new promotions. The fact that the money was tight was reflected in the use of coupons, with 12 per cent more issued. The average face value was up by 25 per cent and redemptions by the same amount. The overall value of coupons redeemed was up by more than 50 per cent.

BY ROYAL COMMAND

A good time for all involved in SP was prophesied and correctly so, helped by the 1981 wedding of Charles and Di giving a lift to the whole souvenir industry. The same manufacturers would continue to be grateful with a new royal baby due to arrive in 1982. As you will see, the owners of sales promotion companies got rich in the next few years. Some got fat as well but others kept their weight down with personal trainers in their home gyms and heated indoor swimming pools.

You may not know this, but it is illegal to reproduce illustrations of the royal family without specific permission which is rarely, if ever, granted for commercial purposes. However, you can illustrate items which carry pictures of the Royal family and this allowed Persil to feature Princess Diana on pack for a promotion at a time when she was probably the most famous woman in the world.

It did this by arranging for the Crown Agents to sample, at no cost to Persil, 17 stamps from 17 countries - most of which were very small and not exactly well known but one, the Falkland Islands, would achieve world wide fame in the next few years. Sales of their stamps to collectors, which of course were never used, provide a useful income for the issuing governments. They were all taking part in the Princess Diana 21st birthday stamp bonanza. The rest of the sets could be purchased so the whole scheme was a self liquidator. Sometimes everything seems to be going your way and this was one of them. The timing of Prince William's birth during the run of the promotion, gave it a major boost and it won an ISP gold award. Well done Charles.

This was a period when companies were discovering the joys of joint promotions. One of the major attractions was that they provided more scope for the imagination and more bang for your buck. Most links were fairly obvious, but not all. How about a deal between St Ivel and the Post Office? Post Offices in Britain were hanging posters that drew attention to a National Giro transfer form on which they could place orders for clotted cream to be sent to any location in the nation.

Another very successful and regularly repeated promotion of the decade linked a ticket BOGOF on National Express coaches with a number of large blue chip brands. The essential offer was very simple: a two for the price of one fare in exchange for proof of purchase.

Organised for National Express by Masterguide, the offer appeared on Mars bars, Pepsi cans, PG Tips packs and several other major brands. National Express did not charge for the tickets but the promoting company had to spend an agreed amount, usually around £250,000, on advertising the promotion.

One particularly surprising occasion had the brand manager requesting his opposite number at the agency to come down to the Victoria Coach Station, not a part of London he visited frequently, preferring to use his company Mercedes when travelling. The client wanted him to see travellers buying 10 Mars bars to get the proofs of purchase required for their two-for-one ticket. They were taking off the wrappers and giving the bars away. It's a rare instance of a promotion where the product is bought purely for the reward. It happened with Hoover, but that is a very different story.

TOP OF THE POPS
The use of music premiums, which had begun in the previous decade, increased rapidly in the Eighties. Improved manufacturing meant records and cassettes were cheap enough to be given away free against a reasonable proof of purchase. However, great care had to be taken in the selection of music in order to avoid copyright problems. The music industry is notoriously quick to call the lawyers. On one occasion a compilation album was being offered on a Kellogg pack and towards the end of the promotional period one of the tracks on the LP went out of the agreed copyright arrangement. Two days later Kellogg received a letter from the musician's lawyer. However, music was a big craze at the time. During the first year or so of the Eighties, music was used by, among others, Beecham, Volkswagen, Pioneer, Gallaher, United Biscuits and Levi Strauss. This also led to a proliferation of small companies offering to package suitable music and outflanking the major record producers.

This was also a time when SP consultancies began to feel that they were really in a profession. At the end of 1982 Alan Toop came up with a set of basic rules. He only managed six, but perhaps he should have gone a bit higher up the mountain. They probably apply today, make sense and, to be fair, several are pretty much self evident, but they are still worth a look. His homily went like this:
When it comes to the statement of objectives, many companies are not realistic in terms of sales promotional briefs. Problems that have proved resistant to large advertising budgets and the best efforts of the sales force are expected to be solved by a single sales promotion. The sales promotion 'commandments' include:

1. Do not ask for miracles - have only one, achievable objective.
2. Recognise the value of brands to survive, as well as their fragility, and the ability of sales promotions to support and enhance the identity and individuality of the brand.

3. Make sales promotions as original as possible but always consistent with the brand's personality.
4. Make a real effort to sell the brand.
5. Do not rush promotion developments.
6. Do not launch a promotion unless it is really needed.

Number 4 was really pretty obvious but we particularly like number 6, coming from a sales promotion consultant who we suspect would be happy to launch any promotion for which the client was prepared to pay a fee. Or are we being too cynical?

This was when The Institute of Marketing, based in the bucolic Thames Valley splendour of Cookham, decided it needed to become Chartered and hence the CIM. New media was a new phrase and people were getting a bit worried about it, in particular the TV remote control which, combined with a VCR, allowed consumers to fast forward through the ads. The airwaves were shared by the BBC and ITV, but a fourth channel was on its way and satellite broadcasting was on the distant horizon. Clive Sinclair launched his home computer, the ZX80, priced at £99.95. Apparently press ads in the News of the World produced exactly the same percentage of responses as the Sunday Times. BA was promoting Concorde with a cut-price offer of one way to New York for £830. It also had a special deal for two family members travelling together that went to the trouble of stating that in-laws counted as family.

Abbey National was very daring for a financial institution, running a lottery of all things, to entice investors to tuck their savings away in an account with a lower interest rate than was available elsewhere. Not everything was novel. Someone remembered the personality promotions of the mid-Sixties with men and woman in ever more outlandish costumes roaming the suburbs and startling unexpected housewives. This time it was the McVitie's Money Maids, in leg-revealing costumes. They called on 100,000 homes and handing out a fiver to anyone one with three or more McVitie's products. In all they gave away £75,000.

LOYALTY IS IN THE AIR
May 1981 saw the launch by American Airlines of the world's first frequent flyer programme. It started what is probably the biggest single promotional technique in the world if you do not count money off. For convenience sake let's call them air miles. In just 25 years more than 130 airlines issued air miles and 120 million people were members of the various schemes with 14 million flights a year paid for with the currency. Based on an average value of around 3p a mile, The Economist worked out that the global stock of unredeemed miles was worth around $7billion. There are so many outstanding miles, and they are growing by 20 per cent a year, so if the airlines stopped their programmes immediately it would take at least 25 years for them to be used up.

You may think you have clocked up a few miles, but an American property developer purchased a painting at auction for £2,478,000 and paid on his Amex card, earning one air mile per pound. Here is one last little problem for serious air miles collectors to ponder. Imagine what would happen if the Treasury decided that miles used personally but earned on company business were payment in kind. Collectors could find themselves being taxed at top rate for those air miles. Doesn't that sent a shiver down the spine?

After years of saying it would never enter the frequent flyer market because of the accounting problems and tax issues, British Airways finally succumbed towards the end of the Eighties. Unlike every other scheme, initially it did not issue miles to its own customers but sold to third parties for promotional use. This is very cunning and profitable. The airline is paid upfront for points which may not be used for some time, if at all. Secondly, computer systems allocate a certain number of seats on each flight for redemption purposes with more seats on unpopular flights and few, if any, for the more attractive destinations at more attractive times. It is unlikely these seats would be sold, so effectively BA was being paid in advance for seats they would not otherwise sell.

A few years later BA decided it had to compete with airlines that were giving their customers points and so set up two separate operations, one for its own frequent travellers and one for anyone else. BA now has almost two million frequent flyers in its Executive Club and it is one of the most popular methods of purchasing flights.

WHERE'S MY LILO?

This was still a period where major FMCG companies had large sales forces calling on supermarkets and independent stores. This was the period of the 'dealer loader', which we have previously described. Nowadays of course, it is all controlled, regulated and centralised. Risk taking has been replaced by totally risk adverse activity. This was very much a product of the slump in the more brutal 90s. "Better safe than sorry" has become the motto when previously it was often "Why not?" Agency staff in the Eighties were expected to turn their hands to anything but today's account manager would be horrified if asked to write copy and scamp (?) a layout for a sales presenter, if they knew what a sales presenter was.

The Mintel survey of 1980 covered 46 companies. It put KLP just ahead of The Sales Machine, followed by IMP, Cato Johnson, Promotional Campaigns and Marketing Solutions. Further down were Purchasepoint, Communications in Selling (CSL), and a final group made up of Marden Kane, Glendenning, Clarke Hooper, Lansdowne and Underline.

The following year provided the first financial list, followed by a similar list in 1982. Many companies appear in both of the lists but there is quite a variation with several, apparently successful, companies appearing who were not even mentioned in the 1980 survey. CSL had morphed into Tim Arnold Associates. At the time Tim was the first chairman of the ISP as it was reconstituted from the SPEA. Typically, the change was made up by Mr Arnold in advance of the AGM where it was to have been debated.

TALES OF THE RIVERBANK

Taking into account the companies who participated in both years, there is 25 per cent growth. FKB posted billings of £6.1million in 1982. It was the first major breakaway in the industry, having separated from International Marketing & Promotions (IMP). Co-founder, Chris Killingbeck remembers "the sales promotion whirlwind" of the time. FKB started with six people from IMP and three from KLP - the SP version of Chelsea and Manchester United of the time. Setting up in February in a leaking stone and granite warehouse in Fulham, they were in profit within weeks. The junior account executives had the unusual job of collecting sacks of coal from the Esso station to burn in the tortoise stove that was the centrepiece of the office. To cope with the business, FKB took on staff at a rate of knots and Killingbeck claims that FKB had by far the best looking agency staff in town.

Work hard, play hard was the rule of the day, and with the founders being the only married staff; it was fun, fun, fun plus some original perks. On a hot summer's day the company would block book the outside area of the now defunct Crocodile Tears Brassiere in Fulham Road where staff would eat and drink until five before going back to the office and working till eleven. A trip to see the solstice at Stonehenge and a staff outing to Le Mans were other perks. FKB even used to take group of 20 people to play cricket against New Beckenham CC on Sundays following heavy Saturday nights in the local pub.

Despite all the fun and games, it attracted some great clients including Whitbread, NatWest, Yellow Pages, United Distillers, United Biscuits, Stowells of Chelsea, The Daily Telegraph and Shell. The riverside location required an annual Boat Race party to which clients and their families were invited. Upstream in Barnes, Masterguide, who were five years old and about the same size in 1982, were doing much the same thing in their much more elegant Georgian office and there was a certain amount of competition as to who had the biggest and best party.

This was the beginning of spectacular success for FKB with a successful floatation on the stock market and a great deal of money sloshing around for a time. Unfortunately, it all ended in tears and serious financial problems and as we shall see they were taken over by the Carlson Group in 1990.

The list of winners of ISP Gold Awards in 1982 included companies not in the top 20, including some advertising agencies. The Grand Prix that year was won for Guinness with a promotion called 'Watch the Birdie', organised by an agency called Grocer Jack which apparently disappeared soon afterwards. Other winners were CBH and Partners (two Golds), Aidap Marketing, Promotional Campaigns (three), Masterguide, Creative Strategy, Kirkwood Sales Promotion (two), The Market Square, The Sales Machine (two), Marketing Solutions, Marketing Events, and, with probably the longest credit in the business, Butler, Dennis and Garland in consultation with Brown McGurk Turner.

There was massive inflation in the number of awards available. Whereas 1983 had 14 categories, the 2007 Awards has an initial list of 31 plus two Audience Awards, a Service Partners Recognition Award, an ISP Promoter of the Year Award and The ISP Agency of the Year Award, as well as the Grand Prix. This enabled agencies to enter the same promotion in several categories which increased their chance of picking up a gong. It also increased the income for the ISP, but surely that was not the objective was it?

PAPER TIGERS

Vouchers were growing fast, a trend that has continued to the present day, although it would be 15 years before the Voucher Industry Forum, later The Voucher Association was formed. E F MacDonald, founded in 1922 in the US, had been in the UK since 1960. Bonus Plan had vouchers acceptable at 44 retail and hotel chains. The business was, however, dominated by the retailers such as Boots, Debenhams, Dewhurst Butchers, Peter Dominic, Dolphin Vacation Vouchers (due to morph into TLC), Ellerman Travel Bonds, Embassy Hotels, Habitat, W H Smith, Woolworth and Victoria Wine.

Another valuable bit of paper was coupons, although misredemption was a big issue. Jeremy Sandys-Wynch, a greatly respected SP manager at Kellogg was quoted as saying that up to 40 per cent were redeemed illegally. A smaller proportion came back from retailers, who were cutting them out from unsold newspapers and magazines. Handling houses got a bit suspicious when 40 or 50 coupons, all neatly clipped and in pristine condition came back from one retailer. The real problem was the major grocery retail companies, who accepted coupons from customers whether or not they had actually purchased the product. This running sore goes on to the present day. It is little wonder retailers are slow to tackle misredemption. Not only do they get the face value of a coupon, but they also get a useful handling fee on top.

CHARITY BEGINS ON PACK

The success of the various Heinz charity promotions led to a number of other brands jumping aboard the feel-good bandwagon. Weetabix enlisted Cliff Richard to help raise £250,000 for children's hospitals. It upped the contribution from 2p on standard packs to 8p on a giant pack and 4p on the mid-size. It printed in quite large letters the fact that it was paying the cost of all administration, advertising etc. This was something that cropped up in previous research carried out by Heinz and Weetabix must have had a similar message.

Mother's Pride loaves carried a promotion that funded Carshalton Children's Hospital radio station, Radio Lollipop, with £35,000. It roped in Radio 1's Peter Powell to front the programme. The money was sufficient to kick-start a whole chain of very successful Radio Lollipop stations in the UK and around the world.

Meanwhile, Andrex launched a £100,000 appeal to train 1,000 puppies to become guide dogs for the blind. The presenter was Barbara Woodhouse, famous for training dogs and her catchphrase "Walkies". Andrex boxes had a 5p seal attached and in a neat twist, KLP arranged for collection boxes to appear in stores so that the seal could be deposited before the pack had even reached home. Some five million seals were collected and Andrex achieved its biggest brand share to date. It was the first time that Andrex had allowed its packaging to be used for promotions and started a trend that continues today.

Heinz launched its own heavyweight charity promotion. Once again, thanks to Ian Fryer's archive collection, we are fortunate to have a complete set of documentation to trace the promotion from the original brief.

In May 1980 Heinz was considering its promotional activity for the next year and evaluating its previous charity promotion 'The Schools Foundation'. In January 1981, agency Clarke Hooper was asked to come up with some new ideas. True to form, it presented three initial proposals.

1: Rerun the schools promotion, this time entitled the Heinz Youth Foundation with a total budget of £1,030,000 and approximately £350,000 media spend. The target was 45 million labels with £450,000 donated to the youth activities. This was the agency's preferred proposal.

2. A charity promotion where the consumer chose which one of 12 British charities got their money. The total budget was £1,185,000 with £400,000 to the charities and £240,000 spent on advertising. The big-money went on a 16 million door drop planned to cost £370,000.

3. Help Your Local Hospitals with Heinz. The budget here was £900,000, and the target reduced to 35 million labels with £300,000 on media.

However, determined to give value for money, in the same month Clarke Hooper came up with four more extreme ideas including a Metro car-a-day scheme, but upped the ante from 57 to 100. Even after this they came up with more ideas. The additional ones were a hospital League of Friends scheme, 57 mini-buses for schools, and 'How many Beans Means Heinz', which was based on estimating the average number of beans in a can to win £57,000, plus vast numbers of 57p vouchers. With an unexpected sense of humour, not common in researchers, the report also included a cartoon, related to the "How many Beans" proposal.

By October 1981, after considering and extensively researching at least 10 proposals, Heinz went for Number 2 on the initial list, the tried and tested 'labels equal cash for charity' but with a twist. The consumer was given a choice of 12 charities. This was a typical example of the classic 'three proposal' approach. Idea 1 would be very original, but possibly risky. Idea 2: a variation of the programme run last year that produced acceptable results and an acceptable fee and Idea 3, a very safe, unexciting proposal in case the client got cold feet. In each case the fee was rolled up with research, design and artwork and was standardised at £50,000

However, dull as it might sound, it had a lot of appeal to the Heinz consumer as they sent in a massive 35 million labels, which must have made the handling house very happy. Heinz handed out £500,000 to the charities, in proportion to the labels dedicated to each by the public.

The research for this promotion may well have been unique at the time. Even such high-powered companies as Mars, Lever Brothers, Van den Bergh, or Kellogg rarely carried out much research. There were no budgets for serious research and secondly the time constraints rarely allowed for it. As far as post-promotion research was concerned, it usually amounted to two questions. What effect did it have on sales and did it come in on budget?

As the business moved towards the 21st century, there was more research taking place. However, it is often driven by a risk-averse attitude. If the Eighties attitude was "Can do", after the millennium, it became "Might do, but not until six people have signed it off, we have researched it to death and purchasing has been over it with a fine tooth comb". Agencies' ideas are tested to destruction, driving promotions back to tried and tested methods with a small, creative tweak.

There have been various levels of research, ranging from showing an idea around the office to hiring a market research agency to conduct an in-depth survey. An interesting example of a short, sharp piece of research was used by Branston Beans for a launch in 2005. It had initially planned a straightforward experiential sampling campaign but tested the testing on 250 adults in a pub in Hertfordshire. They were offered the opportunity to taste alongside the brand leader, Heinz. The drinkers in the pub went heavily for the new brand so Branston went ahead with a straightforward blind taste sampling campaign without any more research. Everyone thought this a good idea, apart from the experiential agency that lost some lucrative business. The brand got an amazing seven per cent of the market in three months on the back of the campaign; Branston should perhaps have bought those 250 adults a couple of drinks.

GREEN SHOOTS

The economy was looking a little more cheerful at the beginning of 1983 with high street spending up 4.5 per cent in the first three months of the year compared with 1982, and the forecast of further growth. On the other hand, inflation was likely to increase into 1984 but happily, expected discretionary spending would continue increasing faster than overall consumer spending, with a strong rise in durable goods and a lesser extent in clothing and alcohol. A lot more cars were sold, so things were looking up.

On 21 June 1983 the ISP, in conjunction with Marketing held a seminar entitled 'Promoting Sales: What Motivates the Retailer and the Consumer?' at the Institute of Directors. The object of the exercise was to unveil the results of a research study incorporating both quantitative and qualitative work. There were a relatively small number of speakers as the conference started at 2pm and finished with drinks at 5.45pm when they probably needed them. The research identified an important general change in the attitudes to sales promotion at the time. Brand managers for packaged goods were looking eagerly for marketing techniques that added value at the point of purchase and also shifted product.

The economy was tight, TV advertising rates were inflated and trade prices were being cut to the bone. Most of these comments would apply today. Sales promotion was also being tried with success by a number of non-traditional businesses, including financial services, public utilities and durables manufacturers. Even in 1983 it was estimated that total expenditure below the line exceeded the amount spent in the media. Research was also beginning to play a more important part.

The researchers tried hard to find out what the public thought about SP, along the lines of previous research for the Advertising Association, which said that three out of four people thought advertising was pretty much okay. In 1966 one in three people were not in favour of advertising, but by 1980 it was only one in five. Sales promotion got the same thumbs up with only 18 per cent being against it. Reactions to different types of promotions varied considerably, but the only really strong negative was cigarette coupons. Oddly enough, the next least desirable offer appeared to be free gifts, and the most desirable was money off (surprise!), followed as equal second by coupons and trading stamps. Stamps have long gone but they would translate as electronic card collection schemes.

The consultants who were questioned were also quite enthusiastic about sales promotion, which is hardly surprising. They felt that it had become more complex with an increasing need to specialise. The consultants also reckoned that promoters were becoming more sophisticated and setting more relevant objectives but they still saw the classic all purpose brief: "Sample non-users, switch consumers from my competitors, increase volume of purchase and reward loyal buyers", to which might be added the other ongoing cry: "Find something new, really different, excitingly original and, ironically, tried and tested".

Asked for their views on the future of SP, consultants said that there would be more competition and they would be forced to work harder to be creative, but they were generally upbeat. They anticipated a growth in non-grocery markets; more interest in retailers' needs; more spending on above the line support, and an interest in new techniques and new technology.

Another comment, which may have been wishful thinking, was that they saw themselves becoming involved with more senior personnel in client companies. They were now talking to marketing directors rather than assistant product managers. Respondents also predicted, quite accurately as it turned out, a reduction in coupon usage, mainly because of misredemption. Coupons, they said, were losing popularity and were expensive to handle. Forecasting was difficult and they felt that retailers did not like promotions unless they were their own.

THE PROMOTERS' AND RETAILERS' VIEWS

Promoters were keen on the SP, which they thought had a strong psychological effect, whatever that meant. However, its emphasis had changed. Ten years before, SP was designed to increase purchases by the consumer, but in the early Eighties considerably more attention was paid to motivating the sales force, a team of workers now almost non-existent in FMCG. The promotions were designed to sell in rather than sell out and brand managers of second-line products were terrified of being delisted, which is still the doomsday scenario. They felt that a good promotion kept the brand on the right side of the buyers and was therefore a worthwhile investment.

Promoters' views on the future of sales promotion were quite encouraging. They felt that in a tight economy SP was bound to prosper and that when budgets were cut the money would move below the line as it was seen as less expensive. There was disagreement on the effect of sales promotion on a brand in the long term. Some thought it unlikely that brand loyalty could be achieved without advertising support; others were more optimistic about the advantages of strategic promotional campaigns. Promoters were worried that sales promotion was developing so fast that it might cease to have an impact on the consumer.

They expected promotional consultancies to work harder to come up with creative and exciting ideas and manufacturers intended to take more care to monitor and measure returns on promotions. Finally they realised that they would have to work more closely with retailers - and how right they were.

Finally we come to what retailers thought about Sales Promotion. It is interesting to see how many of their concerns apply today. First of all, the things they liked. Promotions designed and executed by the store group; promotions that raised the 'authority' of the retailer; promotions that improved the image of the store; promotions that concentrated on a product category; promotions that encouraged consumer loyalty to the store, and tailor-made promotions in general. And of course price reductions, price reductions and more price reductions.

Then what they did not like. One thing that was a given was any promotional activity that they had to pay for. They were most dissatisfied with national promotions run by manufacturers and not specific to their store group, and point-of-sale material that did not fit their strict design policies. Then came competitions and coupons. Competitions were felt to be a waste of money and coupons were difficult to handle at the checkout. They also felt that advertising that promoted the store was preferable to backing specific product promotions. In a competitive environment they had no intention of telling researchers the techniques that they considered effective.

On the future of Sales Promotion, they envisaged retailers and manufacturers working in partnership; campaigns for imaginative and innovative ideas; building societies, banks and holiday companies using SP, and a revision of coupon usage to avoid misredemption. Just read that last one again. Retailers really said that? They should have been politicians.

GIVING THE 18-30S A MUSICAL LIFT.

Back on the shop floor, Thomas Cook was giving away Top 10 LPs to anyone who booked a 'youth' holiday with its Club 18-30 operation. Students of street slang may be interested to know that its 1984 radio ads featured Lenny Henry describing the offer as "wicked" and "totally crucial". In the same year a promotion for Mateus Rose wine won an ISP Award. This may evoke nostalgia in those old enough to remember Berni Inns introducing the plonk to the British Public in the Sixties. Puzzled by the novelty of ordering wine, millions played safe and chose this compromise between red and white. Its distinctive oval bottle subsequently became the feature of a million table lamps, and it is claimed that Berni, almost single handed, saved the Portuguese wine industry.

This was the year when an agency that is still in the same place, with the same name and owned by the same people was founded. That is very unusual. Simon Mahoney, who co-

Quaker on pack offers in the 19th century.

Green Shield Stamps were the biggest thing in the 70's, turning over more than £10,000,000 a year at peak. They were considered quite glamorous, available everywhere and the Redemption Shops simply metamorphed in to Argos.

Green Shield Shop.

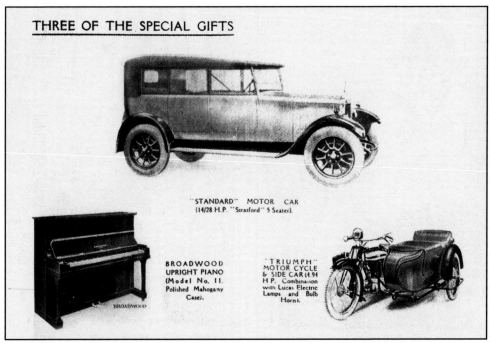

THREE OF THE SPECIAL GIFTS

"STANDARD" MOTOR CAR
(14/28 H.P. "Stratford" 5 Seater).

BROADWOOD
UPRIGHT PIANO
(Model No. 11.
Polished Mahogany
Case).

"TRIUMPH"
MOTOR CYCLE
& SIDE CAR (4.94
H.P. Combination
with Lucas Electric
Lamps and Bulb
Horn).

The Bryant and May retailer collection scheme from the 20's. They must have sold a lot of matches to get a car!

Marathon made the most of the nearly disastrous Apollo 13 Mission.

The Quaker "Toby" Jug, first of a series of promotions that revived a brand.

The very first "proof of purchase for charity" offer that launched a thousand imitators.

This got the buyers on board.

Chivers Goldfish. A free mail that went swimmingly.

OK in 1986 but today distributing lethal weapons might be popular with the local ASBO candidates but not with the local police.

It took over 2 hours of his stand-up show to produce just enough acceptable jokes to fill a minidisk and 90% of these would be banned as "inappropriate" in the 21st century. His act made the "edgiest" thing on current TV sound like a Vicar's tea party.

Barbara Woodhouse of "Walkies" fame started the Andrex puppy on a very long walk.

The Cadbury's Crème Egg that had lots of people digging in lots of wrong places

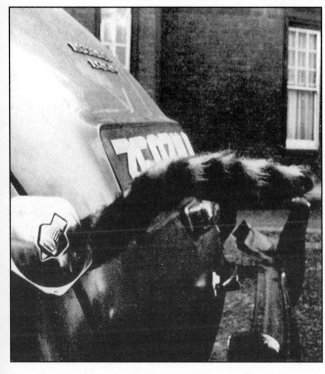

The Esso Tiger Tail, a promotion that wagged the adverting slogan's theme into a world wide success.

The Heinz Build a Children's Home promotion. This was the first of a number of Heinz Beans blockbusters with charity themes, raising large sums from proof of purchase. That lifeboat really launched something.

Simple but very effective. Shell Make Money is considered by many to be the best promotion in modern times.

Thanks to a printing fault this Asda promotion went badly wrong. It cost the agency and printer a lot of **their** cash.

Beer at 1912 prices

A selection of the great and the good that sang for their supper and discussed the future of sales promotion. From left to right they are: Geoff Howe, Louise Wall, Graham Kemp, Colin Lloyd, Our Editor, Andrew Marsden, Ed Downey.

The sexist Grand Prix winner ever with the most unsexy title-. "The government message on unprotected sex".

Who would believe that thousands of ladies [well maybe some men as well] would go to the trouble of knitting little woolly hats with the unlikely, in fact ridiculous, aim of keeping Innocent Smoothies warm in the refrigerator?

founded SMP, started as most leading practitioners did, by working in sales. In his case for Aspro Nicolas, where he worked or, as people who know him think, talked his way up the ladder to be a key account manager with Boots and Superdrug. He then moved into marketing and became a brand manager, a position where he was exposed to both advertising and sales promotion. In his words he thought "sales promotion was really good, as it was about scribbling things down on a pad and giving away crap stuff like sponges".

This led him to join Tim Arnold & Associates as an account executive, one of just five at that time. Simon stayed with Tim for three years and reached the dizzy heights of board director. His major clients at the time were Bowater Scott and the London Rubber Company (LRC), the makers of Durex, and he was responsible for annual revenue of £1.5million. In those days, Simon comments: "Every day when we came in we seemed to have started a new company, nearly all with 'Worthy' in the title." They were all part of the Arnold Worth Group, with TAA the SP agency, backed up by Praiseworthy (hospitality and conferences) and Praiseworthy Personality Marketing, Artworthy (studio), Newsworthy (PR) and Worth Marketing which seemed to be a sort of advertising agency. This proliferation may well have been the undoing of the TAA Empire, as after Simon had moved on it got into financial difficulties and closed its doors.

Why, when everything seemed to be going well, with a strong central agency, Worthy subsidiaries, a good client list, good staff and a good reputation, did the whole thing collapse? Tim's answer is short. "I was pretty good at what I did, but I have since learned there are other issues around managing companies." In reply to a supplementary, about what he would have done differently, his initial reply was even shorter: "I would have taken more money out." After some thought, he expands in typical Arnold fashion: "Given what I know and where I am now, I would not have done anything differently." He admits that this sounds a bit trite and adds that the entrepreneurs who start companies are not always the best people to take them on.

On a lighter note, and in typical eccentric fashion, Tim's response to a request for the best promotion he conceived was one that never ran. It was an idea for match maker Swan Vesta. Working on the fact that some sad people collect match boxes and lots more are keen on birds, he suggested that it produced limited editions with various birds illustrated on the reverse, under the theme Duck Vestas.

The boxes would become collectors' items in themselves, and there would be a self-liquidated poster available showing the full set of ducks. Tim remembers the marketing manager shaking him by the hand and saying it was the best promotion he had ever seen. This may have been because it was free, apart from a fee to Tim of course, but for reasons best know to the board, it was turned down. For the best one he actually ran, he names an ongoing programme for Spar, where TAA took up the cartoon character Hagar the Horrible and his long-suffering wife Helga and attached them to every merchandising scheme the group ran, so that they became synonymous with the store.

PUPPY LOVE
With unusual modesty, he suggests that his all-time favourites are the long-running Andrex Puppy promotions started by KLP. Every offer reinforced the brand, but with a number of twists. In a more philosophical mood, he mused that all promotions have two aspects. Firstly, how it is structured and the nature of the offer, and secondly, how it is communicated. "The best offer, badly communicated will fail," he says. He is critical of the way in which the ISP Awards in the Eighties became heavily reliant on results which, in his opinion, are not all that mattered.

Here he is at odds with Promotional Campaigns' Keith Bantick who says that results are everything. Tim disagrees, a not unusual position for him. and offers this slightly bizarre proof of his view. His promotion for the Dewhurst chain of butchers tried to sell turkeys in February and didn't. A similar scheme in late November and early December was staggeringly successful. We suppose his argument is that both were good promotions, equally creative, perhaps award winners, but timing made all the difference. This proves something but we are quite sure that it is a mistake to try and sell turkeys after Christmas, a not particularly staggering concept.

Tim also has his own, very short definition of sales promotion: "Any marketing activity that promotes sales". Perhaps we should have included this in the introductory chapter. He also disagrees with the dictum that no one pays an agency to tell them to cut prices, citing Jack Trigg, SP manager for Lyons Tetley in the Eighties who would happily pay agencies to come up with different ways of expressing price cuts such as 'Double your Money' and 'Make a Note of It', a cash back scheme. Tim's view is that this was not just a neat headline, but part of the brand's image or persona. "Make a Note of It" came from the brand theme of the time, 'Tetley Makes Tea'. In Tim's view, the offer aims to reach the promotional objectives or, as he prefers to call them, targets but also has to take into account and promote the brand objectives. In other words, integrated marketing.

A BAD DAY AT THE OFFICE
One day Simon Mahoney at TAA presented what he considered to be an exciting scheme to his Bowater Scott client, Chris Simpson, to be told that it was "crap". When he asked the client for a more detailed explanation he was told that it was "f...ing crap". Oddly enough, a week later the same client suggested that Simon might consider going into business on his own. Well, not exactly on his own as the man who was suggesting the idea was proposing a partnership. When he arrived home he told his wife who said she thought it was a good idea so, naturally, he did as he was told. It obviously was a good idea. They roped in Jim Parrock as a third partner and asked the 'Listening Bank' for a start-up loan. It replied: "You must be joking", but luckily Simon had a friend who was an accountant and was able to let them have £10,000 to get going.

On this budget, smart West End or even central London offices were out, so the trio set up in Tunbridge Wells High Street. The initial start was a little hesitant as SMP was about to launch a new medical product for LRC. Unfortunately it was refused a licence and bang went the first job. Things looked up from then on with lots of work for LRC and a steady stream of other clients. More perceptive readers may have noticed that initial customers were the same clients as Simon had worked with at TAA. The same perceptive readers may guess how Tim felt about this.

In time SMP acquired new clients, such as Bristol & West Building Society. The marketing director, Ian Kennedy, was a real character with a rather unusual sense of humour whose idea of a joke was throwing SMP's boardroom chairs out of the window. These were the days when lunch with the client was rather more than bottled water and a salad sandwich on organic brown, and could well run into the afternoon. The problem Kennedy set the agency was to promote the society's mortgages nationally. The difficult bit was that it had different mortgages in different parts of the country and it was not practical to show all the alternatives. The geniuses in Tunbridge Wells came up with a campaign that had staff outside Bristol & West offices handing out packets of 'money tree' seeds to passers-by. The clever twist was that the money tree that grew in Chelsea, perhaps a pension mortgage, would be different to the Cardiff money tree which was probably a 100 per cent mortgage.

All went well until one day Simon received a call from a lady living in the West Country complaining that her son had eaten the seeds from the money tree packet and what should she do about it? Convinced that this was Mr Kennedy setting him up, he told the lady that she should not worry until her son was seven feet tall and looking over the neighbour's fence with a bright yellow face, at which point she could call him again. There was a very stony silence at the other end of the phone, followed by a very irate call to Bristol & West, followed by an equally irate call to SMP from Ian Kennedy and the agency losing the business. We think that is called being too clever by half.

As part of its search for new clients SMP found itself pitching to L'Oreal, on a product called Freestyle Mousse. The presentation was made to a French executive who had come over specifically and SMP was convinced that it was going to get business. It had done a very good deal with Foster Grant sunglasses where, if you bought two of the products you would get a free pair of the rather trendy glasses. After the presentation, the beautifully dressed French executive sat for 30 seconds before saying: "Non"

The problem was in the title for the promotion which SMP had worked up as 'Set the Style with L'Oreal'. It was then explained that under no circumstances would L'Oreal use the word "set". Had they got the business? "Non." The presentation team then departed only to find that their car had collected a parking ticket. The consensus of opinion was that they had not got it quite right on this occasion.

THE HISTORY MAKERS

John Farrell

Alan Toop

Edwin Mutton

Simon Mahoney

John Greenaway MP

Mike Leeves

Stuart Macmillan-Pratt

Kevin Twittey

Joe Flanagan

Roger Hyslop

Peter Kerr

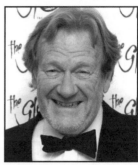

Mike Preston

CHAPTER ELEVEN

The Eighties, Part 2

We're in the money!
The numbers game – how agencies went public
The rollercoaster stock market ride
Life after flotation
Death after floatation

Given the amounts that agencies were claiming to be making in the first years of the decade, it was not a great surprise that some decided they could cash in by floating their company on the stock market. The junior market was then called the Unlisted Securities Market (USM), now transformed into the Alternative Investment Market (AIM). First up was KLP as it was possibly, or at least claimed to be, the biggest independent. In the end, four companies had a life of their own in the public arena although they have all become part of bigger outfits, usually, with the exception of KLP, after running into financial problems. If you are not interested in money (or just dislike lots of numbers) skip this chapter. The figures may seem small change compared to the banker's bonuses of the 21st century but they we pretty good at the time and even now, for anyone in the real, as opposed to the financial, world would be nice to have.

In 1983 KLP was 'placing' (i.e. selling) 747,000 5p nominal value shares for £1.15 each. Of these, 473,256 were sold by directors; the rest were newly issued. To save you reaching for your calculator, this would net £544,000 for the owners and around £200,000 extra capital for the company. It valued the company at £4,700,000. To justify this valuation, KLP showed a steady increase in gross profits from £201,000 in 1978 to £408,000 in 1982. The turnover had moved from £1,966,000 to £5,231,000 during this time.

FINANCIAL TRICKERY

Now, here is an interesting but perfectly legal financial twist. The launch prospectus showed that the profit for shareholders after tax, etc went from £135,019 in 1978 to £180,019 in 1982. However, these figures had been adjusted upwards by writing back extra payments made to the directors, over and above their salaries, under their service contracts. These would not be paid in future to directors of a public company. In other words, the value of the company was based on a notional profit which was considerably higher than the real profit left in the company because the directors had perfectly legally and, as a private company, perfectly reasonably, helped themselves to a fair chunk of the income over those years.

The prospectus also told what the new salaries for the names over the door would be. K got £42,000; L was on £48,000, and P received £45,000. Michael Price, who ran the design side of the business Lloyd Ellerton, was also on £42,000. Now of course they had pocketed some £550,000 by selling some of their shares, plus the money they had already paid themselves but which was in theory, although not in reality, being put back into the company. Not only that, but they still owned and could, in due course, if they wished, sell a large proportion of a company worth more than £7million and rising. Nice work if you can get it and they, together with pretty well everyone else who launched their companies during this period, managed to do just that.

If we move ahead to the end of 1986, we can compare these figures with those of Clarke Hooper which floated at that time. Its gross profit had increased from £52,000 in 1981 to £1,986,000 in 1986. Its turnover had increased from £1,459,000 to £7,350,000. It placed 2,100,000 5p shares at £1.30 per share. Of these, 1,560,500 were sold by existing shareholders and another 539,500 were new shares raising £480,000 for the company. The directors pocketed well over £2million. They also did the 'pretend to put the money we have taken out back because we are not going to do it in future' trick to legally inflate the profits on the previous years. The years 1983, 1984, and 1985 saw unnamed directors take bonuses of £30,000, £40,000 and £48,000 respectively, which were charged against staff costs.

Having just collected £2million between them, the directors continued on quite reasonable salaries for the time with, Messrs. Clarke and Hooper each collecting £60,000 while Colin Chamberlain, the deputy chairman received £45,000 on a fixed term contract to early 1987. Colin had been with the company since 1982 and had come from Heinz which, by some strange coincidence, was a major client of Clarke Hooper. Alan Penson, finance director, was the lowest paid with £35,000 and another director, Denzel Hughes who had been with the agency since 1985 got £45,000. Of course the two founders had also retained a fair number of shares and at the launch price of £1.30, both Clarke and Hooper's shares were worth more than £2million each. At first things went swimmingly with 1986/87 witnessing turnover of £9,350,000 and pre-tax profits of £1,020,000. The company was now worth £9,530,000 but, as we shall see, there was serious trouble on the horizon.

VALUATIONS MAY GO DOWN AS WELL AS UP

Looking back some 20 years later, John Hooper explains what happened. "Like many others, Clarke Hooper was savaged on Black Monday in October 1987 when the share price virtually halved. It never recovered. I resigned from the board in 1990, served an honourable year exclusively on client business and left in mid-1991. To the best of my recollection, the Plc went into planned receivership in late-1992. Colin Chamberlain and I tried to buy the still very profitable UK sales promotion business, but the shell-shocked local management team preferred the AMV offer. Barry and I were left with worthless paper. He stayed on as chairman of the AMV subsidiary some years and then the Clarke Hooper name finally disappeared, some thirty years after its creation."

Why did everything go wrong? There were a number of reasons, several of which also applied to FKB. John lists the key contributory factors as follows:

a) Pandering to City demands for more and more acquisitions.
b) Paying too much for these, due to competitive pressure (Saatchi/KLP/FKB etc).
c) Putting the CEOs of acquired companies on the main Plc board.
d) Opening up too many US offices, from California to New York, Chicago and Houston.
e) Trusting untrustworthy Canadians.
f) Splitting a winning management team geographically. (Me in Slough; Barry in the US).
g) Getting the debt: equity ratio wrong and borrowing at 16 per cent.
h) Putting the wrong people in key roles.
i) Having far too many b****y accountants on central overhead.
j) Allowing one account to dominate (40 per cent) and then losing it.
k) Spending too much time on diversifying into areas such as direct marketing and design.
l) Spending more time on our own business than that of our clients.

He also has strong views on the relationship with advertising agencies. "Sales promotion people were always seen as the 'country cousins' by those arrogant dilettantes. Sadly, although we won many battles, we lost the war. They couldn't beat us so they bought us."

LIFE AFTER SP
But life goes on. In 1995 John became director general of the Incorporated Society of British Advertisers (ISBA), the 'Voice of British Advertisers', serving six years by agreement, leaving in December 2000 just after his sixtieth birthday.

This is how he describes his time running what might be called the 'Advertisers' Trade Union', and a far cry from the coalface of sales promotion. "I had a great time, thoroughly enjoyed the challenging role, learnt many new skills and believe, perhaps immodestly, that I radically changed the organisation for the better. I could probably drone on for hours about my experiences with the senior clients with whom I had regular contact.

"But my overwhelming impressions were that they were overworked, spread too thinly across the many demands of the marketing portfolio, beleaguered in the boardroom and constantly assailed by financial colleagues demanding greater accountability, confused by the rapidly changing media scene, insecure in their personal positions and by and large unconvinced that their agencies were truly adding value." So it's not all long lunches and chauffeur driven Bentleys.

1985 also saw Holmes & Marchant joining USM with a value of £12million. Towards the end of 1987 its paper value was £44million, but at its lowest point in the early Nineties, the company was valued at around £3million. How are the mighty fallen. At the same time, 1987, FKB was worth £29million, KLP slightly less at £27million, and Clarke Hooper at £18million. They were on staggering price-earnings ratios: H&M at 32, with Clarke Hooper on 34. FKB was a little lower on 26 and KLP, which in fact turned out to be the most soundly financed, on a relatively modest 17.

Holmes & Marchant was founded in 1971 and made up of a number of companies, most of which were not pure sales promotion but heavily weighted towards the design business. It made a profit of £674,000 in the year 1983/84 on sales of £2,600,000 but it was hit by Black Monday and the general problems that made life difficult for the other quoted companies in this area. It did manage to keep afloat into the next century when it finally became part of a PR group and dispensed with its sales promotion arm to concentrate on graphics. It was then spun off and still operates independently in a striking Georgian office block in Marlow.

INTERLUDE FOUR - IT SEEMED LIKE A GOOD IDEA AT THE TIME

Crafty consumers, dodgy doings
Simply collect seven million points for your free jet fighter
Free flights with your pudding
A revealing car launch
Staff who helped themselves a bit too much
Corporate entertainment, Manchester style

When you have been working in sales promotion as long as the authors, you begin to feel that nothing can surprise you, which is usually when something really makes you sit up and take notice. Often, it is something the consumer does but at other times it is something that an individual in the industry does. In this section we describe some fairly unusual events. For various reasons it is probably a very good job that they are unusual.

Although consumers can be bloody-minded at times and amazingly stupid at other times, some of them are extremely smart and should not be underestimated. One prime example was a young man in the US who took a long hard look at the small print in a Pepsi promotion 'Buy Pepsi - Get Stuff'. Consumers amassed points by buying Pepsi and could buy merchandise such as T-shirts, caps and jackets with it. However, some copyrighting genius came up with the idea of including a Harrier Jump Jet for 7,000,000 points. A Mr John Leonard of Seattle, who was not only extremely smart, but also extremely persuasive, got together with some of his friends and somehow or other, raised the required points.

When Pepsi received his application it probably did not know whether to laugh or cry, and pointed out that it was only a joke - these things cost $23million. Mr Leonard did not get the joke, but he did get a lawyer. What else, this is America. In court, Pepsi claimed that it was quite obviously a joke, pointing out that the advertisement showed a teenage schoolboy arriving in the aircraft. As part of the judge's 42-page opinion (US lawyers expect value for money) he agreed with the suggestion that a boy of that age would probably not even be trusted with the keys to his father's car. He found for Pepsi, but to be on the safe side, Pepsi then put the points value of the jet fighter up to 700 million.

DON'T TOUCH THAT DIAL

Mr Leonard was not the only consumer to sue a promoter who had not provided the prize they thought they had won. Shannon Castillo of Bakersfield, California, took part in a contest organised by a local radio station Play 103.9. The object was to come up with the correct mileage accumulated during one week by the station's two Hummer H2s. The prize for the correct answer was apparently a Hummer H2. Anyway Shannon got the correct answer, which by a strange coincidence was 103.9. She and another prize-winner arrived at the station at 6am to find that she was not about to collect a $60,000 muscle machine but a toy version. Very funny, but the radio station was promptly hit by a lawsuit for $60,000.

Radio stations do have a reputation for being a little careless in the promotions they run, possibly because the fast-talking DJs do not have to have their scripts approved by a lawyer or the ISP's Legal Advisory Service. In May 2005, a certain Norreasha Gill was the tenth person to call a station known as Hot 102 after 'DJ Slick' (real name Jason Hamman) announced that the station would be giving '100 grand' to the tenth caller. Ms Gill's prize was not $100,000 in cash but 100 Grand brand candy bars from the Lexington based station. She is suing the owner, Cumulus Media Inc, for the $100,000. Although you might think that the chances of these two ladies winning are slight, stranger things have happened in US court rooms.

Another lady, Jodee Berry, took part in an incentive scheme run by a brewery to see who could sell the most beer in a month. The prize was a new Toyota, or so the Hooters' waitress thought when she was led blindfolded into the car park to receive her award. With an excruciating sense of humour this turned out to be a 'Toy Yoda', a doll of the Star Wars character. While everyone else fell about laughing, Jodee got on the phone to her lawyer who succeeded in successfully suing for breach of contract and fraudulent misrepresentation. The amount paid out was undisclosed but one of the delighted law team said that it enabled her to pick out any model of Toyota she wanted.

Some other consumers who won without resorting to the legal profession were those frequenting a chain of home electronic stores called Silo. In an effort to be hip, it advertised on TV a very nice stereo for 299 "bananas". It seems that 'bananas' is a slang term for dollars. A number of consumers literally took them at their word and turned up with the appropriate number of bananas worth approximately $40-$60. In the end Silo handed out 32 of the stereos and donated the bananas to local zoos.

Another crafty consumer was a certain Klaus Hilleprandt, a reader of the German magazine Bunte. It ran a promotion showing a French pop star of the period, Mireille Mathieu apparently floating in thin air. The caption read: "Naturally, there is a trick about it. Whoever spots it wins a trip to Las Vegas." Bunte meant to say that the first person to spot the trick won the trip but this slip was quickly spotted by Klaus. He claimed that he also deserved to go on the trip as well as the official first prize winner. He won his case and the judge said that he was entitled to a flight to Las Vegas and a three-day stay at a luxury hotel. The publisher was terrified that thousands of other competitors would claim, but some kind of statute of limitations saved them. Now you know why defence lawyers work so slowly.

IN FLIGHT MEALS
Many people can become quite obsessive about collecting frequent flyer miles but the undoubted king is David Phillips who managed to convert $3,150 worth of Healthy Choice

puddings into 1,253,000 million miles. Not only that, but he claimed a $815 tax write-off. Visiting a local supermarket, he noted a promotion offering 500 frequent-flier miles for every 10 barcodes from Healthy Choice products. The closing date was 31 December and if you responded quickly you could double the mileage up to 1,000 miles for every 10 labels. David, a civil engineer and good at maths, recognised what a great deal this was. The puddings cost $2, and in no time at all he had filled his garage and his living room and ordered 60 more cases from his local outlet, taking him to a total of 12,150 puddings.

With the deadline rapidly approaching he had to remove all the barcodes and mail them in. Quick thinking solved this problem as he trucked the packs to two local food banks and the Salvation Army organised the removal of the barcodes in exchange for the food. He sent off the barcodes and waited with understandable trepidation for the promoter to find a technicality that would disbar him from collecting the miles. He need not have worried. It was not an insurance company.

The mail delivered 2,506 certificates, each good for 500 miles, making the total of 1,253,000 miles. The terms allowed him to use these with any airline account but he put most of them with American. This had the added benefit of giving him 'Aadvantage Gold' status for life with priority boarding, upgrades and even more bonus miles. Because he gave the product to charity, he could deduct the original cost from his tax bill and save himself $815.

Now here is a good bit if you are in the promotional marketing business. The promoter, Healthy Choice, considered that it did very well out of the whole deal. It was only paying the airline a maximum of two cents per mile. Ten bar codes @ $2 = a retail price $20, with, say a wholesale price of about $16. It cost them at most $10 to buy the miles so the costs were controllable and related directly to sales. The company would only say that the promotion "met and exceeded expectations". In addition it got a vast amount of excellent publicity at the time in 2000, because it mailed out the certificates without a quibble. As an end note, in 2002 this true story was the basis for an Adam Sandler film called Punch-Drunk Love.

A cunning but rather less successful punter was a clerk working at Air Canada in London who earned himself an unusual holiday by misusing frequent flyer points. Nine months in jail in fact. He had given five million frequent flyer points, worth £33,000, to himself and his friends. In Germany there was a hot election issue over how MPs could spend their Lufthansa air miles and two prominent politicians, accused of spending points earned in work-related travel on their personal trips, were forced to resign. If everyone who collected air miles in this way was caught there would be mass unemployment in the executive ranks. Something similar has cropped up in the UK, with the then Speaker of the House of Commons using air miles earned on official business to send his wife on holiday.

Another example of crafty travellers occurred in 1979. United Airlines was recovering from a major strike and needed to recapture customers. Someone, presumably with grocery marketing experience, came up with a 'money off next purchase' coupon. A voucher gave a 50 per cent reduction on the next United flight, anywhere, with the first flight purchased. It brought the customers pouring in, mainly because it had an enormous loophole. Customers were buying the shortest, cheapest flight, New York to Washington for example, and then immediately booking more costly flights at half price. There was even a rumour that the US government was buying up vouchers to fly staff all over the country.

SMILE!

This was not the only US airline promotion to be miscalculated. In 1985 TWA teamed up with Polaroid, which offered a 25 per cent discount on TWA economy flights to any destination as long as they bought a camera or some film. Polaroid had already done something like this successfully with both United and Delta, offering $100 discounts or two-for-one flights. However this time it made a small but disastrous mistake by omitting to limit it to one application per customer. Across the US, travel agents looked at the scheme and rushed out and bought up all the Polaroid cameras and film they could lay hands on. A 25 per cent discount on a long flight was a lot more than the cost of a Polaroid camera and travel agents were able to pass it on to their customers at no cost and still make a margin. Fortunately for the airline, IATA rules would not allow it to operate on transatlantic flights, but the expected redemption level of 100,000 to 150,000 was exceeded by more than 300 per cent. Shades of Hoover.

On one occasion Lever Brothers found to its cost that retailers can spot a loophole if it is to their advantage. Lever persuaded a number of other manufacturers to provide money off coupons in a book that was included in Persil packs. It was inexpensive for Persil and an inexpensive way for other brands to get targeted coupons into the market. However, the promoters made one cardinal and expensive error. Lever was so successful in rounding up partners that the value of the coupons added up to more than the trade cost of a pack of detergent. An awful lot of small but sharp shopkeepers noticed, slit open the packs, removed the book of coupons, resealed packs with tape (or even just emptied them into plastic bags) and then sold the Persil at a discounted price. They then redeemed all the coupons and got face value plus the handling allowance, making a very useful profit. Of course the consumers had not actually bought the products for which the coupons were redeemed but when has that worried a grocery retailer - not in living memory.

It is often surprising that the best laid plans go astray. Brian Palmer, one-time sales promotion manager at P&G tells of a late-Fifties margarine promotion called 'The Big Dig'. Prize-winners were offered a variation on the trolley dash in which they started with £25,000 worth of silver coins, a shovel and a bucket. They were given a limited time to shovel coins into the bucket and dump them into a container. Everything in the container was their prize.

The agency responsible was very careful. First of all it discovered that £25,000 in coins was very heavy and checked that the floor would take the strain. Secondly it opted for a relatively small spade, shaped like a scoop to give the winner a reasonable chance. It wanted to have some idea of how much was likely to disappear so hired a couple of navvies from a nearby building site to test it. The amount collected was not unreasonable and everything was put back ready for the event. At this point it was decided to recount the money. Surprise, surprise, there was a fair bit less than £25,000 remaining. It seemed that the hired diggers had deep pockets, and by the time the count was completed the local building site had finished and the diggers had disappeared elsewhere.

In today's digital electronic climate, numbers can cause problems, as Sainsbury discovered when it ran an online promotion. This included a £10 voucher sent to customers whose orders arrived more than an hour late. It turned out to be rather more generous than intended, because the e-mailed vouchers carried codes, which more switched on customers realised could be used time and time again by opening a new account. No figures have been released, but one crafty character claimed to have ordered up to £5,000 worth of free goods before the loophole was closed.

More worrying is the discovery that some bright hackers have found a profitable, rather then annoying, use for their digital skills. The ISP had to issue a warning that online competitions were proving a useful source of income for these clever folk. There were two methods in use. One was to write a computer programme that would make multiple entries, and we mean multiple, as they run into thousands, and so collect lots of prizes which they sell on. A variation would be to make a large number of entries in various names, or to be accurate, various e-mail addresses and so greatly increase their chance of winning. Both are bad news for the promoter as they greatly devalue the programme.

STAFF INCENTIVES
Sometimes problems arise within an organisation, created intentionally by members of staff for their own benefit. Over the years, print buyers have acquired a questionable reputation, and several have ended up in jail having conspired with their suppliers to make a very healthy living over and above their salary. Obviously, the vast majority of them are absolutely honest, although in the past their offices at Christmas could resemble the local branch of Threshers wine merchants who seemed to have gone bust at the time of writing this book. One of the biggest, if not the biggest rip-off had nothing to do with backhanders in brown paper envelopes from a friendly printer. This particular scam ran for more than six years, and succeeded in diverting something like £9million into the bank accounts of fraudulent prize

winners. The company that suffered was McDonald's, which has a reputation for very big and very successful promotions.

It ran two cash prize games of Monopoly, followed by Who Wants to be a Millionaire? The answer to that question turned out to be the security director of its supplier, Simon Marketing. He was the man responsible for seeding winning tickets on a countrywide basis. What he actually did was pass them on to the various members of his gang, who would then claim the prizes and split up the cash. When this activity came to light, the agency lost its two biggest accounts (the other being Philip Morris), and with them several million dollars of turnover. We don't know what happened to the security director, but we suspect he is somewhere with very good security!

On a smaller scale, a very subtle scam took place in, of all places, the stately homes of England. A number of the larger locations set up a cross merchandising operation. If you went to one such home, you received a voucher that gave you a discount when visiting some other delightful residence. This might be worth a pound or so off your entrance fee and ticket office staff would send a number of their vouchers to their opposite numbers at another home, who would return the compliment. When the visitors paid the full fee, the crook behind the till inserted the voucher and pocketed the value. The tills balanced, so it was hard to spot, until someone wondered why such a large number of vouchers were turning up. There were soon new faces on the gates and, probably, in the local Magistrates Court.

THE MAIN EVENT
Corporate entertainment is a close relative to sales promotion and has a major crossover with motivation. Nowadays, it seems that everyone is in need of a boost, unlike the old days when a sales director could proudly boast that the only incentive he needed was called "The Sack". Generally speaking, motivation requires expensive locations with a generous food and drink allowance for existing clients, prospective clients or members of staff. Whatever the reason for the event, the opportunities for cock-up and embarrassment are legion.

The first example involves the launch of a new high profile car with a major roadshow travelling around the country and ending on a bleak, overcast, sleet-filled day in Edinburgh. This meant that a good deal of cold and murky water had been trodden into the exhibition area and the floor closely resembled an ice rink. The typical 'reveal' would involve yanking covers off the car. This was to be done by female dancers, clad in Lurex body stockings and not much else, who before the event, were doing their thing around the vehicles.

This would have been great, if the floor had been dry or if the body stockings had been a better fit. In this instance, one of the dancers, who would have given Jordan a run for her money in terms of her endowment, lost her footing and actually slid beneath the car canopy, only to emerge seconds later and continue her performance. What a trooper! However, much to the delight of the audience and the chagrin of the producer, her endowments had appeared above the top of the costume and were performing an unplanned and a very energetic routine of their own. Eventually the producer was able to persuade her to leave the stage, amidst loud jeers from the audience. It gave a whole new meaning to the word 'reveal'.

YOU'VE GOT TO LAUGH

An example of an unfortunate choice for corporate entertainment comes from Whitbread. It decided to put some effort behind its Mackeson brand with a relaunch and needed an in-pub promotion to gain lapsed and new drinkers. The advertising positioning was along the lines of 'You'd be surprised how good Mackeson is' with the strap line 'The Mackeson Surprise'. At the time record companies were developing 'flexi-discs' as a sampling product. Also at this time the TV series 'The Comedians' was popular, with the eponymous Bernard Manning delivering his 'unique' sense of humour to the masses. Whitbread's agency KLP teamed the two innovations together as a free flexi-disc called 'The Bernard Manning Mackeson Surprise'.

Bernard Manning was at the time linked to Granada Television, so the agency negotiated with it to record his talents. His demands were cash on the day with the recording to take place in his Embassy Club in the back streets of Manchester during a normal Friday night show. He would provide six minutes of jokes to fill one Flexi-disc. The client decided to attend the show and meet Bernard. Big mistake! On arrival at the Embassy Club, Bernard was busily writing on his hand, his material for the evening. The tables were covered in plastic gingham oilcloth with cigarette burn marks. Just the place to entertain good clients and their spouses. Not realising what sort of nightclub it was, the wives had dressed for the occasion in high fashion frocks. They were not impressed by the ambience. Bernard introduced himself and cracked a few jokes, which were a bit near the mark. Then the punters arrived.

In they poured, strictly segmented by gender. It soon became clear that Friday night at the Embassy was the stag/hen night capital of the North West. The tables were soon covered with a brewery of beer and Babycham and the oilcloth was smoking nicely. The place was heaving and there was not a couple in sight, apart from Whitbread's clients who by this time were questioning their sanity. On came Bernard, but his first one-hour stint did not provide a second of acceptable material. The client was dumbstruck and the wives spent a lot of time hiding in the ladies. After much negotiation with Bernard, who had no idea what the problem was, he agreed to tone down the second half of his show. His version of toning down and the client's were somewhat removed from each other. However, after another hour it proved possible to scrape together six minutes of material that could just be used without being prosecuted for obscenity. Despite the evening's debacle, and to everyone's surprise and delight 'The Mackeson Surprise' beat all its forecasts.

It is an old acting adage to avoid working with children or animals, and the same applies in sales promotion. Kevin Peake, who in 1992 was SP manager at the TSB Bank, ran into problems with an animal of sorts. The plan was to run a Christmas charity promotion linked to the NSPCC and at the time Sega game consoles were the top Christmas list item. Kevin's agency came up with the bright idea of offering an exclusive Sonic the Hedgehog poster from all TSB branches in exchange for a minimum donation of £1 to the charity. To publicise this, a nationwide tour was organised with the giant spiked hedgehog visiting major branches. The first appearance was at TSB's head office, and proved a great start as the local newspaper ran a photograph of Sonic, with his costume head removed, having a quiet fag. Not great PR, although at that time smoking in public had not become a capital offence.

The agency then provided a minder to keep control of Sonic. The next major appearance was at the huge Meadowhall Shopping Centre in Sheffield, heavily publicised and attracting press, TV, thousands of kids and the TSB marketing director. Nothing could be allowed to go wrong, but everything did. Firstly, the minder called to say that the actor inside Sonic had been rushed to hospital with food poisoning, blaming a curry and beer session in Liverpool. The minder was told to bring the costume to Sheffield, at which point he revealed he could not drive. This became irrelevant, because the costume was last seen in the children's ward of the Liverpool General Hospital, and never made it to Sheffield. Kevin Peake is still working, but not for TSB.

Mock animals of this type can occasionally be a good thing, and provide more than the original plan. Knorr Soup was running a panda ad campaign and supported this with a tour of supermarkets. This required one poor soul to prance around in a panda suit with a minder dressed as the zookeeper. On one occasion, as the pair was outside getting some fresh air, someone tried to rob the store. They heroically tackled the robber and wrestled him to the ground. That would be a police report to read, and the robber has probably never lived it down. This, and the following story, comes from Diane Rowe, who was formerly sales promotion manager at Unilever.

On another occasion she was working on Andrex and landed the job of looking after all the puppy photographic shoots. She describes it as "always interesting". Apparently it is very hard getting a seven-week old puppy to run, sit or lie down on cue. The length of the shoot is linked to the time it takes for the puppies to be fed and watered, checked by the vet, have their naps, and generally enjoy themselves, which usually took almost the whole of an eight-hour day, and often provided only around 10 minutes of actual photography. On one occasion, the team had to sit in silence for nearly two hours, waiting for a puppy to fall asleep, so that they could get the snaps they wanted but this was not as bad as a four-day shoot during a heat wave when all the puppies got mites and the whole crew was scratching as much as the dogs by the end.

PROBLEM, WHAT PROBLEM?

Timing can cause problems, as Clive Mishon discovered one day in the Eighties before Black Monday, when everyone was buying and selling shares. He had to respond to a Guinness brief and at that time it was one of the favourite stock market shares. Instead of offering some kind of widget, the proposal was that prize winners should 'Own a Share in Britain's Greatest Companies'. Naturally, one of these was Guinness. On his way to the presentation he heard a radio news item about the DTI raiding the offices of Guinness and it was suggested that there were some irregularities in their merger with the Distillers Company. He thought it might cause a problem, but as the news had just broken he did not think it would ruin his presentation, which after all had required hours of work, so he put it to the back of his mind.

When he arrived at Park Royal there was no mention of the news item and the meeting went ahead as planned. At the end, one of the client team asked if today's news would affect the promotion. This produced some blank stares around the room so Clive, wanting to show he had his finger on the pulse, told everyone that this was a small inconvenience and finished with the prophetic words that "When this promotion breaks in four months time this event will have been forgotten".

This proved to be as about inaccurate as one could get. What followed was a major City scandal that changed the face of Guinness as a company forever and affected the lives of a number of people, including an executive who was given a term in jail, but famously became the only known case of a patient recovering from Alzheimer's!

CHAPTER TWELVE

The Eighties, Part 3

Onward and upward
The new wave of break away agencies
Dial-a-promotion - the next electronic revolution
SP Down Under
Payback time – SP agencies earn a pretty penny
The return of the Magnificent Seven

Moving on in the decade, what was happening in the real world of 1984 as opposed to the slightly unreal world of sales promotion? It was Los Angeles Olympics, although the Eastern Bloc wasn't playing. The final Jacksons' tour was big news. Nearer to home, the late and not much lamented Robert Maxwell had bought the Daily Mirror and was personally on the telly extolling the first ever £1million guaranteed newspaper bingo prize. It was also the year of the miner's dispute, three million unemployed, and the 5-0 'blackwash' of England's cricket team by the West Indies.

In SP, The Premium Show took place at the Wembley Conference Centre. It was the 11th event of its kind, although the name had changed. The visitor promotion was the chance to win a 125bhp, 120 mph Colt Turbo. It was also announced that the BPMA would henceforth be called the British Promotional Merchandise Association. It had, since its 1964 foundation, had the same initials, but at the time no one seemed to remember what they stood for before the change. In fact, as mentioned in a previous chapter, it was the British Premium Manufacturers Association.

THE BREAKAWAYS BEGIN
By 1984 Bob Bayley had moved on from Marden Kane and was a big wheel at the highly successful agency The Sales Machine, where there was some possibility of selling out to Saatchi & Saatchi. It didn't come off and a coven of his senior executives persuaded him to break away and set up shop as Option One. The name started as the code name for the planned breakaway but stuck. The move left the chairman of The Sales Machine, Alan Toop, in a rather difficult position having just lost five of his senior staff and a fifth of his headcount. Apart from his managing director Bayley, he also lost Colin Jones (operations director), Charles Lauber (finance director), plus account directors Robin Ford and Diana Toombs.

Alan Toop managed to put a fairly upbeat spin on the situation, saying: "For some time I have been aware that there have been too many chiefs and not enough Indians in the agency so I'm taking advantage of the situation. I will not be replacing them, but will concentrate on building up a strong middle management." He added: "By losing some heavyweights I will be by reducing my overheads which have always tended to be high." He also pointed out increased turnover from £1,430,000 in 1982 to £2,757,000 in 1984, not mentioning that these figurers were achieved before all the rainmakers left. Good try Alan.

The new business started with 19 people and required almost no financial input from the founders as they were backed from the start by clients. As in most breakaways, these were mainly clients from the previous agency. To avoid the possibility of one person dominating the others, as had happened previously, the directors each had 10 per cent of the equity. They also brought in Doug Goldie, who had been an independent operator and Ken Vaughan from General Foods, an ex-client. Doug did not last long as he had a different understanding of how an agency owned by a number of shareholders worked financially. When he acquired a piece of business with a fee of £2,000 he claimed that this was all his. This did not go down well with the other directors and he was soon waved a not too fond farewell.

The 1983 ISP Awards Grand Prix winner was the 'Pint Size Guinness Book of Records', the second year that a Guinness promotion had achieved the top award. It went on to win silver in the European Federation of Sales Promotion Awards too. It was entered, not by a SP specialist, but by the now defunct advertising agency, Alan Brady and Marsh. Other winners included Creative Strategy, Clarke Hooper, Senior King, CBH and Partners, KLP, Masterguide, Endacott RJB, AMA, The Sales Machine and Impulse. It is also interesting to note that four awards were won by promotions designed, operated and entered by the client.

THE FUTURE'S BRIGHT
What else was the ISP up to in that year? Apart from its golf tournament at Wentworth, where Keith Bantick came second, the big news was the publication after two years' work of two major research projects. One entitled 'Promoting Sales: What Motivates the Retailer and Consumer?' was referred to as a Delphi study or 'Futurology'. The researchers asked such interesting questions as whether competitions were more popular than self liquidators and why both retailers and housewives disliked low value coupons, which doesn't sound a very difficult question. It ran to 75 pages and cost £20. In November 1984 the result of another massive research project was announced at a conference called Sales Promotion – Tomorrow's World. The research was carried out by the Cranfield School of Management plus NOP Research and the resulting paperwork was roughly the size of an average telephone directory. The conference set delegates back £69, including a copy of the report, worth £25.

Such crystal ball-gazing can be a dangerous hobby unless you can make sure that no one remembers what you got wrong. In retailing, the report predicted late-night opening to increase and that Sunday opening, if allowed, would be adopted slowly. The multiples were expected to continue to grow to a national market share of 75 per cent by 1990. It also thought that sales promotion would extend out of groceries into insurance and professional services. Pretty good so far. As far as SP agencies were concerned, they were expected to be operating Europe-wide by 1990 and that most of the large ones would have gone public by 1994. This was hardly earth-shattering insight, as KLP had floated successfully while the research was underway.

Cranfield also thought that advertising agencies would take over SP agencies in order to protect their spheres of influence and share of budget. In terms of promotional techniques, there was nothing very exciting. Predictions included a decline in competitions, trading stamps and in-press coupons with growth for free gifts and mailed or in-store coupons. The 42 people surveyed (23 consultants and 19 promoters) were asked when they thought certain things would happen. The soothsayers could foresee a four-day week by 2000; EEC harmonising sales promotion by 1992, and that sales promotion would become more influential with the average market director by 1988. Not so good!

The second half of the research project by NOP questioned a cross-section of consumers. The first half of the questions asked what they thought of sales promotion and the second section asked which promotional techniques they liked or disliked. The good news was that consumers tended to approve of SP, particularly the 15-24 year olds. An encouraging number of consumers claimed to buy an item on promotion with half doing so at least once a month and 70 per cent doing so at least once every three months. However, the older and more affluent were less enthusiastic about SP. Unsurprisingly, the most popular promotions were those offering price reductions, together with those where everyone was rewarded. These included BOGOFs and label or token collection to obtain reductions on a future purchase.

Competitions and games were very popular among the heavy users and with the younger users. Participation in these appears to be one of the major discriminators between those who like promotions and partake regularly and those who don't. The least popular promotions were trading stamps, collecting labels for charity and in-store demonstrations. The time taken to receive anything tangible from trading stamps was a deterrent and charity offered no obvious material benefit. Despite this, there have been an awful lot of charity promotions since this research and trading stamps have become electronic and are very popular.

There was no significant agreement with a suggestion that sales promotion saved money and makes shopping fun, but 80 per cent did agree that it gave an opportunity to try new products and brands. Consumers generally considered that games or competitions were run fairly and there was no indication that promotions were losing favour with consumers. Surprisingly, consumers were not enthusiastic about newspaper promotions, with 51 per cent against them. This was a time when the tabloids were throwing £1million promotions in all directions.

In summary, it seemed that at this point in the development of the industry, consumers were prepared to accept sales promotion and were generally in favour. They were prepared to accept promotions in new areas such as insurance and even legal advice. It was also clear that the consumers aged 15-24 and from C2 households were the most prolific users.

DIAL-A-PROMOTION

It was around about this time that the telephone, the old fashioned landline of course, was considered a dynamic, low-cost method of communicating a promotion. Phone-ins were big news, just as text-to-win would be some 20 years later. British Telecom had a business in phone-in services, such as Dial a Disk where you could listen to pop tunes over your telephone. Sound familiar? Such services received more than 100 million calls a year. The speaking clock got 320 million calls a year, so there were obviously a lot of people without a watch.

With 80 per cent of homes linked to the phone network, most of the consumers of interest to promoters could be involved. There were two types of phone promotion, live and pre-recorded. The former was popular for competitions where answers, names and addresses were required to be collated. Voice recognition was yet to be invented and there was no pushing buttons to record your options. Pre-recorded messages were convenient and easy to update as necessary, not to mention cheaper. BT was the big provider of the mechanical side of the service and there were a number of commercial companies who would hire equipment and staff. Here are some call levels from promotions at the time.

KP Mystery Phone-in	900,000
KP Dial the Stars	1,300,000
Persil Mickey Mouse Phone-in	400,000
Persil Auto Dial a Programme	500,000
Unigate Prize Guys	600,000

This was a period of massive competition in the tabloid press, mainly between The Sun and The Mirror. As well as cutting cover prices, they were throwing million pound promotions at each other. These were mostly variations on bingo. The Mirror cut its price to 17p which, with daily sales of 3,500,000 copies, was something it could not afford to keep up for long. The paper, led from the front by the later to become notorious Robert Maxwell, ran a unique roadshow which consisted of Mr Maxwell and a group of his writers travelling the country, meeting readers and no doubt charming them into keeping buying The Mirror.

EMPIRE BUILDING

Meanwhile, the rapidly growing and expansionist agencies were adding numerous specialist services to their basic consultancy package. Most had artwork studios and print departments and they were taking on PR, conferences, AV production and even a travel agency or two. Anything that could turn a reasonably honest penny. Not everyone thought this was a good idea and Alan Toop spoke out against it, even though he had a subsidiary studio called Brass Tacks.

Roger Hyslop of Marketing Triangle was similarly not in favour, claiming that 90 per cent of its business was either on contract or retainer and that it would buy any specialist skills it did have in-house. FKB, on the other hand, was expanding like a blowfish on steroids. From 1982 it had added a field promotions company, a telephone selling company, a print works, a design studio and a PR consultancy called Jervis Read. Brian Francis was also on the lookout for a conference production company. In 1981 Promotional Campaigns had its own studio and had added an advertising division with at least three clients, including Safeway and a Portuguese table wine. (Probably Mateus Rose.) Meanwhile, Tim Arnold's TAA had almost as many tentacles as an octopus and the five-year-old Le Conte Gale let it be known that it was considering collecting an ad agency, a travel company and a market research firm.

Mintel was doing one of its regular surveys into sales promotion and ran into the problem that everyone has had before and since: how dto you define sales promotion? It came up with a market size of between £1billion and £5 billion which gave a reasonable amount of latitude. However, after eliminating what it referred to as "price dealing" it produced a best estimate of around £2billion. This compared to the ad spend of the day of around £4billion. Mintel also concluded there were about 100 specialist SP consultancies operating at the time, of which 25 were "important". It did not name them, and it is hard to put much faith in the research as it considered that lotteries or sweepstakes were competitions and completely ignored free draws, tailor-mades, multibrand schemes, share outs, and banded offers, not to mention money-off coupons and premiums. Hopefully no one reading this book actually paid for the Mintel survey.

Sales promotion gongs were also being handed out Down Under in 1984, by the Australian Sales Promotion Association, which was founded in 1979. It is now renamed The Australian Promotional Marketing Association, showing how up to date it is. The Grand Prix went to Promotional Campaigns' work that linked the Variety Club and Nissan to a sugar refining company and handed over A$50,000 for Sunshine coaches. A major award also went to CSR for something involving jam pots and raising money for children, Cubs and Scouts. Between them these good causes got A$110,000.

ASPA had 20 consultancy members, compared to the ISP's 60 consultancies. Fourteen of these were in New South Wales, around Sydney. The lifestyle was beginning to exert an appeal and the industry was run almost entirely by British expats, with familiar names like Purchase Point, The Sales Machine, Promotional Campaigns and IMP having outposts with apparently no financial or managerial involvement.

Mike DaSilva of Mike DaSilva Associates in Sydney reckons he was the man who founded the sales promotion industry in Australia in the early Seventies and has a good story to tell. He went on to be the 2007 president of the global body for sales promotion agencies, the Marketing Agencies Association Worldwide, and had always wanted to get into advertising. On leaving school in Adelaide, he got a job with Esso at the time that Australia was in the throes of the 'Tiger in Your Tank' promotion. It arrived Down Under in 1966 and Mike's job was a highly responsible one, taking the Tiger suit around to petrol stations to be part of local promotional activity.

Rather than try to get into a Sydney ad agency, he packed his bags and took off for London in 1969, where he promptly failed to get a job in advertising. On the strength of his vast promotional experience in petroleum marketing, he contacted Castrol who were impressed and offered him a job as senior credit controller, something for which he was totally unqualified. This was a stepping stone to becoming assistant to the publicity manager at Burmah Castrol at a time when high profile forecourt promotions were a massive business.

When he went back to Australia in 1974, there was no such thing as a sales promotion agency, so he decided to launch one. At that time, promotional activity was carried out in-house and the sector was about 10 years behind the British experience. To drive income, he initially attached himself to an ad agency which generously offered to pay him A$6,000 a year. When his first promotion made a profit of A$36,000, he was promptly offered a 10-year contract. However, he was determined to go it alone and started his own agency in 1975. In 1981 he merged with two other companies and became Purchase Point, a name which one of the partners had seen on a visit to London and appropriated without mentioning it to the British owners. The combined effort was the biggest SP company in the country. In 1984 it sold out to McCann Erickson which had the Coca-Cola business and wanted to get its hands on the below-the-line programmes and start charging commission. Until then SP in the agency had been subsidised by the commission on media.

Mike DaSilva's favourite promotion from the many that he has run is very different, due to its prize structure. Qantas needed to promote its business class cabin but it would take 12 months to catch up with the competition in terms of seating arrangements, so required something in the meantime. Mike persuaded the Columbia Business School in New York to allow five Qantas business class prize winners to attend one of its high-profile and very expensive senior executive courses for free. Qantas paid for the prize, worth around US$34,000. He could not resist calling it 'Win a Business Class'. It was very successful and was repeated with other clients and other business schools.

BUILDINGS DOWN, SALES UP

Sales promotion has always been a 'can do' profession. In its earlier days it would occasionally work on the basis of "The answer is yes, now what exactly was the question?" In their enthusiasm, agencies would agree that they could do something and then work out how. What follows is a pretty good example of this approach. This promotion is so typically macho and Australian that it had to be included. It could have ended in the disaster files, but against the odds, it didn't.

The product was Nestle Crunch and the campaign ran in the mid Eighties. It was based on a TV commercial in which a kid was eating a Crunch bar on the shore of Sydney Harbour. As he took a bite, the houses on the other side of the harbour shook. With a spark of inspiration, the agency suggested to the client at the briefing that they could have winners in the five states making a real building go 'crunch'. The client bought it on the spot.

At this point the agency suddenly started to think of liability, legal approvals and a possible PR backlash if anything went wrong, but they went ahead anyway. It couldn't show any real examples of the buildings because they had no idea how, when or where they would make the buildings go crunch. But they had 12 months to negotiate these five events.. The promotion finished and the five winners were selected, but there was little budget to spend on the prizes, and the cost was unknown.

The agency started to drive around building sites. It phoned departments of planning and demolition companies and eventually found an old wharf on Sydney harbour. Mike put on jeans and a shirt to meet the die hard union site managers. Having told the manager what he wanted to do, he was asked what was in it for the workers. A promise of cartons of beer, supplied by another client, did the trick. The next day, the 10-year-old winner, the client, and a TV news crew descended on the site. The site manager was ecstatic and the beer was hidden while the whole site stopped. Four wooden corner beams were attached by a line to a bulldozer.

The kid sat next to the bulldozer driver and put his foot to the pedal whereupon the whole wharf shook and gave way, crashing to the ground. Everyone, the TV Crew, drivers passing by the wharf and one of the Royal Australian Navy Frigates, were covered in a wave of dust. The site manager said: "S..t that was good. I've always wanted to do that." The pictures made the 6pm news and helped secure the other four events. They used a ball hammer to knock down a block of flats, an enclosed bulldozer to drive through an old shopping centre and two blasts to bring down chimney stacks as each site manager tried to outdo the others.

SALARY LEVELS

On a more prosaic theme, how did the money look in the UK at the time? A product manager in a large company could earn around £12-13,000 a year with a company car. Marketing directors in FMCG companies were earning an average of £41,000 a year. Their equivalent in a construction company would earn around half that amount but had better job security. On the agency side, account directors were around the £35,000 mark and account managers got £18-22,000. Just about everyone got a car in those days, before the tax system made it much less attractive. To put this into perspective, in 1983 Lloyds offered an 'extra interest' account paying 13.25 per cent gross interest. The rate of inflation was higher than this, as were mortgage rates.

In 1984 there was a product launch that demonstrated the power of below-the-line marketing. Showering had a new product called Cherry B as a competitor to Babycham, which was the only serious product in the female pub drink market. Babycham had 70 per cent of this baby bottled drink business. Originally a Britvic product before being acquired by Showering, Cherry B was a British made grape based wine with imported cherry juice and had an alcohol content of 13.5 per cent which was probably rather more alcoholic than many of the drinkers realised.

These drinks, which do not taste alcoholic but have a hidden kick, were known in the trade as KDs or 'knicker droppers'. Cherry B was also competing with Snowball, a ready mixed Advocaat and lemonade, and Pony which was a cream sherry. It was launched entirely below the line with a massive £10,000 budget. Each drink came with a cocktail stirrer and flag as proof of purchase. The flag included a competition entry form which the handling house complained were often stained with fluids, not always Cherry B. As part of the promotion the company ran party nights at various discos, and this successful launch developed many variations on the theme and increased the budget to £200,000 a year, selling £8million worth of product.

It wasn't all debauchery though. There was a growing healthy living bandwagon in the early Eighties which the cereal manufacturers leapt smartly aboard. Kellogg launched Bran Flakes, harking back to the Sixties when, as noted earlier, All Bran spent years claiming to cure constipation. At the same time, after the years of being told how good full cream milk was, suddenly semi skimmed milk was heavily promoted. Political correctness also reared its head when Ken Livingstone, then boss of the Greater London Council, banned Robinsons jam from

London schools because it featured a gollywog, deemed to be racist. In time Robinsons bowed to this pressure and closed one of the longest running promotions in Britain. He also threatened to ban Kit Kat because the manufacturers refused to give the GLC details of its employment policies towards minorities. He was not bothered by the fact that Kit Kat was produced in York, not London

BUSINESS BOOMS BELOW THE LINE

SP consultancies were on the up, and in 1985 a survey showed a considerable increase in their use. Drinks companies, consumer finance and tourism were making greater use, although retailers seemed to be reducing their dependence on outside consultants. There was a suggestion that they expected suppliers to pay for promotional activity and also for the consultants who were planning and operating it.

Agencies showed a considerable enthusiasm for expanding overseas. KLP and Cato Johnson had offices in no less than nine countries and IMP International had affiliates in seven. The MD in charge of that operation was Jerry Postlethwaite, later of KLP, and IMP did have a few international clients such as Atari, where it promoted Pac Man, a McDonald's Big Mac promotion and the Pepsi Challenge. FKB was looking good at this time. In March 1985 it was employing 90 people and making £859,000 pre-tax profit but was only interested in working with English-speaking countries, looking for tie-ups in Australia, Canada and the USA. Like some of the other publicly quoted agencies, with the exception of KLP, this enthusiasm for overseas links, particularly North America, proved its undoing. Meanwhile, The Sales Machine came up with an original thought. It planned to design 80 per cent of a promotion and allow the locals to finesse the final 20 per cent.

One event of almost earth shattering importance which took place around this time was banks opening on a Saturday morning. In a fit of generosity Lloyds opened 75 branches at a time when customers might actually be able to get to them and was considering opening a total of 200 nationwide. The reason was increasing competition, not least from building societies. This effectively broke up a cosy old boys' cartel and led to the introduction of some serious marketing. NatWest came up with the sophisticated NatWest Piggybanks programme, one of the first serious promotional efforts in the banking industry. Naturally, being a bank, it did not want to spend much of its own money so generously offered a piggybank for every child's account opened and then rather less generously deducted a pound from an initial deposit. If parents continued to invest they would ultimately acquire four more piggybanks to get the complete family. A minimum of £100 was required to get the second and so on. A fascinating piece of research by the bank claimed that parents disapproved of children getting something for nothing, hence the £1 charge. It's good to see such a socially responsible approach, is it not?

An unexpected consequence is that these money boxes have become collector's items. At the end of 2006, Jenny Wright, the lady responsible for collectables at Wade Ceramics, which made the piggybanks, found that a complete set would now be worth around £240 but some do even better. In 1998, NatWest revived the idea with a new design called Cousin Wesley. Only 5,000 were made and they have become so collectable that they are a prime target for forgers. Not many premium items achieve that distinction.

Other financial institutions woke up to the need for promotions, which was good news for the BPMA, as almost all the promotions involved giveaways. Depending on where you chose to deposit your pennies, you could collect luggage, a personal organiser, a desktop calculator, a carriage clock, a radio alarm, a hardback A-Z of London, car tow ropes, ballpoint pens, telephones or desk clocks. Research showed that almost 50 per cent of all financial advertising included a premium offer. There were a few more imaginative ideas around, including an early points collection scheme by Barclaycard called 'Profile' and a joint promotion in The Sun from Norwich Union and Cigna, offering £10,000 insurance cover in return for proof of purchase over one year. More than 600,000 people took it up.

SP'S GOT TALENT

In April 1986 there were 68 companies on the ISP consultants register and there was a shortage of qualified staff. For possibly the first time, agencies were paying head hunters to assist in recruiting, backed up by a considerable amount of advertising in the trade press. SP agencies were also complaining, not for the first time, that they did not get the recognition they deserved. Unlike advertising agencies, they were not considered glamorous, they were not dealing with top people, were considered a short-term weapon and had to pitch for every scrap of business. Despite this whingeing, there was an increased interest in sales promotion agencies and the idea of a Sales Promotion Register was floated, to be based on the same lines as the Advertising Agency Register (AAR), which allows potential clients to study the agency's show reel without letting the world and the incumbent agency know that it is looking around.

The ISP was not enthusiastic about bringing this particular idea into the SP business as it had tried once and failed, in 1972. One of the problems had been that consultants did not keep their information up to date. Brian Francis thought the whole thing was a complete waste of time but more importantly Heinz's Ian Fryer did not see much merit. The AAR had looked into it and turned the idea down because the sales promotion business is much more fluid than advertising and clients did not ask them to find SP companies. However, it did to set one up for public relations.

1986 was a very busy year for Ian Fryer as he helped Heinz celebrate its 100th anniversary.

It had spent 18 months researching promotional effectiveness because it was set to spend £3 million. It did not do anything groundbreaking and stuck to what it knew worked, but did it bigger and better. An interesting part of the research was that consumers were given a questionnaire in the form of a scratchcard, which could be completed in under a minute. This worked because there was a 60 per cent response from a sample of 30,000 participants. For the first time Heinz used TV to support its 'A Car a Day for 100 Days'.

HEINZ IN A PICKLE
It also did a toy version of the Heinz turn-of-the-century Pickle Van which proved very popular. In fact consumers were hit by a non-stop stream of Heinz Centenary promotions. And boy, did they work. Seven promotions produced 14 million labels, with the 100 Cars push on top garnering 5,900,000 of these. 'Feed Baby Free' was next pulling 3,500,000. Heinz also ran a number of SLPs, one of which, for a fleece run on Big Soup, produced 49,000 redemptions at £6.99 each.

This was the time when mobile phones began to really take off. Initially they were known as car phones because, apart from some great heavyweight portable numbers, they were universally fitted in cars. The two major competitors were Vodafone and Cellnet, a joint venture between BT and Securicor, later renamed O2. Having a mobile or car phone in those days indicated some considerable wealth or a generous company as they cost upwards of £1,000. A connection would cost you £60 and you had to pay a minimum of £25 per month subscription with the cost of calls on top. The average subscriber was spending around £750 a year which might explain why there were only 170,000 in the UK. However by 1999 there were 19 million and the numbers were growing by thousands per day.

A company called Excel launched what it claimed to be the UK's first pocket-sized mobile. You would have needed a very strong and deep pocket, as it weighed over a pound and cost £1,900. Hand portable units, often requiring a large case with an accumulator, had 15 per cent of the market with 20,000 units in use.

On other technological fronts, the first mass market word processor, by Amstrad, was the PCW 8256 which cost £460 and had a 120kb memory. Twenty or so years later this sounds like something out of the Bronze Age, but it introduced many to the mysteries, delights and frustrations of word processing. Sky was also beginning to make ripples as a minor media owner, about on par with taxi sides and ads on parking meters. Another innovation being discussed in 1986 was the possible introduction of bar-coding coupons, although it was felt this might take up to five years.

There was another promotional war on the forecourts. BP was spending £5million on a scratchcard promotion linked to the Dallas TV soap while Shell was sticking to the tried and tested free glasses. However, deciding change was required. Don Marketing was employed, and came with up with 'Make Merry'. This was followed by 'Bruce Forsyth's Lucky Deal' by Saatchi & Saatchi. Don Marketing was somewhat upset by this as apparently it had presented a similar proposal to BP the previous year. You win some, you lose some. However, there were now fewer forecourt sites on which to run promotions and therefore presumably less business for the agencies. In 1962 there had been 50,000 or so sites but this had reduced to less than half by the mid-eighties, with about 1,000 or so per year still closing.

By now, more than 40 per cent of British homes had a VCR so pre-recorded video tapes became the big premium. The first campaign featuring video was run by Smirnoff in 1986 when the retail value of a tape was around £20. This meant that they were almost always self liquidating as there were very good margins. Initially, such promotions tended to be music based and audio versions were often available at the same time. Smirnoff's campaign offered the audio version for £2.99 and the video for £12.99, plus proof of purchase.

The 'Men from the Pru' found themselves the target of an incentive at this time. The insurer had around 13,000 agents still working door to door selling policies and collecting cash. The scheme was put together by Grass Roots, and boss David Evans organised 426 different breakfast meetings at various branches. We are not sure if he had the full English at them all. However, his efforts produced a 50 per cent increase in business generated and probably expanded his waist line.

If you were feeling generous, you could send your top sales people to Richard Branson's Necker Island at a cost of $5,500 a day or about £3,600. Another surprisingly popular destination for incentive travel was Israel, with direct charters by Monarch and the now defunct Dan Air, better know to its passengers as Dan Dare. Those waiting to jet off from BAA airports could take advantage of a promotion run by IMP, offering spirit doubles at the price of singles. It must have been extremely popular with nervous flyers in need of some Dutch courage.

In case you thought going green was a new idea, in 1986 Lever Brothers got behind a government campaign called 'Get More for Your Monergy'. This was run by FKB, which organised a massive nationwide leaflet drop offering the chance to win £50,000 worth of energy-saving homes (missing word ?)and linking with all sorts of exciting partners such as the Solid Fuel Advisory Service. It was backed by a £5million advertising campaign. An unusual angle was that it was intended to persuade consumers to buy less, not more of the various products.

Despite the apparent slow growth, by 1987 SP in the UK was on a roll. Publicly quoted FKB, KLP, and Clarke Hooper were whizzing backwards and forwards across the Atlantic armed with large cheque-books buying up associated businesses. KLP began with the acquisition of Comart Associates, claiming to be the third largest promotions agency in the US. This was added to acquisitions across Europe and Australia, the Middle East and Cyprus with associate companies from Sweden to Brazil and Japan. It was aiming to be the world's largest sales promotion group by 1990. Clarke Hooper, a public company for less than 18 months, was buying in Canada and California and had affiliates in the Far East and Australia. Europe was on the cards for next year and John Hooper expected to enlarge the £20million capitalisation to £100million within three to five years. FKB was a little behind but was set to announce at least five acquisitions across the US. Its planned expansion would triple its current £47million capitalisation.

Unfortunately for two of the three, the activity would prove their downfall. Both Clarke Hooper and FKB blame their demise on wrong choices across the Atlantic. Only KLP managed to control its far-flung empire and prospered. The fourth quoted company, Holmes & Marchant had a different strategy. It followed KLP on to the then junior Unlisted Securities Market in 1985 and decided against overseas expansion. It was capitalised at under £40million and felt the need to reach £75million before it could make significant acquisitions. In the next few years it picked up a number of UK companies, including Catalyst which had recently purchased Masterguide. H&M had problems but struggled on as an independent quoted company through the Nineties before being taken over.

It is quite interesting to look at the US at this time. There were no national groups. The largest agency was Frankel, based around McDonald's business in Chicago and about twice the size of FKB or KLP. It employed 200 people but was an anomaly - only about five agencies in the US employed more than 100. They were unlikely to IPO (Initial Public Offering) and use their paper to fund acquisitions. For British companies it should have been easier to expand in the US than in the rest of the world. The laws regarding promotions were similar, it was a huge and expanding market, growing faster than advertising, and they speak a very similar language. The table below from Marketing compares the size and rate of growth of sales promotion in the two countries. You can see why the go-getters in the UK wanted a slice of all that action.

YEAR	UK £bn.	% +	US $bn	% +
1980	2.71	11.5	49.0	-
1981	3.00	10.7	58.1	19
1982	3.5	16.7	63.5	9
1983	4.0	14.3	71.7	13
1984	5.0	25	83.7	17
1985	5.5	10	94.4	13
1986	6.0	9	106.7	13

1988 was also the year of the Big Prize Draw. There was something of a stampede into this particular technique with major promotions from Cadbury, Rowntree, Nabisco, Duracell and Arthur Bell among others. We think it is fair to say that the pioneers in this area were Heinz, who had been celebrating their centenary in 1986 by giving away a car a day for a hundred days. This was so successful that they ran it again at the end of 1987. The car was a Metro City, the prize fund was claimed to be £660,000 and they were also giving away hampers and other items.

Never one to go for novelty for novelty's sake, Ian Fryer of Heinz was quoted as saying that in any company internal boredom with an idea arrives before the public gets bored. He also believed that the consumer often understood a promotion better the second time round. Why do we consider the car a day promotion to be a breakthrough? Well, prize draws have been around for a long time, led perhaps by "The Reader's Digest". The technique is governed, as we expect you know, by The Lotteries and Amusement Act 1976, although this changed in 2007. Simply, it is illegal if entrants have to make a purchase in order to participate. The Digest's technique is to send two envelopes in which to return your prize draw tickets. YES if you want to buy, NO if you don't and will we trust that the NO envelopes are treated as fairly as the YES.

Petrol forecourts and high-street outlets gave scratchcards to anyone who cares without purchase, a route not open to manufacturers. The Heinz breakthrough was simple but effective; the "plain paper entry" and the magic words "No purchase necessary" which has kept us all going until the new rules came out with the 2007 Act. Variations on this theme have been with us ever since for good reason. Retailers love it, consumers love it (no tie-breaker to complete), manufacturers love it and most important of all, it moved the product.

The 100 up seemed to be catching. Rowntree gave away a hundred bouquets of day and Kit Kat holiday breaks with 1,000 2-week holidays for two were drawn over a 100 day period. Nabisco Shredded Wheat had a variation with 60 pairs of tickets on the Orient Express and Clark Hooper for some reason chose to go with 79 pairs of BA tickets, anywhere on their routes, plus £1,000 cash.

The agencies were making some money in 1988. Here is a Marketing table of the top 10 by profit in that year. However, out of the 46 listed and giving turnovers and some other information, 17 did not include their profit figure for various reasons (not making any perhaps?). The no shows included IMP, the largest by turnover, Tim Arnold turnover £5 million and SMP who turned over £3 million.

	AGENCY	PROFIT (Pre tax)
1	Promotional Campaigns	£2,140,000
2	FKB	£1,500,000
3	Clarke Hooper	£1,160,000
4	Holmes and Marchant	£639,000
5	KLP (London)	£497,000
6	Option One	£474,000
7	BLP	£389,000
8	DCBA	£280,000
9	The Marketing Store	£269,000
10	The Marketing Consultancy	£226,000

In 1988 the ISP's decision to update its awards caused ructions. It decided that none of the judges could be a current member of either the ISP Management Committee or any of its subcommittees, nor a Fellow currently practising, or anyone who had been a judge in the past five years. In other words, almost anybody who really knew what they were talking about.

Ian Fryer decided that he would not allow any Heinz schemes to be entered that year. In a letter to David Drakes, who was taking responsibility for the ISP's decision, he said: "I feel that you are depriving the industry of much of its accumulated wisdom, knowledge and experience of what actually constitutes an effective promotion. To be judged by your peers in your industry is better than being judged by people who know two-thirds of nothing about that industry." John Hooper was equally unhappy about the fact that the Awards Gala was to be supplanted by a lunchtime meeting and that there was a reduction in the number of awards. Given that this would undoubtedly reduce the number of entries, which were a major source of income for the ISP, he had a point.

PROMOS ACROSS THE POND
The ISP awards give a good snapshot of activity at the time, but for a change let us look at the US equivalents, the Reggie awards. The Promotion Marketing Association of America's gongs derive their name from a cash register. Only 10 gold Reggies and one Super Reggie, are handed out. The 1989 Supper Reggie went to Seagram and the agency was Siebel/Mohr. The promotion 'Send the Family' covered the cost of travel for one family member per athlete

participating in the 1988 Seoul Olympics and some 500 people benefited. One neat move that stretched the budget was to allow consumers to donate a refund on a case or half case of Seagram's Wine Coolers to the fund rather than keeping the cash for themselves. Meanwhile, the ISP Grand Prix for 1987 went to the Tetley Teafolk Biscuits and Barrel campaign by Geoff Howe & Associates. How very British!

One Reggie winner that really caught the eye was 'Singin' in the Shower' for Lever Brothers. This was a multibrand operation across five brands of soap. The POS unit resembled a shower stall and a consumer-activated voice box sang the soap contest jingle. Even with Lever Brothers' clout, it is hard to see such a thing in today's supermarket aisle. Radio activity had listeners sing 'shower songs' incorporating the brands on air. There was no premium line telephone voting, so the DJ decided who were the winners, who grabbed trips to Jamaica, shower proof radios and rubber ducks. Then there was a roadshow consisting of three 'Singin' in the Shower' sets, featuring running water, a 15 foot bath, a branded curtain, a stage and a sound system. Consumers were invited on stage and winners were sent to Hollywood or scooped cash prizes. It is not clear whether or not they had to get wet.

AGENCIES UNDER SCRUTINY

Yet another conference in October 1989 was called 'Promoting for Profit' (what else would you promote for?). The most entertaining section was a possibly unique double-hander with Ian Fryer and his opposite number at Kellogg, Jeremy Sandys-Winsch with the title 'We Are Talking to Six Agencies. Buying Ideas or Management?' Essentially this was an interesting insight into the way two major promoters used, or didn't use, SP agencies. Jeremy thought that they were pretty much a waste of space although Kellogg used them occasionally, preferring to do the work in-house and buying directly from suppliers. On the other hand, Ian had a 15-year relationship with his agency.

Jeremy had a list of grievances including accreditation presentations, fees, artwork charges, confidentiality, communications and overheads. He was appalled when up to four agency executives arrived for a speculative half-day visit to Manchester, estimating the cost at £800-1,000. If he did pay for agency services, he achieved great value for money. When Kellogg ran the first British Rail Free Tickets promotion he paid a fee of £2,000. With 800,000 applications it worked out at 0.25p per application.

By contrast, Ian Fryer felt he was buying a blend of creativity, marketing counsel and common sense built on a foundation of an extended working partnership. Eighty per cent of Heinz promotional volume went through Clarke Hooper which created continuity, consistency, efficiency, congruity, curiosity, confidentiality and last but by no means least, creativity. He was happy to pay for all that. Nice alliteration Ian. In Heinz fiscal year 1990, Clarke Hopper earned £785,395 and Senior King got £504,756.

Things were still looking pretty rosy for agencies. Marketing's 1990 league table of agencies had IMP on top with turnover of £27.81million in 1989, up from £23.1million in 1988, but it was coy about profits. Second and third place, being public companies, had to show all. Clarke Hooper turned over £18.98million, up by almost £7million on the previous year, while FKB went from £10.52million to £12.72million. CH made a pre-tax profit of £2.03million with FKB just behind on £1.8million, an impressive margin of more than 14 per cent, which must have interested their clients.

Surprisingly, KLP was down to eighth with a turnover of £6.7million and profit of just £200,000. The fourth public company, Holmes & Marchant, only included figures of its SP arm H&M Promotions, and showed Masterguide, which it owned, separately. Added together, it would have been in seventh place. On its own it showed a turnover of £5.08million and a profit of £678,000 and was twelfth. For the record, the others in the top 10 at the end of the decade were Promotional Campaigns (4), Equator (5), Option One (6), WLK (7), Marketing Triangle (9) and Core Group (10). Out of the 46 names on the list, only five seemed to be operating under the same name in 2007.

Determined to grow and get the top spot, FKB was on an overseas buying spree. In its 1989 two volume annual report, it boasted eight acquisitions in the US in the past year plus two in the UK. The FKB Group consisted of a staggering 32 companies. It's a wonder it found time to do any promotional work, although employing 759 staff may have helped. However, it is no surprise that in the next few years it took its eyes off the ball. The directors paid themselves £709,000 that year, with the highest paid (unnamed) getting £159,000 and three others getting around £125,000. In addition, they got a dividend that was worth £110,000 to F, £121,000 to K and £148,000 to B. B also sold 64,875 shares netting him around £130,000 and K picked up more than £500,000 in the same way. In total the three names over the door made almost £1.5million. It's as well they got the money out while the going was good, because the next decade would not treat them so well.

About this time Marketing magazine ran a feature on the millionaires in marketing which featured a number of SP entrepreneurs towards the top of the list. This was based on the value of their shareholdings in March 1989, and ignored cash squirreled away. FKB's Duncan Baines was at five with £7.84million, while Chris Killingbeck at six was just ahead of Martin Sorrell, a situation that has probably been reversed since then. Brian Francis was number eight and John Holmes at nine, well ahead of Colin Lloyd who was at number 23, with John Sandon of H&M at number 31. He was followed by Barry Clarke at 35 and a little lower was John Hooper at number 39 with a meagre £2.17milion. However, it was not to last.

THE MAGNIFICENT SEVEN RIDE AGAIN

In such a close knit industry, the principals of the top agencies had been a tight peer group from the Seventies birth of many of their agencies. However, the regular dinners that had birthed the SPCA, among other initiatives, fizzled out in the mid-Eighties due to pressure of buying, floating and selling businesses. However after a few years Colin Lloyd had a call from Brian Francis with the idea of reviving them for a select few. Thus Francis, John Farrell, Keith Bantick, Roger Hyslop, John Hooper, Bob Bayley and Colin found themselves having dinner two or three times a year for the next decade.

For one brief interlude the seven became 14. It was decided that a group of blokes meeting regularly was a tad sexist and that they should at least embrace female promotion leaders, who by then had shattered the glass ceiling. Each member invited a senior female agency head to an evening in the Dorchester Club and was staggered when these highly-talented ladies agreed to spend an evening with what was becoming the geriatrica of the business – the ever youthful John Farrell excepted.

Colin Lloyd had the unenviable duty of introducing everyone and trying to kick start the discussion with something remotely intelligent. However, thankfully this was ignored pretty quickly and they got on to more interesting industry gossip and decent champagne. The ladies were magnanimous enough to say that they enjoyed it and one even agreed to organise the next get-together, which of course never happened. They were, however, kind enough to make the offer and let us down gently. For the sake of ruining exemplary careers we resist the urge to name names.

The Seven continued with enthusiasm until John Farrell decided to cross the Pond and make his fortune. Six did not quite have the same ring about it. Brian Francis is sadly no longer with us and is really missed, not least because no one else in the business had a haircut like his. So it is probably right that the remaining six leave a small epitaph to his genius and conviviality.

In the early Nineties the economy went through the worst recession in recent times and marcoms suffered more than most. Companies went bust and downsized and budgets shrank. At one of the dinners the Seven challenged each other on what was needed for an agency to survive recessionary times. John Hooper catalogued these words of wisdom and thankfully a copy survived, for future plagiarism. They may seem like common sense, but in tough times common sense can be the rarest commodity. As for the Magnificent Seven, they have probably ridden into their last sunset, but generally in very nice cars.

HERE ARE THE 20 COMMANDMENTS FOR SURVIVING A RECESSION WRITTEN IN 1992:

1. Love your clients to death; at a senior level.
2. Don't be dependent on any one client.
3. Prize ideas and innovation above everything.
4. Never resort to price cutting.
5. Look after your people, particularly in lean times.
6. Strive for total communications integration.
7. Cultivate talented advertising people; they've a lot to teach us.
8. Keep on keeping it simple.
9. Protect the margin. Income minus cost equals profit.
10. Cash is still king. Be totally cash conscious.
11. Sell ideas that sell. Be a salesman first and foremost.
12. Listen and respond. Give your customers what they want.
13. Trust your instincts. Gut feel rather than reason.
14. No excessive borrowing.
15. Hype the business. Achieve positive PR.
16. Demand the best: of your people, your suppliers, and your board.
17. Redefine creativity and recognise it in your people.
18. Speed of reaction. Capitalise faster on opportunity.
19. Run a better business as good as your clients.
20. Love the business every waking hour... and in your dreams!

They would apply equally well today or 150 years from now, and were certainly tested to destruction in the following decade.

CHAPTER 13

Hoover: the best of times, the worst of times.

Who sold you that then?
First Europe, then the USA
The media get involved... and the lawyers
The aftermath
But the Government had a bigger disaster

Mention Hoover to almost anyone connected to SP and they will start backing away, making the sign of the cross and reaching for the garlic. The Hoover 'Free Flights' promotions (there were two) began as spectacular successes and ended as disastrous failures. It is probably the most appalling SP failure ever, rivalled only by a small problem in the Philippines when Pepsi inadvertently put winning numbers under the lids of millions of bottles. UK customers reached for their lawyers, whereas in the Philippines they wielded guns, petrol, matches and death threats. But to paraphrase Mr Chamberlain, this "was in a small country, far away about which we know little".

Hoover was on our doorstep and most people know somebody affected. With considerable help from Harry Cichy of the Hoover Holiday Pressure Group, we think we have put together the definitive story of this fiasco. It all started with a chance meeting at a marketing event early in 1992 between an unnamed Hoover marketing executive and a husband-and-wife team called Neils Wetterlin and Jenny Axelson who ran JSI, a small travel agency with offices over a shop in Shaftesbury, Dorset.

JSI had been successfully selling a basic free flights promotion for a number of years, mainly to timeshare marketing companies. They explained the concept to the man from Hoover who, at that time, was under pressure to shift a vast backlog of goods that were threatening to close a factory in Scotland. He loved the idea and after some further detailed discussion, agreed that JSI would provide two free flights to Europe with a wide choice of destinations to anyone who spent £100 or more on a Hoover product. At the time £100 bought the basic vacuum cleaner.

The travel agency would receive a fixed fee of about £100,000, and was responsible for all redemptions. This seemed a reasonable arrangement to all concerned but unfortunately it was based on a number of fallacies. Possibly the biggest was that JSI signed up to the fee based on the sales they were told would be likely. Unfortunately, the deal was open ended and would run on everything Hoover sold. However, it seems that JSI was not just naïve or even deliberately misled in allowing this, possibly with no idea of what could happen, but was playing a few games of its own. Hoover, on the other hand, did not bother to look at the agency's balance sheet and see what it could afford if redemptions exceeded the estimate.

Maytag, the giant American company that had recently purchased Hoover was demanding increased sales, so having fallen in love with the free flights proposition and thinking it had a perfectly safe financial situation, Hoover really went to town with support. It produced massive point-of-sale material and backed it with heavy media advertising including a powerful TV commercial with the simple, bold and very effective statement 'Two Return Flights Free – Unbelievable'. The public did believe it and started to buy products on an unprecedented scale. Suddenly, rather than having to just move stock from stacked warehouses, the factories were going on to extra shifts and supply could not meet demand. The marketing men were the heroes of the day and, basking in this unaccustomed situation, promptly decided to go one better with a second promotion. This offered two free flights to the US with a choice of New York or Florida, for the same minimum purchase of £100, or with extra goodies if you spent £300. What had been unbelievably good seemed to have become unbelievably better.

A factory that had been threatened with closure was running flat out and so was every other part of the manufacturing operation. Hoover again backed the push with advertising and lots of point-of-sale. It found another small but eager travel agency called Your Leisure. It is thought that it was paid a fee of around £500,000 to run the US offer. Your Leisure also had a small office over a shop, based in Warwick. Meanwhile JSI's Shaftesbury office was also going flat out, but not nearly fast enough to keep up with unprecedented demand. No one at Hoover or Your Leisure seemed aware of the massive problem that was looming on the horizon.

The first rumblings were a number of telephone calls to the Hoover head office in Merthyr Tydfil, from customers wondering where their free European flights had got to. In time a large number of staff was working in the offices handling these calls. The lack of information and the general reluctance of Hoover to recognise that it had a problem aggravated the public further. Around the same time Your Leisure, already committed to handle the US operation, went to Shaftesbury to see how things were going. It was a rude awakening. To reach the upstairs office they had to climb over piles of black bin liners full of unopened applications. This was despite JSI having taken on extra staff, more office space, and 40 new phone lines.

A TSUNAMI OF REDEMPTIONS
However hard JSI worked, it fell further behind and more people were complaining. At its peak, 30,000 applications a week were coming into the office, which made a mockery of the

original estimate of 7,000 in total. To make things worse, the single line telephone number to deal with complaints was published widely. Getting through was almost impossible and because it was the only number around, JSI was even getting calls about Hoover spare parts.

At one stage Hoover consulted about over-redemption insurance. PIMS-SCA was one of the few companies offering cover but by the time they were asked it was too late.   In any case, managing director Mark Kimber did some simple mathematics on the offers and considered them uninsurable, even if the information he had been given was correct, which it was not. He had some sympathy with Hoover because the travel company could have put together a workable promotion that made financial sense and still had a success on their hands. The US offer had absolutely no chance and Kimber's back of the envelope calculation suggested a £20million loss. He declined to quote and in effect told Hoover that it would be crazy to run the promotion. In fact, £20million proved a considerable underestimate.

It soon became obvious that action was needed, but at this moment the roof began to fall in as the media got in on the act. John Nairn, a journalist with Scotland's top selling tabloid The Daily Record, ran a small story on the number of complaints. His story included complaints that JSI had changed the rules to add more hurdles and that customers were being asked for credit card numbers before they knew the cost of accommodation, car hire and insurance. In no time his paper was running regular front-page stories on Hoover. A circulation battle with The Mirror fuelled lurid headlines as the papers sought to outdo each other.

Just before Christmas 1992 Hoover raided the JSI offices in an attempt to salvage all the outstanding applications and do something with them. At this point JSI was effectively out of business. In the long-term the two owners lost not just their company but also their houses and almost everything they had. They just about avoided being made personally bankrupt. There was no suggestion that they were ripping off the public: in fact we think that they were effectively, although not intentionally, ripped off by Hoover, and we will look into the various reasons later on in this chapter.

The trading standards people also got involved and although they did their best to help, they were handicapped by a legal opinion that Hoover had not breached the Trade Descriptions Act. The QC concerned found there were insufficient grounds to prosecute the company under the provisions of the Act of 1968. The investigation showed that Hoover did not deliberately set out to defraud customers, just grossly miscalculated the likely take-up. This was quite accurately described as naiveté, a lack of realism and a failure to accurately forecast the response.

The campaign was called an unmitigated disaster but no criminal offence had been committed. The important aspect was, that under that law, false statements had to be made knowingly or with criminal recklessness which, in these circumstances, would have been very hard to prove. So no action was taken by trading standards, which surprised irate customers. Many launched their own legal actions with varying degrees of success, but these were generally based on breach of contract which is a civil matter. To give an idea of trading standards' workload, the Mid Glamorgan office, the nearest to the Hoover factory, received more than 2,000 complaints and was still dealing with them in July 1994.

The tide of publicity meant that many customers who might otherwise have given up, continued to fight for their rights and the Scots were particularly keen. John Nairn travelled to Warwick to visit Your Leisure and was not impressed to find it running over a dress shop. His view was that Hoover had been taken in by a couple of smart salesmen. Nairn asked Hoover for details of the airlines it was using and contacted BA and the like who confirmed they had not booked seats for the promotion.

This gave him several more good stories, despite the fact that the sensible plan was to book seats as requested by consumers rather than pre-book. The 144-point front-page headlines screamed 'HOOVER HAS NO FLIGHTS!' triggering mass panic. The Daily Record was happy to record that 1,332 people, all trying to obtain flights, had phoned its office. At this stage the media agenda was firmly set and Hoover could do nothing right.

WATCHDOG BITES

TV, and in particular the Watchdog programme, got in on the act. At this time Watchdog was a relatively low-key consumer programme, but it is fair to say that it built its popularity - not to mention the career of presenter Anne Robinson who took over in 1993 - when the Hoover story was just moving into overdrive. Watchdog reckoned it received more complaints about Hoover than any other consumer problem. On the other side of the coin Hoover was getting market share figures beyond its wildest dreams and, amazingly, extended the US promotion for another month.

In the early part of 1993 both promotions were being handled by two agencies. Your Leisure had been taken on for the US promotion but resigned its ABTA membership in July 1994 when there were still a lot of outstanding flights. Hoover had recruited a larger operation Free Flights Europe, based in Watford and part of the well-established travel promotions agency Brevis to handle the flights.

In Warwick the first applications for US flights arrived in January. The number grew each day and by mid-February everyone realised that the numbers were going to be huge and the system had started to produce the final booking forms. The bosses at Your Leisure realised that redemptions were going to be far higher than previously discussed. Having done a few quick sums they told the Hoover finance director that the cost could easily reach £20million, which probably did not make his day.

Meanwhile a Watchdog undercover operative, Hilary Bell, was doing some secret filming in Watford. As an aside, the hidden camera used by Hilary rapidly ran down its batteries and she had to disappear into the ladies to change them. She wondered if the rest of the staff thought she had a medical problem. The material she produced allowed Watchdog to put together some very nice 'Shock! Horror!' exclusives. She was employed to ring up customers who had booked flights to try and sell them extras, in particular the not greatly overpriced but profitable accommodation, which would provide the largest margin to set against the cost of the flights.

She claimed that the policy was to make flights available to people who had signed for extras but to make it as difficult as possible for those who had not. People who wanted Glasgow flights were offered departures from Gatwick and vice versa. Anything, in fact, apart for what they wanted. It was presumed the same thing was happening at Your Leisure although it claimed it had not been told to do this by Hoover. As the instructions to the travel agents were to reduce costs to a minimum by either avoiding having to provide flights or producing enough income to cover the cost, they were possibly acting on their own initiative in order to meet their client's requirements.

The media soon claimed three high-level scalps because immediately after Hilary Bell had taken up a new job, the vice president of Hoover Europe, the director of marketing and the marketing manager were all sacked. This led to more headlines and Maytag sent one of its senior people, Richard Rankin, to appear on Watchdog and make fulsome apologies. His title was the New Labour-sounding Co-chairman, Free Flights Task Force. Despite this, three months later the majority of applicants had still not received their flights. One or two decided to take matters into their own hands.

CONSUMER POWER

One of the first and the most publicised took place at High Seaton, Cumbria where David Dixon impounded a Hoover service van when an engineer had come to mend the washing machine, purchased in order to acquire the flights. After two weeks of massive media coverage and a High Court order, Hoover got its van back. TV news featured it being towed away as the battery had gone flat. Questions were asked in Parliament, particularly by one MP who was trying to get flights for himself and his family.

A rather more conventional attack was made by a Scottish headmaster and ex-commando, Sandy Jack who took the first of many legal actions against Hoover. He lost on a technicality related to when and if his various bits of paper arrived at the travel agents. Recorded Delivery had been used and the action persuaded Royal Mail to change the way items were recorded and signed for. The media coverage of the action included a leader in The Times. Meanwhile, a pressure group was started by Harry Cichy in Hemel Hempstead. In no time it had 8,000 plus members and it took up his life for the next six years, including two trips to the Maytag head office in Newton, Iowa.

The first of these was in 1994 when Harry and two companions, one of whom was Sandy Jack, were able to ask questions at the AGM after purchasing Maytag shares. Maytag later admitted that it employed a private eye called John Nolan to shadow the Pressure Group team around town until they left the country. It seems likely that Harry was also watched for some 18 months by someone working for Hoover. He was back again in Newton 10 years later for a re-enactment set up by the BBC which really got its money's worth from the promotion. At least someone did.

On the second occasion, Maytag had long since sold Hoover Europe (they still owned the US Company), and claimed it had no further interest in the affair. Things have not gone well with Maytag over the years with financial problems and a depressed share price. It was finally bought by Whirlpool in 2006 and it is likely that the operation in Newton will be closed. Even in 1998 it was still haunted by the spectre of the free flights promotion and could not close out the disaster. Part of its listing with the SEC in the US, which made news in the Washington Post, included the fact that it might still have a liability for 350,000 flights having already spent $72million to fly 220,000 people. Harry Cichy is still involved in the consumer complaint side of the industry acting as a consultant to companies such as MKM when they have problems with travel promotions.

As 1993 went on, Hoover was getting its act together and its travel agents had arranged for 160,000 people to fly, but there were larger numbers still waiting. In order to shift this backlog, Hoover began to charter planes. Apparently the sole topic of conversation on board was how people got their flights and comparing the Hoover goods they had bought to qualify. Despite this, Hoover managed to shoot itself in the foot yet again when sending out what was supposed to be the final 30,000 flight offers. By either conspiracy or cock-up, these were mailed on 23 December 1993 and in order to get flights the forms had to be returned by mail before 5 January 1994 – an obvious impossibility. Moving on, in June 1995 the very last planeload of free flight travellers left for Orlando but, true to form, this flight was delayed for 28 hours.

THE LAWYERS GET INVOLVED

Hoover thought it was all over but the pressure group was just gearing up to take it to court to obtain compensation for flights which, it claimed, had been unfairly withheld. It had details of thousands of customers who were convinced they had been cheated. The basic claim was a variation on breach of contract and several of these cases appeared in 1995's Current Year Law Book. Hoover sent teams of lawyers around the country fighting every one of these cases. It employed an expert witness, Mr Graham Aiken, who was flown from court to court. His claim to be an expert and unbiased seems a little thin because a) he now worked for Your Leisure, and b) his previous job had been in gentlemen's outfitting, with no previous travel trade experience.

Hoover won some and lost some, although with lawyers' fees it might have been cheaper to pay for flights. The highest compensation, as far as we know, went to a consumer in Gateshead who collected £1,058. Harry Cichy and the pressure group thought that up to half a million people might still be claiming for flights. In 1998 there were still 900 outstanding court cases across the country. To try and bring the operation to an end, it was agreed by both sides that 10 test cases should be used to settle all the outstanding cases. If Hoover won the majority they could walk away from the others but if the pressure group won, Hoover would settle the other 890 out of court.

The tally went backwards and forwards like a tennis match. Hoover won four in a row and by the last day there were three cases to be settled. At this point the best that Harry and his team could hope for was a five-all draw at which, under the agreement, Hoover could ignore the remainder of the cases. Six years after the original launch, it was a black day for Harry and Co. but he says he would do it all over again. In fact the real ending was a year later when Maytag sold Hoover to Candy and the new management has nothing to say about the whole affair. You have to hand it to the pressure group; they did keep trying and in 1998 sent a formal petition to Her Majesty the Queen, requesting that the Royal Warrant should be withdrawn from Hoover Ltd. They were politely told by Christopher Pickup of the Royal Warrant Holders Association that this was a matter for the Lord Chamberlain, who is probably still considering the said matter. In the meantime Mr Pickup had this to say on 8 July 2004.

Dear Mr Cichy,

A Royal Warrant of Appointment does nothing more than acknowledge that a satisfactory trading relationship, in terms of both the quality of the product and the associated level of service, exists between the Grantor (In the case of Hoover Ltd, that is The Queen and of course The Queen Mother) and the company concerned. Warrants are cancelled only when, for whatever reason, that trading relationship ceases. So far as Hoover is concerned, for the time being, they are still supplying The Royal Household - presumably in a satisfactory way. That aside, I am sure that you will understand that The Queen, as Head of State, cannot be seen to involve herself directly in any kind of commercial let alone legal dispute. And, so far as The Royal Warrant Holders Association is concerned, again we cannot afford to involve ourselves in disputes that may, from time to time, arise between our members and their customers. This is not our role or remit which, by virtue of our Royal Charter, is effectively to police the Royal Warrant to ensure that Warrant Holders abide by The Lord Chamberlain's Rules. These, however, refer to how Warrant Holders may display their Warrants. They do not cover the essentially private relationship that exists between company and client.

I am sorry not to be more helpful

Yours sincerely

Christopher Pickup

The media is still interested, particularly the BBC who made meal of the whole business. After Watchdog and Anne Robinson had gone on to new heights, it made a 30-minute TV documentary narrated by Tom Baker. It was for the benefit of this programme that the BBC arranged for Harry and Co. (without Sandy Jack who had died two years previously) to make a return visit to Newton and face the Maytag directors in their annual general meeting den. In August 1995 Radio Four included it in a series under the title of An Unfortunate Turn of Events to which co-author Ken Spedding contributed. It then resurrected it in 2006 for another series Trouble at the Top. The advertising industry has not forgotten it either as, during a May 2006 debate held in the House of Commons, the chief executive of advertising giant Publicis, Grant Duncan, very unfairly cited it as being reflective of sales promotion. Having traced the history we can look at the various fallacies that caused the disaster to happen and hopefully learn something from them.

DISSECTING THE PROBLEM

The first fallacy or mistake was to expect that the level of redemption compared to the number of vouchers distributed would stay much the same as the previous experience. People attending slightly dodgy timeshare presentations were not surprised to find that their free flight voucher was not all it seemed and did not try too hard redeem it. But in 1990, a survey showed that a majority of people considered Hoover to be a trustworthy company. With the Hoover name attached, consumers did expect to get their flights, even before the media egged them on.

The second fallacy was Hoover's estimate of the number of flights that would be required, based on their estimated sales. These at the time were low and, even allowing for an increase in market share, it only expected to require up to 7,000 European flights which would give the travel agency an income of around £15 per flight based on a £100,000 fixed fee. Based on its experience, the travel agency probably did not expect it to be even that high. The £15 figure would not cover the cost but add ons such as accommodation, car hire and insurance would contribute. It seems that there was an estimate of at most a 10 per cent take up, but in the end it reached 35 per cent. But 35 per cent of what?

The third fallacy was that the fixed fee was based on the number of units Hoover expected to sell. Unlike an on-pack promotion where there are a finite number of opportunities to redeem, Hoover went on to sell every machine that it could make, which meant a vastly increased number of opportunities. JSI had naïvely accepted a fixed fee on an open-ended offer. This might not have been quite so disastrous if the number of sales on which the 10 per cent had been based had been accurate. In reality, it was exceeded many times over, and JSI ended up trying to fulfil applications that were several thousand per cent up on the figure on which their fixed fee had been based.

The secret of success for these promotions, as far as the travel agency was concerned, was the number of hurdles which it put in the way of the potential flyer. The second promotion offered two free return airline tickets from London Gatwick, Manchester or Glasgow to either New York or Orlando for a stay of one or two weeks if you spent £100 or more on any Hoover product, plus a £60 car hire and accommodation voucher when you spent £300 or more with Hoover.

The terms and conditions makes interesting reading. It has 12 paragraphs and runs to 700 words of around six point type. Note that the tight deadlines were based on dates controlled by the issuing agency, not by the consumer, and so hard to prove if there were any arguments, which of course there were in spades. The Sandy Jack court case was determined by this aspect. Here is the list of steps an applicant had to take and the timescales applied.

CUNNING CONDITIONS

1. The application form had to be stamped with the authorised dealer's stamp and the original receipt, not a copy, had to be enclosed and received at the handling house not later than 14 days after the date of purchase.
2. The handling house had 28 days to return a registration form and this had to be returned to them to arrive within 14 days of the registration form's issue date. This timing includes being handled twice by the Post Office.
3. Unless all details on the application and registration forms were completed in full and returned in the time limits they would be invalid and Hoover could reject any that it deemed to be received outside the time limits. Anything deemed by Hoover to be lost, incomplete, illegible or damaged would also be dead in the water. Obviously you needed a very quick turnaround, a very efficient Post Office and your very best handwriting to have a chance.
4. Your voucher would be posted to you within 28 days of the receipt of a correct registration form and you then had 30 days from the date of the voucher to nominate your preferred travel dates and airports. No guarantees of course, but book early to avoid disappointment!
5. If you do not wish to take up any of the seats offered on your first three nominated flights,

or the agency, which in this case was Your Leisure, cannot match your requests, you can nominate three more flights. If none of those can be provided by Your Leisure, it would provide three alternatives but if those were not acceptable for whatever reason, you've had it mate!

This may seem pretty complicated but there was more to come. The question of accommodation suddenly reared its ugly head. You did not have to buy accommodation, insurance or other services from Your Leisure but if you didn't, proof of payment and confirmation of address and dates of the accommodation were required before the airline tickets could be released. This meant that you had to either book the flights and then try and get the appropriate accommodation before you got your tickets or alternatively book the accommodation and hope you could match it with the flights. Obviously it is much easier to buy accommodation from the people who provided the tickets, and customers were sent quite attractive brochures with not greatly overpriced hotels and followed up by a hard sell on the telephone.

Paragraph 6 had a neat little sting. This prevented you using your free flight voucher with free accommodation or free ownership offers unless authorised by Hoover. There was no indication of how this authorisation could be achieved. Anyone hoping to stay in their own property, a timeshare or with friends and relatives would not be able to use the voucher. The offer was only valid for purchases between 1 November 1992 and 31 December 1992. It is amazing how many people did manage to buy Hoover products in this period, although it was helped by the fact that the promotion was extended for another month. Finally, paragraph 11 said that any queries in writing could be dealt with by Mrs Ross Hamilton, who was based at the handling house in Sutton-in-Ashfield. If Mrs Hamilton actually existed she was probably taken away by men in white coats very soon after this promotion was launched.

BUYING THE PROMOTION, NOT THE PRODUCT.
For the financial success of the promotion, these rules and conditions had to discourage or disqualify the vast majority of applicants. It had worked for the timeshare salesmen and it might have worked for Hoover, but for a combination of its respected brand name, the low entry point of £100 and the media furore. It was also driven by the fact that people were buying two tickets to Europe or the US and getting a free £100 Hoover product. Promotions are supposed to work the other way round. If the Hoover machine had not worked, consumers would have taken it back and complained and they felt they could do the same with the tickets.

Proof of this comes from an anonymous independent retailer who was selling as many of the £100 Hoover vacuum cleaners as he could get his hands are. He had to persuade the salesman for his area to scrounge a few hundred extra from someone else's supply. The majority of the purchasers did not want the cleaners and were planning to resell them through small ads or car boot sales. When he discovered the situation, the retailer would offer to buy them back, at a discount, subject to the packaging being in pristine condition. Usually they had not taken the box from the shop so it was an easy transaction. He then recycled the goods to the next customer looking for their two free flights. You might consider that he was being green, not greedy, but if many people were doing this it must have distorted the figures even more.

To sum up, Hoover sold a great deal of product, far more than it expected, but this was more than cancelled out by vast over-redemption, with no insurance cover and a fixed fee that bankrupted the agency. The promotion is still getting serious media coverage nearly 20 years after it was launched; the published cost to Hoover has risen to $72million which excludes the admin and legal costs. In the end 220,000 people actually flew; Hoover was taken to court more than 1,000 times and paid out compensation in a number of cases; three senior executives lost their jobs and one large, well-established and famous company was sold at what was reckoned to be a knockdown price. Maytag seems to have gone downhill since the promotion which, even though it was not in the US, received considerable bad publicity there. In the end it was taken over.

Shall we ever see its like again? Let's hope not!

FOOTNOTE – if you thought that was an expensive failure...
$72million is a lot of money, but it seems that the British Government managed to spend more on a failed promotion but without ending up on Watchdog which is a result of sorts. The scheme was the Connections Card and was intended to encourage young people to attend school on a regular basis, instead of bunking off. This points collection loyalty scheme offered discounts on youth brands such as Blockbuster, Top-Man/TopShop, 3 Mobile and National Express. Launched in 1999, with 600,000 cards distributed, it was quietly closed after five years due to the minimum redemption levels. It was reported in Marketing Week to have cost the tax payer around £100million which, at present exchange rates, is about $170million, comfortably beating Hoover. It was run by a services company, Capita, not a well known name in the sales promotion business. Despite having already been paid £66million, a fee that would make any SP agency turn bright green with envy, it is still seeking compensation. However, as far as we know, no one has lost their job.

THE HISTORY MAKERS

Annie Swift

Clive Mishon

Louise Wall

David LeBond

Graham Kemp

Geoff Howe

Chris Killingbeck

Randle Stonier

Iain Fergusson

Keith McCracken

Vince Sottosanti

Bob Bayley

CHAPTER 14

The not so nice Nineties

Black clouds
The internet, Sky, texting and green promotions
Meet Harry the Lime
Cash that didn't come back
We're still standing

As the Eighties drew to a close a number of black clouds appeared on the horizon. The dreaded phrase 'negative equity' became common parlance as, for the first time in living memory, house prices went down. While prices were heading south, interest rates were spiralling to 15 per cent by the end of 1989, with inflation even higher. A general recession led to other new phrases like 'downsizing' becoming commonplace. It all had an effect on sales promotion and highfliers of the mid-Eighties were to have their wings clipped.

The decade seemed to be starting well enough. Tim Berners-Lee, a particle physics scientist at CERN in Geneva, had just been launched something he called the worldwide web. Sky launched a satellite network with all of four channels and avoided bankruptcy by merging with British Satellite Broadcast to become BSkyB. By 1992 it was paying the massive sum of £304million for the broadcasting rights to Premier League football. This was also the year that launched a thousand promotions as the first text message was sent, although there was only one word at a time on a small screen attached to a very big handset.

The financial figures published in 1990 showed that the past two years had seen growth across the board for SP agencies with turnover and profits up. It must have been a more leisurely time as big hitters such as Alan Scaping, Ian Fryer, Jim Addison, Peter Le Conte, John Farrell and Brian Husselbee, could put aside two days for a conference in March entitled 'Getting Maximum Mileage Out of Your Sales Promotion'. The event was launched by ISP chairman Roy Piercey, who worried about the definition of SP. At the time the ISP, SPCA and ISBA all had different definitions.

Ian Fryer, who seemed to be a permanent fixture at conferences, won the prize for the longest title with 'Maximising the Role of Sales Promotion and Fully Integrating It into a Tight Financial Environment'. Speaker evaluation forms (see, they do have a use) showed that Richard Millett's riveting session on VAT avoided being rated lowest by attendees. That honour went to Alan Sheridan of The Retail Group with 'Exploiting the Benefits for Retailers in Using Sales Promotion'. It must have been his delivery.

Everyone had only just recovered from all this excitement when they found themselves at another two-day event in October 1990. The Second Annual Sales Promotion Conference at the Portman Intercontinental boasted a few familiar names, including Tim Arnold and John Hooper, although they managed without Ian Fryer.

GOING GREEN IS NOT SO NEW

Jim Addison also took another two days off from his day job for a piece entitled 'Save the Coupon, Save the Planet'. There was so much 'green' advertising at the time that ITV was demanding proof on ads making spurious claims. Jim held forth on green promotions and many of his comments sound familiar today. "The truth is that environmental issues have crept up on us and from being a cause supported by apparent fanatics, it is now the single most important factor that we have to face in the coming decades," he prophesised, adding, "You currently have the most motivational promotional message of all time available to you. 'Buy this product, if you don't want to die'." And this was almost 20 years ago!

He named some of 1990's green promotions such as one for Barclayloan. It was printed on recycled paper with a prize draw with every entry resulting in the planting of a tree, up to £100,000 worth. It did slightly blot the copy book with the offer of a gas guzzling Land Rover Discovery as the top prize. Meanwhile Andrex was actually running a promotion that did not have a puppy in it, but backed trees. There is a connection between trees and puppies but it probably wouldn't have worked on pack. Mind you, the name 'The Woodland Relief' conjures similar images, although the actual aim was to get up to £250,000 worth of trees for the Woodland Trust.

Trees were definitely very big at this time. Persil was 'Planting a Tree Free' and the Co-op had 'David Bellamy's Tree Spree'. Jim thought the drive was so strong that the sales promotion manager of the future would be called the environmental communications manager. The urge to be green has been in and out for a lot longer than you may think and it crops up again and again in the next few years.

This was the year in which the ISP appointed its first director general, David Williams. A management consultant, he was chosen ahead of 40 other applicants despite no direct experience of the business. However, he was president of the Institute of Management Consultants. Stephen Callender, the man behind the working party that came up with the idea, said that Williams' lack of SP experience would be an advantage. "He is not wrapped up in any of these sales promotion industry politics," he said. The experiment turned out to be a dismal failure and he soon parted company with the ISP.

Promoting to the older generation was identified as a challenge in 1990. There were going to be a lot more grey wolves or empty nesters. This was defined as anyone over 55 and IMP had done a survey which came to the interesting conclusion that the older generation were more likely to be affected by promotional marketing. As usual, the survey came up with a number of blindingly obvious conclusions, such as the idea that there is more than one set of predictable attitudes and the difference in attitudes was related to personal circumstances. The rich are different from the poor. Amazing!

Ethical schemes such as environmental promotions did have some appeal but more on behalf of children or grandchildren. The survey discovered that older people do not like to be patronised, but then who does? They also like quality, expected good service and were very doubtful about offers that appeared to be too generous. Fancy that. Finally, IMP told the world that older people's lifetime experience had taught them to say "Where's the catch?" Interesting, but not particularly useful or surprising.

ITS SHOW TIME

September saw an exhibition called PROMOTE, the Autumn Incentive and Business Gift Exhibition at Earls Court with some 240 exhibitors. To give some idea of prices, you could buy hats and aprons for 75p each, sweatshirts for under £2 and sweaters for less than £5. Someone was offering a mohair sweater for £100, which is unlikely to have been for a mass market promotion. One company claimed to have sold an agency 200,000 T-shirts from a contact at the exhibition, which must have made the salesman's day, if not year.

Coupons and couponing were big news in the trade press during 1990, triggered to some extent by the launch of The Coupon Book. This had a massive 10 million circulation and was based on the American free standing insert (FSI). Coupons and vouchers are such a big subject and play such an important part in sales promotion that they are addressed in a separate chapter. However, in 1990 with a recession well underway, they proved extremely popular. According to Nielsen Clearing House, five billion coupons were issued by UK manufacturers in 1989, with a total value of more than £1billion. Around 300 million were redeemed, so the consumer benefited to the tune up around £80million. The figures were a 23 per cent increase over the previous year.

No one knows how much retailers benefited from misredeeming coupons. The perennial subject of retailer rip-off cropped up, but no serious attempt to eliminate it was to appear until 2006 when the ISP tried to stir things up. Whether this will have any effect remains to be seen. The ISP did do some research on coupons and possibly the most useless bit of information that came out was that the least susceptible coupon user was a 19-year-old female living in Scotland, which seemed to suggest that the view of the penny pinching Scots is unfair unless they start once they reach the age of 20.

Sales Promotion agencies do not usually spend much money on press advertising but an ad cropped up in 1991 that was a little unusual. Run by Option One, it claimed the lowest turnover of staff across the top seven agencies. The ingenious boast was that only 12 per cent of senior staff left, whereas on average 39 per cent of the staff at its competitors left over the same period. We're not quite sure what this proves. Did it mean that they earned more money at Option One or that it was such a wonderful place to work that no one wanted to leave or, perhaps that they could not get a job anywhere else?

THE BLACK CLOUDS THICKEN

By the middle of 1991 the recession was deepening and this was impinging on sales promotion, which normally does well when times are hard. First of all the new chairman of the ISP, John Farrell, was disappointed by its drop in the Institute's operating profits - down to £1,519 in 1990 from £6,000 in 1989. Awards income was down by more than 50 per cent to £9,643 but education was up and it managed to make a remarkable £110,000 from recruitment. Oddly, no one can remember any money-earning activity in that area. It was also the year that Philip Circus became the legal adviser to the Institute. We are sure that there is no connection between these facts.

Meanwhile the highflying Clarke Hooper issued its first ever profit warning, and the first for any of the publicly quoted SP agencies. Chairman Barry Clarke blamed the "large and unforeseen" drop in main client business during the third quarter for a 50 per cent pre-tax profit fall. The agency had to go back to the Stock Market for cash, a total of £2.74million. They actually found people to take up the offer which they probably lived to regret. The cracks were beginning to show. In October 1990, its accounts showed potential liabilities for acquisitions of between £8.6million and £11.6million that would fall due before the end of 1993. It would send shivers down the spines of most financial directors and get shareholders thinking "Sell", which would have been a wise move.

One particularly interesting table from Marketing magazine is reproduced below. What had the retailers been doing for the past five years to create a situation where two to one consumers mistrusted them?

Agree 1986%	Agree 1991%	Promotions.	Disagree 1986%	Disagree 1991%
15	23	Save you money	13	11
9	12	Make shopping more fun	30	26
10	17	Encourage you to try new products	21	17
18	12	Competitions are fixed	21	22
47	45	I prefer no frills	4	6
39	39	Saving packs is not worth it	11	15
28	24	Manufactures are not to be trusted	7	26
n/a	22	Retailers are not be trusted	n/a	11

October 1991 saw the Third Annual Sales Promotion Conference. Delegates spent two days in the Cafe Royal. Despite the overdose on conferences, speakers' notes, courtesy of Ian Fryer, provide a real in-depth indication of what was happening and what the movers and shakers were thinking at the time.

John Farrell's keynote address was entitled 'How We Retain Our Hard-Won Respect'. He was followed by SP's tame MP John Greenaway, on how the government viewed sales promotion. Day Two was chaired by Ian Fryer and also featured Philip Circus taking over from his partner in Lawmark who had addressed the two previous conferences.

John Greenaway's section entitled 'It Shouldn't Be Allowed' quoted a 1990 report by the Director General of Fair Trading, Sir Gordon Borrie, who said: "I want to see consumers, as much as possible, in control their own lives - making decisions, exercising choices and having real influence as buyers and users over matters which directly affect them." Does the present Labour government have the same view? He then referred to the publication of a European Sales Promotion Code of Conduct in 1989 which was driven by the UK. In his view the chances of the British approach to sales promotion being adopted elsewhere was unlikely, and he has been proved correct.

An interesting aside came in Ian Shepherd's 'Will It Work at Retail Level' presentation. The marketing communications controller for Asda posed the question: "Retailer power, does it really exist?" He went on to answer by saying it was a myth and that although the major multiples had 65 per cent of the market, the only person with real power was the shopper. Has anyone told Tesco?

A WINNING TASTE

There was a relatively low key promotion in 1992 that had a lot of unexpected consequences. It was an instant win, with a prize budget of just £25,000 made up of five top prizes of £5,000 each and was run by Ribena on its carton drink. It was called 'Find Harry the Lime' and worked by putting a lime flavoured drink in the winning packs, with no exterior indication. Your first thought might well have been that you were being poisoned but hopeful you would then realise that, as you were tasting lime, you had won a prize. This was the forerunner of a stream of promotions using the product to indicate winners. A great deal of creative energy went into thinking up new ways of doing this, including warming, cooling and microwaving, dipping into vinegar, holding behind the product to read the message and so on. All of these bright ideas appealed to the client and got the business for the agency but probably did little for the customer, who just wanted know if they had won by the simplest possible means. Finding a £20 note in a packet of crisps for instance.

The year 1994 saw four successful new brands emerge. The National Lottery was a triumph, not least considering the problems governments have had with IT systems. Well done G-Tec. Equally successful was Orange, with the WCRS slogan, 'The futures bright, the future's Orange'. Amazon got underway, although its first sales were in 1995 and Yahoo! opened to the public, working up to 33 million visitors a month before 2000.

GUILTY!

In 1995 a very rare event took place concerning a company called Interactive Telephone Services (ITS). It was found guilty of running an illegal lottery and an unlawful competition. This TV game, Telemillion, had a £250,000 top prize, and ran for three months after a launch in January 1994. Entry was by a 24-hour premium rate telephone line backed up by a free postal entry to a PO Box. This free entry method only appeared in very small print and for a short time in Telemillion ads. The Crown Prosecution Service was asked by the Gaming Board to look at the case because it felt that it undermined existing controls over lotteries.

The legal question over the scheme hinged on two issues: whether it was a game of chance or whether questions made it a game of skill, together with the point about the postal entry making it free to enter. Having gone to all this trouble, the court only fined ITS £250 plus £7,500 costs, which probably did not bother them as much as being forced to scrap the programme. ISP legal adviser Philip Circus, told the media that the result was consistent with the advice the ISP had given on competitions but in the past there had been a general attitude of "Who cares?" because of a lack of enforcement.

The 1995 ISP Awards broke all records with a total of 910 entries. Under the chairmanship of Peter le Conte, this required 196 judges, an awards committee and a vetting panel. There were 31 categories with every category considered good enough to be awarded a Gold, Silver and Bronze. The 1995 Grand Prix was won by IMP with a promotion for IDV's Southern Comfort. It was called 'When the Band Strikes Up You Are a Winner'. An electronic device attached to the bottles and optics caused lights to flash and Dixieland tunes to ring out, when a shot was dispensed. Different songs corresponded to different spot prizes. It obviously worked as the sales went up by 100 per cent at participating outlets. There was also the strong possibility that pub staff were heading for a nervous breakdown by the end of the promotion.

1995 was the year that industry maverick Ford Ennals turned up as marketing director of British Airways. This was his fourth job in not many more years, having been with Reebok, shopping channel Q2 and Fruit of the Loom. He will be best remembered in the SP industry for his time at Lever Brothers, where he ran a number of high profile promotions on Persil and Domestos. He then moved to Mars, where along with Masterguide, he set up what many consider to be the UK's most successful sports sponsorship programme, the Mars London Marathon. At that time he was actually brand manager on Marathon, which later changed its name to Snickers. He was not given to elaborate briefs and simply told the agencies "Come up with a marathon promotion".

In a classic example of "It's who you know", Masterguide MD Graham Morse was married to the daughter of Sir Walter Winterbotham, recently chairman of the Sports Council, who knew everyone in sport and also knew that Gillette was about to drop its sponsorship. So Masterguide got the business and Ford got the marathon promotion of all marathon promotions. It was, for some time, going to be called The Marathon London Marathon, which caused endless discussions as to whether anyone would actually call it that. In the end it was taken over as the first ever total multi-brand company programme under the Mars banner. A personal note from co-author Ken Spedding; the race was won by Charlie Spedding, who went on to win an Olympic Medal. This caused an upset for Ken's wife who was a guest of Mars and wore a name badge. When congratulated on her son's success, the offended lady point out that she was only 10 years older than the winner.

GETTING HIGH
Promotions & Incentives magazine supplemented one of its regular salary surveys in 1996 with the question of whether respondents had taken illegal drugs in the previous six months. Surprisingly 35 per cent of female respondents claimed they had, compared to only 19 per

cent of males. Results showed that at almost every level, female staff were earning less than their male counterparts which may have had something to do with this apparent excess, but one wonders how they could afford them.

The 1996 ISP Awards, with Nick Wells as chairman, broke yet another record with almost 1,000 entries in 34 separate categories. It proved a triumph for Triangle with its blockbusting 'Watch and Win with Coronation Street' promotion collecting five Golds and the Grand Prix. Cadbury's was sponsoring 'Corrie', and printed one of 25 symbols on chocolate wrappers, which appeared at various times in the credits. If your wrapper matched, you had won a prize ranging from £25,000 to a glass tankard. Triangle claimed a staggering 35 per cent increase in sales.

David Gilk, then marketing director of Kimberly-Clark Europe, gave a client's perspective on deciphering agency speak to "Promotions & Incentives" magazine..

The agency says...	The client thinks...	David's advice...
I'm currently talking to BA, Coca-Cola and Nestle	He's left a message for the brand manager to call him	Not credible even if true. Say something concrete, or say nothing
We have a new and exciting proposition	Tell that to the Marines	Make sure it is new. Research and develop it properly. It is the key to success
So that overheads go towards client service, we currently use freelancers	Oh my God, artwork by an out of work art student	Implies a lack of control. Trust is the critical aspect
My old agency got too big/lost its soul/disagreed over a matter of principle	He couldn't compete with the new talent/got fired	Don't slag off your old company or don't try to appear principled. You will just look impetuous
We've done some project work for Mega Co	The client hated the work they did for them	Project is a bad word. Speculative work that It says short term relationship

The national press were promoting very heavily around this period with the tabloids getting into aggressive price cutting which effectively cancelled out each other's efforts. There was lots of direct marketing, door drops and short-term reduced price trials, so papers could not afford really serious offers and were running relatively modest promotions such as free garden seeds, restaurant vouchers, discounted days out and suchlike. There were some more high profile efforts by the more middle and up market publications such as a Daily Express promotion which gave one reader a house and car and £10,000 a year for life. They probably hoped it would be won by a 90-year-old.

The Independent on Sunday was offering a reader the chance to fly to New York and back for £10, having come to a very lucrative arrangement with United Airlines. The Daily Mail was giving away IPC magazines and two for one main meals at Brewers Fayre, plus even lower cost flights with Buzz, the KLM subsidiary. When the tabloids stopped cutting each other's throats they got back into the more cost effective approach. The Sun linked with Ryanair trumpeting a million seats at "ludicrously low" prices.

The same paper was distributing free Budweiser and even went a little more middle class with free 1999 Rugby World Cup tickets. More in keeping with its readership were other RWC linked promotions such as one involving Guinness as a major supporter of the game and Fantasy Rugby with generous prizes. If you read the small print you would have discovered that these were funded by premium phone lines. You could also get free golf lessons from the Express and free sunglasses from the Mail. By the end of the decade some of the newspapers were experimenting with promotions on the internet but with slow data transfer speeds, these were extremely crude by contemporary standards.

MONEY MAKES THE WORLD GO ROUND

Salaries for people in marketing at the end of the decade were looking quite healthy. Brand managers would earn around £33,000 and their boss, the marketing director, £50,000 plus. Company cars had not yet been taxed out of existence and the brand manager would probably get a VW or an Audi while the marketing director would expect to drive BMW, a Merc or, if he was not that senior, a Rover. In agencies an account director would expect around £35,000 and account managers earned on average £22,000.

Surprisingly, some 13 or so years later, the salaries advertised had not gone up that much. Marketing and Account Directors at £80,000 with special qualifications adding another £10,000 or so. Marketing, Brand or Account Managers from £25-£55,000, entry level Executives around £25- £30,000 and Business Development Manager (a posh name for salesmen) £30-£50,000 plus the "Opportunity to earn a possible £120,000 and uncapped". They wish!

The gap between male and female pay was still enormous, working out at 43 per cent in men's favour. This seemed to be a matter of supply and demand as there was a lot more woman than men working in the industry. A company trying to get a gender balance had to pay more to get the rarer creature. A business lunch was still a big part of business and two per cent of marketing directors admitted to having a business lunch almost every day. Of course, at that time, the first rules relating to what you could ask for in an applicant came into force and have got steadily wider since. It soon became illegal to even hint that age, gender, sexual orientation, ethnic background or just about anything else could affect the possibility of getting a job offer.

THE CASH BACK SCAM

Around this time some 300 companies across Europe found themselves in trouble because they had bought into a very successful promotion called 'Cashback'. It was successful because it offered the purchaser of high ticket items, such as cars, 100 per cent cash back on the purchase price in five years time. They even sent purchasers a post-dated cheque. The supplier company was called Intervest Capital but, unfortunately for everyone holding the cheques and the companies running the promotions, it was wound up by the DTI towards the end of 1997. The cost to the promoters had been high, 15 per cent of the purchase price, but it seemed so attractive that companies such as Apple, Honda and many others thought it worthwhile. Apple had £50,000 in cheques outstanding and Honda more than £300,000 when everything went pear shaped. Of course the consumers expected the sellers to pay up.

The DTI said that it closed the company because it had been unable to confirm the financial status of the US company due to honour the cheques and could find no evidence that a fund had been created for that purpose. Despite the name, it did not have any investments or any capital and had simply taken the money and run. The man behind this scam, Charles Gordon-Seymour, had an interesting history, having been associated with Victoria Insurance of Georgia which went bust in 1988 owing $20million. He was accused of shipping $10million of Victoria's cash to a London bank, while claiming that he had brought the fraud to light.

At this time the loyalty card get began to play a larger part in promotional activity. Tesco reckoned that 28 per cent of its customers participated with Club Card, with Sainsbury claiming 24 per cent, Boots 17 per cent and Safeway 16 per cent. WH Smith, Homebase, BP and Shell were all in single figures with Shell scoring lowest on 3 per cent. The cards were more popular with women, with 68 per cent using at least one card. Only 58 per cent of men took part in one or more of these schemes. The most likely users were 35 to 45 year old ABs.
  Things moved on. For instance, by 2009 the Tesco Club Card was 15 years old, had 15 million holders with 9 million variations of statement, tailored to customers apparent interests, and was sending out £400 million of vouchers a year. Despite this success they still decided to do a relaunch with a £150 million budget.

Things were beginning to move rapidly to greater and greater use of technology, ready for the millennium. Telephone bookings were booming but were about to be overtaken by the internet which, in 1998, was available in just 15 per cent of homes although more than 60 per cent of all businesses had a website by this time. Easyjet was expecting to do 30 per cent of its business online although, at this point, 87 per cent still came by phone.

With the millennium coming up, the EU was once again thinking that it should be doing something about SP rules across the continent. Its latest wheeze was 'mutual recognition'. This had the seemingly sensible idea that companies could carry out promotions in the target country as long as the scheme was legal in the country of origin. Like every other plan to date, this produced a great deal of hot air but no changes. It was far too sensible to ever happen.

COLLECTING FOR THE KIDS

This was also the year when one of the most successful schemes benefiting schools launched. 'Walkers' Books for Schools' linked with The Sun, The News of the World and The Times, with a target to distribute 15 million books which, by a strange coincidence, came from News Corp publisher Harper Collins.

More than 350 exhibitors turned up at Incentive World in the less than glamorous surroundings of Wembley. The usual large contingent of voucher companies were worried by the changes in the tax situation. Harriet Harman, then Secretary for State for Social Security, did the dirty deed and made vouchers taxable. They would now be treated as remuneration and so attract a national insurance contribution related to the face value.

They would also be taxable as income, which led to all sorts of complications. Companies soon worked out that rewarding their staff with £50 worth of M&S vouchers on which they might have to pay £20 income tax was not a great incentive. In the end, an arrangement was made with the Revenue to cope with this, much to the relief of the voucher companies. Judging by the steady growth in sales since that time, it seems that the NIC contribution, now upped by Mr Brown to 11 per cent, did nothing to dent their customers' enthusiasm for vouchers of every type.

Two companies at least latched on to the growth in computer games. Kellogg gave away a CD-ROM computer game, Mission Nutrition, on 400,000 packs of Frosties and Van den Bergh's Peperami took a similar route. They probably weren't serious competitors to Grand Theft Auto. The first prepay mobile phones appeared at this time, which caused a rapid growth in ownership and also caused the more technically minded agencies to start looking at ways of targeting the 19 million phone owners. The SMS revolution was on its way.

Grolsch came up with yet another novel way of telling people that they had not won in an instant win. An ingenious agency came up with 'sensitive time reveal wrist cards' that actually took 30 minutes to tell you whether or not you had collected the prize. Never mind, customers could buy another drink while they were waiting. Meanwhile McCain had customers microwaving game cards. We don't think they were intended to eat them, but you never know.

COMPERS

The large number of competitions now being run had produced a growing number of enthusiastic competition entrants or 'Compers' as they like to call themselves. They held conventions where it was not unusual for 150 enthusiasts to meet in such salubrious surroundings as the Pudsey Civic Hall. Stories circulated, such as the lady who won seven bikes in one year, or the regular who managed to win a holiday every year for seven years, and another who won three cars in 10 years. Magazines dedicated to this activity emerged. Co-author Colin Lloyd's first job was on the first one -Competitors Journal, and one of them, Competitors Companion calculated that there were at least 60,000 'Compers' in the UK. There was a brisk trade in books designed to help you win a steady stream of cars, holidays and household goodies. They had titles such as How to Win Any Consumer Competition and Great British Prize Winning Slogans.

This semi-professional approach produced a few people who took it very seriously. Some actually took issue with the results of competitions. The best known was an ex-RAF pilot called William Freitag who took on Douwe Egberts, Courage and Coca-Cola. In 1999, he went to court with Douwe Egberts over a 1992 (the law moves very slowly) competition where the object was to identify the position of an aircraft flying between two coffee plantations. His arguments were that firstly, the promoter had not accurately measured the distance between the two airfields and, secondly the independent judge wasn't. He won his case and was awarded damages but lost his case against Courage and apparently settled out of court, probably because it was cheaper than paying the lawyers.

Another court case of the period was Russell v Fulling and Page. Russell designed a campaign for Fulling and Page intended to be used by independent retailers and he invested a considerable sum in it. Unfortunately it never got off the ground and he was owed money by F and P. He sued them for the debt but when it came to court, the judge decided that the scheme was actually illegal. This meant that Russell could not enforce the debt and the case was thrown out. It was supposed to be an instant win game of some kind but unlike the normal method where prizes were distributed by chance, the Russell version allowed the retailer to decide who would win and it was designed so that hardly anybody would. In addition, there was no acceptable free entry route. Well, at least the lawyers got paid.

Promoters were still running what were at that time referred to as roadshows. A large number of such operations were running in the summer of 1999, including sampling a non-alcoholic drink called Brooklyn Brewed Soda, which failed to catch the public imagination. Other roadshows sampled Volvic and Evian so that the public could discover the great taste of water. Also competing for the public's cash and supermarket shelf space were Sprite, Robinsons Barley Water, Tropicana Fruit Juice, Ocean Spray, Strongbow Cider, Dairy Crest and Yoplait, just to mention a few. It must have been a very good summer for what used to be called personality girls but who soon moved upmarket to become brand ambassadors, a much more impressive title but not necessarily any better paid.

The supermarkets were competing heavily with their loyalty schemes and customers were signing up in droves. Sainsbury's Reward claimed 14 million users, which was the same size as the Tesco Clubcard, and demonstrated a bit of an about turn on its "plastic Green Shield stamps" comment. Even the relatively small Safeway, with its ABC Card, had 10 million customers signed up. However, not everyone was heavily into plastic with Archie Norman, then chairman of Asda, deeming them "a waste of money".

CHANGE THE NAME AND DO THE SAME

With the new millennium approaching, the Sale Promotion Consultants Association (SPCA) under the chairmanship of Clive Mishon gave serious consideration to changing its name but could not then agree on a new one. In time it did get around to becoming the Marketing Communication Consultants Association or MCCA. A few years later the ISP considered a name change but decided that promoting sales was what the members actually did, so stuck with the established title. Clive became chairman of the ISP in 2007 when the tag line "when promoting sales is your business" was introduced, and you will find an interesting interview with him in a later chapter. Even M&S began to get into sales promotion, something which in the past had been beneath its dignity, rather like advertising. It ran a series of instant win promotions on its food ranges giving way up to £50,000 worth M&S vouchers.

The Millennium Dome sparked a few promotional incentives, including one by Ford which sponsored 'The Journey' zone in the Dome. It produced a range of limited edition models, painted bright yellow including a Ka, Puma and Focus. They cost £1,000 more than the standard model and despite the slating that the Dome received might now be collector's items.

The internet boom was building up a head of steam and agencies were investing their cash in internet start-ups. Sir Martin Sorrell however was not that enthusiastic, stating: "I don't want a situation where we get underpaid. It's a bull market phenomenon, what if the market cracks?" Good question Martin. The strength of the internet boom also showed up in the salaries being paid. The average for someone who could claim some kind of expertise in this area was around £70,000 compared to the average for the previous leaders in telecoms and IT of £50,000.

So, onwards and upwards into the new millennium which hopefully would get better after the disappointing 'River of Fire' on the Thames and the disastrous Millennium Dome.

CHAPTER 15

The Noughties – go digital young man!

The big names from the Eighties disappear
A bubble bursts
Air Miles reorganised
Winning the Sex Lottery

Despite the Millennium Bug turning out to be the greatest non-event in history and the dot com bubble bursting in 2000, technology was more important than ever. A general reduction in human contact saw the telephone replaced by voicemail, e-mail, texting. The internet and a whole computer-centric virtual reality lifestyle emerged with blogs and numerous online communities. The Sales Promotion practitioners jumped in with both feet. Viral marketing, text to win, and a whole variety of website based activity became possibly the flavour for the best part of a decade. This was the year that the MP3 player burst onto the promotional scene and just in case older readers wonder where the name came from, it actually stands for Motion Picture Experts Group Audio Layer 3.

Sales Promotion had become more professional, more mainstream, more bureaucratic, less entrepreneurial and probably less exciting than it had been. There were no longer any Sales Promotions agencies quoted on the stock exchange although in time one or two did emerge as part of marketing services groups. Usually they covered a wide range of activities and had built up by merging a number of smaller companies, but they were not at all like the big names of the past.

That is not to say that there were no large and successful companies but they were now either private or parts of bigger groups. The funny money of the Eighties floatations has been spent or disappeared when share values went south. Agencies had their hands forced up their back by procurement departments when it came to negotiating fees and margins but still seem to be making a decent living. The first few years of the decade were a recovery period after the tough years in the Nineties but generally things, including the housing market, were picking up.

The big news story in January 2000 and the rest of the year was the Millennium Dome. It was rarely mentioned without a derogatory adjective preceding its name after starting off on the wrong foot when newspaper editors had to queue to join The Queen and Tony Blair for the New Year's Eve party. Queuing seemed to be a unique experience for them, one which they did not appreciate. After that, the media spent the next 12 months slagging off the Dome in every possible way.

They completely ignored the fact that it had attracted 6.5 million visitors, making it the most successful attraction in the UK. They also failed to notice that more than 80 per cent of visitors thought that it had been a good day out. For the last three months of 2000 it even made an operating profit and its £7million marketing budget was peanuts compared to those of dotcom enterprises. It even opened on time and on budget. Finally in 2007 it became a big success as The O2, a premier worldwide showcase for big international acts. Pity it took so long to come up with that idea.

In business terms, the dot coms were the more irresistible story. To give an idea of the amount of cash swilling around, consider that between March and May 1999 internet-based companies spent £3.2million on advertising and promotional activity. In the next quarter this went up to £7.8million followed, in the next quarter, by an expenditure of £28.9million. By the quarter to February 2000 they spent an amazing £43.5million, despite the fact that the companies had never made a profit. In some cases their total turnover was less than their advertising spend. TV companies understandably rubbed their hands in glee and upped their rates as much as possible. Unfortunately for SP, very little of this flood of cash came its way.

Despite the internet, the world went on. Cadbury's Smash went somewhat retro in 2000 and revived the Martians in an online promotion with a £40,000 top prize. The idea of waterborne conferences had spread to the US where the QE2 had been chartered for a trip and packed with enthusiastic sellers and less enthusiastic potential buyers. Unfortunately the weather was lousy, the sea was extremely rough, and even worse, nobody's mobile phones worked. Apparently the Brits got drunk and enjoyed themselves while the Yanks drank water and made themselves miserable by losing money in the casino.

BIG AMBITIONS

Marketing service companies were beginning to feel bullish again and something vaguely resembling long-vanished quoted outfits such as Clarke Hooper or FKB were being floated on the Stock Market with varied fortunes. One marketing services company decided that growth by acquisition was the way to go, despite the lessons of the past.   Media Square appeared on AIM in August 2000 as a cash shell pursuing what it called "an end-to-end e-marketing solutions strategy". With early acquisitions struggling, it purchased marketing services firm Equanim in June 2002 in a bid to turn around its fortunes. The rescue strategy was to try and buy themselves out of trouble. A triumph of hope over experience, like second marriages.

Their approach focused on the provision of marketing communications and retail marketing services, buying struggling businesses and hopefully restructuring them to make them profitable. Within the space of seven months this boosted revenues from £3million to

£7.6million, contributing to a maiden full year profit of £255,692 for the year to 31 October 2003. Carried away by its success, Media Square raised £17.1million of new equity funding and kept on shopping, acquiring AIM-quoted retail marketing communications Coutts Holdings plc. Shortly after, Media Square announced pre-tax profits of £1.5million for the year to 31 October 2004. It was looking good, so in November 2005 it hooked a much bigger fish, Marketing Services Group, bought from Huntsworth (previous owners of Holmes & Marchant) for £63million. The purchase was funded by new equity of £30million and lots of borrowing. We suspect that Huntsworth were very happy to take the money, and rightly so.

Media Square collected a lot of debt and 16 new companies to try and manage, and from then on things then went downhill rapidly. Shades of FKB who, if you remember, tried the same thing with the same results. Towards the end of 2007 it was "restructuring", its trading performance had been "dire" and it had suffered from an "over aggressive acquisition strategy". In just six months to August 2007 it lost £18.57million pre tax. The previous year it had managed a profit of just £365,000. With unusual honesty Roger Parry, group executive chairman, admitted: "These problems were mostly of the company's own making, rather than as a result of market conditions." It's a useful lesson for budding entrepreneurs.

TREASURE ISLAND

In the first part of the new century UK car buyers suddenly realised that they were paying 10-12 per cent more for their cars than the rest of Europe. The UK wasn't called 'Treasure Island' without reason. All sorts of people got into the business of importing right-hand drive cars which led to an 11 per cent drop in UK sales. It also gave rise to the expression 'Rip-off Britain' and forced manufacturers to start promoting. The Russell Organisation came up with an unusual twist for Honda. The competition prize was the value of the car you were trading in against your new Honda and claimed that this doubled the sales of used Hondas. Honda also promoted the launch of its HRV5 with a promotion called 'Five Go Mad in Newquay' which not only gave you the chance to win a car but also a Nokia mobile phone, health club memberships and other "cool" prizes. Did the executors of Enid Blyton notice the plagiarism we wonder?

Other makers introduced all sorts of cash backs (remember, Henry Ford tried this one) and financial inducements to buy a car in the UK, including a chance to win a week on Richard Branson's Necker Island. Fiat offered £1,000 worth of new clothes to Punto buyers and promoted the oddly-shaped family car, the Multipla, at Chessington World of Adventures and Alton Towers. In the end though, it was not until manufacturers lowered their UK prices to the European level that new car sales recovered. Who would have thought that HMG would be handing out cash to motorists who had their 10 year or older car scrapped and bought a new one, which the 2009 budget introduced. It became know as 'Scrapage'. Speaking of Richard

Branson, a man hard to avoid, 2000 was the year in which he won and then lost, on appeal, the National Lottery.

Still on the transport theme, Air Miles split its operations at this time. Its Executive Club members collected BA Miles while the existing Air Miles would only be available from third parties. This was supported by the first ever Air Miles TV commercial. At the same time Judith Thorn, managing director of Air Miles left the most profitable BA subsidiary for GO, which was eventually sold to Easyjet. Air Miles was originally founded as an independent company with BA as the majority shareholder. In 1990 it became the currency for the Executive Club and in 1994 the airline bought out the minority shareholders.

In 1995 it moved to electronic points, and by 2000 the company had acquired an impressive collection of partners led by NatWest, together with AXA, BUPA, Bol.com, Gateway, Homebase, Marriott Hotels, RAC, Sainsbury, Thistle Hotels and Vodafone. In 1999 it had bought an independent travel promotion company, MKM, but this did not last. MKM soon bought themselves back and floated as a public company in 2002, but by 2009 even Google could not find them.

It seems free flights are even more popular when times are hard. In 2009, when the credit crunch was crunching, BA reported a fourfold increase in the number of people joining the scheme.

HELLO EXPERIENTIAL

At the beginning of the new decade the other big sector below the line was field or experiential marketing. This covered roadshows, trade relation activity and home calling, and was summarised as "Personal contact to further their client's sales and marketing objectives". It included some pretty big companies, in turnover terms at least, but whereas SP agencies had mostly become part of much bigger groups, in 2004 this only applied to CPM, owned by Omnicom Group. It seems that the big ad agency groups had not woken up to the fact that more and more of marketing budgets were moving this way.

These days experiential marketing is more than just handing out samples. In 2000 the agency for Olivio ran 'A Taste of the Mediterranean' roadshow, sampling the product and giving Italian lessons to passers-by. Not surprisingly, field staff or 'brand ambassadors' were now expected to be more than just well turned out, attractive ladies or gentlemen. According to commentators, they had to be "Charismatic, irreverent, with a level of maturity, intelligence and last, but not least honesty". It's doubtful these paragons were paid much more as titles are a cheap way to appear to be promoting someone. Just think how many directors there are in agencies, but few who actually sit on the board.

These remarkably talented brand ambassadors were required to do some rather strange things. Not since the days of White Tide Men in the Sixties had out of work actors had to appear in such weird and wonderful kit. There was a search for people to work as, would you believe, 'Fruit Police' which might have been misunderstood, particularly as they had to wear bright green and pink combat trousers which, in high-tech mode, had a LED panel on the front of their t-shirts. Staff were also needed to work with Badboy Bombay Hot Noodles and KP needed 80 Twiglet men. It's difficult to imagine how an eight-foot high Twiglet managed to demonstrate personality, common sense and charisma but they would certainly need a sense of humour in those outfits.

ONLINE MOTIVATION

With hindsight, by 2003 it was possible to look back at the much-hyped 'future age of motivation' that was launched on the unsuspecting industry at Incentive World 2000. The big motivation players, Grass Roots, Maritz and P&MM (now Motivcom), had all leapt on to the idea of having a packaged, off the shelf, web-based incentive management solution that, they promised, would revolutionise the way staff were motivated and rewarded. It would cut costs, increase effectiveness and efficiency and provide a dramatic increase in productivity.

They came up with trendy names such as GRG Options, Warp and Rewardbanking. Everyone got very excited. Three years later all three were still offering the packages and rivals had been launched by Skybridge, Argos Business Solutions and BI. Unfortunately they did not turn out to be 'the new paradigm' in motivation solutions and old fashioned paper remained the medium of choice for motivation programmes. As we move into the next decade of the 21st century, there is a steady growth in the use of plastic in various forms but it has been much slower than projected.

STAFF WANTED

SP was doing well again resulting in serious recruiting problems. Everyone was expected to have a degree but Sales Promotion did not figure on the radar of many graduates or university careers teams. The one seat of learning that really did take it seriously was Kingston and a large number of its graduates have done very well. Other courses paid lip service.

The Marketing Store Worldwide made an effort to improve its recruitment at graduate trainee level. At the end of the Nineties, using conventional methods, it recruited two graduates but it only had five or six to choose from. The next year it advertised to job hunting grads and took part in the 'Milk Round'. The applications jumped to 400, which were shortlisted to 50, with the final list of applicants spending two days at each of its five UK offices. It ended up with 10 excellent new recruits to add to its 200 UK employees. Other companies might have followed suit given the serious competition from areas such as accounting and the City that offered much higher starting salaries, or dot coms(?) that briefly seemed the route to early retirement in the Bahamas.

In May 2001 Marketing published a list of the 100 people it considered the most influential in marketing. The only name that can be connected to Sales Promotion, if you ignore ad man Sir Martin Sorrell who owns a chunk of the industry, was co-author Colin Lloyd, at number 85. This was probably because he was president of the Direct Marketing Association at the time. By the next year he had left the DMA job and slipped to 95th. By the following year there was no one with an SP background in the Power 100.

Despite the lack of recognition, the industry ploughed its own furrow. The 2001 ISP Awards offered the usual insight into what the great and the good of the industry thought was great and good work. The number of entries, 500, was up 20 per cent on the previous year but only half of those seen back in the Eighties. Some 70 agencies took part and 160 different promoters. The ISP chairman of the year, Randle Stonier, commented that the big increase in entries was in event marketing, cause related promotions and B2B activity. Four new digital categories picked up 10 per cent of the entries.

JOIN THE ARMY
The Grand Prix was won by Saatchi & Saatchi with a promotion for the Army, which usually went in for expensive TV campaigns but with budgets reduced it had to settle for a promotion. It was still intended to produce up to 15,000 new recruits with a much smaller budget, which is not an unusual situation in the promotions business. It ran a competition with a prize of seven nights' training with the Army in Kenya. Please, no jokes about the second prize being 14 nights.

Silver in the consumer awareness class was won by Texaco with a sort of treasure hunt for 'buried' Mercedes SLKs. It turned out that the imaginary number plate shown on marketing material belonged to a real-life SLK owned by someone with no connection to Texaco. He was unable to drive his car on the roads until the promotion was over or risk pursuit by hordes of treasure hunters. Other promotions continued the hunt to find different ways to tell people what they had, or had not won. World Duty Free Stores ran a Valentine's Day promotion giving out cards that were held between the hands to heat-reveal the prize and British Midland incentivised travel agents with a light sensitive card.

In 2002 Randle Stonier had been persuaded to do a second year as chairman and oversaw that year's Awards. The Grand Prix went to Safeway for its 'Viva Italia' campaign which, unusually for a retailer, had next to nothing to do with price reductions. It promoted Italian products and included a whole gamut of activities such as a competition to win a Fiat. It seems that the budget would not run to a Ferrari. The whole programme culminated in a real ground breaker, the exclusive 'Picnic with Pavarotti' event in Hyde Park, attended by 70,000 people. The agency was Storm, a subsidiary of Triangle, dealing with retail clients and it also won Gold in Consumer Trial and Consumer Awareness plus Platinum for Best in Category.

The Andrex puppy, without which no ISP list would be complete, picked up Platinum, Gold in the Premiums category and Gold in Traffic Building. It even got a bronze for Best Complementary Use of the Medium. Agency SMP probably didn't bother to put it on the groaning shelf in its Tunbridge Wells office. SMP had held the Andrex account for some time and rumour has it that part of its original pitch was the claim that in an emergency they could cycle from Tunbridge Wells to the Kimberly Clark offices.It's not known if they actually did so.

ALL THINGS DIGITAL
Electronic and digital media were making an impact and there was quite a bit of fuss about multi-media messaging, or MMS, despite the fact that less than one in 20 mobile phones could cope with it. SMS was fairly limited, with only 160 characters available and a basic screen appearance. A sign of things to come appeared in 2003 when Coca-Cola ran what was said to be the first ever SMS 'Text2Collect' promotion, offering consumers a chance to win exclusive music tracks and tickets to a series of eight 'Red Room' concerts. Coke was giving away the latest picture messaging mobile phones and got 2.2 million entries.

An early known use of free DVDs, which today fall from our newspapers like leaves in autumn, was produced by Honda and included the now legendary two-minute TV commercial. 'The Making of Cog'. This DVD was four minutes long and was cover mounted on several large circulation newspapers and magazines. Over one million people downloaded the same material from the company's website. They should get out more.

Another survey must have given the ISP a warm glow. When promotional marketing agencies were asked about their membership of trade associations, the ISP came top with 85 per cent, followed by the direct marketing people with 55 per cent and the MCCA with 47 per cent. The ISP also came top when asked who provided the best service. The ISP and the DMA were beginning to look like an item in 2003 and had been seen holding hands in public, or at least holding serious conversations, but so far nothing has come of this.

The idea that Sales Promotion and direct marketing were rivals was dismissed by various senior figures but as co-author Colin Lloyd said at the time "Hardly any direct marketing takes place without a Sales Promotion offer at the heart of it or as an add on. Without a strong proposition, DM does not work". The bodies did consider merging but decided that this would be taking their relationship a little too far, so they did not go to bed together but decided to operate in adjacent but possibly linked rooms. At the end of 2006 the ISP and the BPMA did arrange a civil partnership and the widgets people moved into the ISP building on Pentonville Road.

In 2002 the major loyalty schemes were still booming. The Tesco Clubcard was now carried by 10 million customers. Sainsbury's Reward Card had reached eight million. Top of the heap for numbers was the Boots Advantage Card, launched in 1997 and now with 13 million members. But the big news was a new player as in 2002 Sainsbury's Reward Card, BP Premier Points and Barclaycard Rewards were all rolled into Nectar.

This was the handiwork of Sir Keith Mills, the man who successfully persuaded BA to get into Air Miles after years of refusing to have anything to do with frequent flyer programmes. Nectar could now claim to be the largest loyalty scheme by some distance but the launch was somewhat tainted by the fact that its website crashed, resulting in 2.8 million cardholders who were unable to register and 3.6 million cardholders who were using the card but no one knew who they were.

TAKE A DEEP BREATH

Other events worthy of mention around the end of 2002 and the beginning of 2003 include the banning of most advertising and promotional activity for tobacco, the first major step towards committing evil smokers to the outer darkness, or at least the outdoors, which came about in 2007. This period saw the launch of the Committee of Advertising Practice (CAP) Code. These are the rules administered by the Advertising Standards Authority (ASA) covering the content of the UK non-broadcasting communications. Previously Sales Promotion had its own code, as did advertising, but now they had been rolled into one.

In March 2003 the world got very worried about a disease called SARS which stood for Severe Acute Respiratory Syndrome. Unfortunately for two companies they both produced products with the same name. Both were soft drinks produced in Taiwan and Australia. They did not actually link any promotional activity to the disease, but someone else did. A Hong Kong company promised to pay $25,000 to anyone who caught it after a 90-day course of its Vita Gain health drink. Like most scares of this sort, SARS soon dropped off almost everyone's radar. Think bird flu.

April 2003 saw the annual ISP Awards celebrating the best promotions in the previous year. They had a few more panel chairmen and a few more judges and they still had Randle as chairman. What stamina the man had. Weetabix picked up the Grand Prix plus Gold in Interactive Media and of course Platinum. 'The Weetabix House' was an online virtual reality house incorporating £1million of high-value prizes. A few years later it was voted the best promotion ever in a magazine poll. As we have mentioned before we, and a number of other people with long memories, disagree and voted for 'Shell Make Money' on the grounds that the Weetabix instant win was hardly ground breaking. We also think the Andrex Puppy was streets ahead, but what do we know? Democracy has spoken.

This self same Andrex Puppy struck again with two Golds and a Silver. United Biscuits won Gold for what is the most easily misconstrued title of any winning promotion. It launched a new cookie range with the challenge to 'Pass the Oral Sensation Test'. Mind you, the promotion was linked to Ann Summers at-home parties so it may have been designed to be misconstrued. The campaign generated 42,000 entries - make what you will of that.

The magazine Sales Promotion was 25 years old in 2004 and had a few comments on how things had changed over that relatively short time. It highlighted the disappearance of in-house sales promotion departments, or at least managers, and their replacement by procurement departments; the growth in retailer power; the increase in the ability to target consumers, and the enormous increase in the use of digital technology and in particular the mobile phone and the internet. Rules and regulations have changed, tobacco advertising is a thing of the past, alcohol advertising is heavily controlled and advertising to children is about to go the same way.

It is hard to disagree with the introduction, which said: "The basic elements of Sales Promotion remain - Free, Win, Give and Save are still the messages... but what different ways we now have of delivering those messages".

However, SP was operating in a rapidly changing world as one magazine article noted: "Children are much in the news at present. If you believe everything you read you would think that paedophiles lurk on every street corner and in the internet chat rooms, the fast food companies conspire to make our young obese, while television and computer games' producers work together to make them violent". There was growing pressure to control all types of advertising to children, kicked off in June 2000 when Sweden took over the rotating presidency of the European Union and in its ultra-politically correct style, suggested a Europe wide ban on all advertising to children. Strict limitations on advertising and promoting to children are now very much on the cards. This was much in line with all single issue pressure groups who disapproved of something. The first call always seems to be 'ban advertising'.

On the same theme, marketing in schools was a hot topic. There is nothing new about the basic technique of collecting vouchers or proof of purchase that could be exchanged for something schools could use. However it found renewed favour this decade. The now demised agency, The Yellow Submarine, even had a kids' subsidiary with the cringe-making name of The Likle Submarine, which ran a very large scheme in 2000 for Tetley Tea. The official tea of the GB Team at the Sydney Olympics linked with The Daily Express and supported with TV and radio to hand over £18million worth of sports equipment bought by redeemed coupons. As it was not costing the government anything it was endorsed by a raft of politicians including Tony Blair, Kate Hoey, David Blunkett and Mo Mowlam.

WORLDWIDE WINNERS

SP was being lauded on the international scene through the Marketing Agencies Association Worldwide (MAAW) Awards in 2004. The 50 judges considered 333 entries from 26 different countries, making the 2004 'Globes' the largest ever. There were 62 finalists, and six of the Globes (the top award) were won, together with 46 Gold, Silver and Bronze gongs. The whole judging operation was run globally on the internet.

The Grand Prix winner was a World Cup Cricket campaign for Pepsi in India by J Walter Thompson. The Indian cricket team play in blue, so Pepsi produced 2.5 million souvenir bottles in that colour instead of its normal red and put together a massive array of big-brand tie-ins, sponsorships, competitions, instant wins, music CDs and pub screenings, plus a great deal of Team India merchandise.

What else was winning awards that year? Sticking with the Globes, most winners came from the US. These included Callaway Golf, United Airlines and, possibly the most unlikely outfit that would ever consider running a promotion, the American Institute of Certified Public Accountants (AICPA). The accountants' promotion was a programme called 'Catch Me If You Can' by Wunderman that linked to the film about a successful conman turned forensic accountant. The object was not to suggest that students became conmen, but to persuade them to train as accountants because it was not quite as deadly dull as they might have thought. It produced 13,822 registrations and 6,384 leads to potential bean counters. A promotion for Victoria's Secret pushing a new line of knickers made a nice contrast.

The MAAW, which runs the annual Globes, started life some 40 years ago as the Council of Sales Promotion Agencies (CoSPA) with an intervening name change in 1996 as the Association of Promotion Marketing Agencies (APMA). The founding fathers of the body were the promotion luminaries of the day: Stanley Goodman, Art Dietrich, Ron Rosenberg, Bud Frankle, Fritz Siebel and Diego Massi from Italy as the association's first international member.

Entry into the Globes is exclusive to the winning overall promotion in that year from the particular country bodies representing the discipline. Over the years Globes' winners have come from every part of the world, with the latest overall winner a tie in for Macdonalds with the Beijing Olympics from China.

Twice a year the association brings together CEO's and owners of some of the world's leading promotion marketing agencies to share knowledge and hear from world experts. In recognition of outstanding contributions to the business, the MAAW inducts leading global practitioners into its Hall of Fame.

Mike DaSilva, from his base in Australia, is in a position to see what is going on around the Pacific Rim. As 2007 President of the MAAW his view is that until comparatively recently, Sales Promotion was mainly an Anglo-Saxon activity with the UK and the US leading the rest of the world. However this is no longer the case, and international prize-winning promotions are coming out of South America and Asia as well as Brazil, Korea and India.

He says that sales promotion can even break down cultural barriers and cites as an example a Football World Cup promotion in Korea. This was a year in which the games were split between Japan and Korea with both countries having teams involved and, of course, with massive local support. Up to that time it had been completely illegal in Korea to make any use whatsoever of the national flag apart from flying it as a flag. Thanks to the influence of the World Cup promotion, these rules were relaxed and fans were painting their faces with the flag and making other uses of it. They were even taught a few suitable chants in English as part of the promotional package. We don't know which but hopefully they were suitable for a family audience. This won the top MAAW Globe.

Another example he gave was the offer of large granite washing bowls by Dove in India. They were provided as communal sinks in villages and the only commercial reference was an engraving of a Dove in the surface of the bowl. These were a considerable advance on the type of equipment normally available and worked extremely well for the brand. It did not involve ladies in their underwear as in other parts of the world.

Mike considers that the great driving forces behind promotion activity in this area are sport, tourism and entertainment. These are all linked and have become extremely international. Soccer is massive in Asia, as of course it is in most of the world other than North America where even David Beckham's move to LA in 2007 did not have much effect. A typical promotion might use mobile phone technology and the internet for a promotion in Vietnam, linked to a soccer match taking place in Singapore between Indonesia and Malaysia. Cable TV and satellite allow widespread coverage of the game and prizes include travel to Singapore and other similar goodies.

DEAD, BUT WON'T LIE DOWN

In 2004 a headline in Incentive Today said "Hyslop Heralds Death of Sales Promotion". Roger Hyslop, one of the founders of the Triangle Group had just retired and was making the pronouncement in an article. Incidentally, he is now back at work in a new agency called Initials, but at the time, he said that the changes in retailing and consumer needs meant that the business was now something new called 'brand promotion'. His article included such staggering insights as: "People are sophisticated enough to know that when a 30-second commercial comes on they are being sold something".

Fortunately for the industry, the marketing people at Coca-Cola did not read the article because that year it ran what it claimed to be the largest ever on pack promotion. This was linked to its legal downloadable music site, www.mycokemusic.com, which allowed consumers to select from some 250,000 new and old tracks. This pitted Coke against various illegal sites that allowed consumers to download tracks without payment to anyone, least of all the artist or the record company. The instant win ran on 200 million packs with 20 million free downloads available. Other goodies could be claimed by collecting tokens from packs and making online bids, using the tokens as currency.

SEX SELLS

If the previous year's 'Pass the Oral Sensation Test' was risqué, it was nothing compared to the GP winner in 2004. It won Gold in the catchall category of Public Services, Utilities, Environment and Agriculture. There weren't many agricultural promotions but this one might have a link with what Shakespeare called "country matters". (For the less well read, this is a euphuism for having sex.) The promoter was The Department of Health and the winning agency was Iris Promotional Marketing. The title, which sounded drearily bureaucratic, was 'The government message on unprotected sex' but the copy headlines and general promotional material was about as un-bureaucratic as you could get. Not many writers get a chance to pen headlines such as "Do not enter without a condom" to be printed on cards which were hung on the doors of hotel rooms and "Who knows what you just picked up?"

They also worked on scratchcards for 'The Sex Lottery', where the latex panel covered the genitals of both male and female models. The object of the exercise was to try and reduce the incidence of sexually transmitted infections in the 18-30 age groups. The results were hard to quantify at the time, but things do not seem to have improved much since then.

In fact the 2004 winners had a fair amount of sex involved. Nescafe's 'Love Actually' promotion was based on a film that included an episode featuring naked two porn stars. Another winner was Nissan, promoting a new van with the headline 'Fancy a Quick One?' and there was a prize for Impulse Siren with the title 'Where Have All the Young Men Gone?'

Muller collected Gold for "The Muller Love Bus". This was not a mobile bordello but carried teams giving away product coupons, bouquets of flowers and details of a promotion linked to Valentine's Day.

Finally, there was Gold for a restaurant group called Nandos which was promoting two restaurants in Norwich. They really went to town with a series of slogans such as 'Breast or Legs?', 'Looking for Oral Satisfaction?' and 'Are You a Hot Lover?' The entry form claimed that in a matter of weeks the restaurant had shifted from a relatively unknown outlet to be at the forefront of restaurant choice. We are not sure what choice.

Eighteen of that year's ISP Awards were entered into the European Promotional Marketing Awards. Sixteen of the British entries were winners including the Grand Prix (for the second year running) plus five Gold, six Silver and four Bronze. It seems that sex also sells on the Continent as the Grand Prix was, of course, The Sex Lottery.

Other changes taking place around this time included the Triangle group, now almost 30 years old, deciding to unify its various offshoots under the Triangle brand. These included a retail specialist called Storm and a digital communications agency, Preceptor. Triangle boss Kevin Twittey announced that it would now be able to produce integrated campaigns which is pretty much what everyone had been saying for decades. Around the same time the agency CBH decided it needed a new and cooler (!) name and came up with incognito. Names with capital letters became so last century around this time. At least it avoided the dreaded use of a number instead of part of a name. Good4them!

ETHICS IS NOT A COUNTY NORTHEAST OF LONDON.

One set of initials that appeared out of nowhere was CSR, which was corporate social responsibility, a new and extremely politically correct introduction to business. Naturally various experts appeared to lead companies by the hand through the new landscape. You could buy a report from the New Economics Foundation entitled "Corporate Spin: the Trouble Years of Social Reporting". It claimed that what it referred to as "social reporting" had been captured by the marketing departments which of course in the view of many of our readers would probably be a good thing. However, as marketing and profits tend to go together and profits tend to be a fairly dirty word amongst the anti-capitalists, we presume that the report thought this was not a good idea.

Essentially it said that you should consider the ethics of whatever you do, such as how you treat your staff and your suppliers or alternatively of course you could stick with the tried and tested method of spinning with PR, minimising the negative publicity and scrambling through. By 2007 CSR had spread pretty widely and the ISP was seriously considering having a code of ethics built into its membership package. In principle it is a sensible idea. Good and successful companies have always treated staff and suppliers as well as possible on the grounds that it produces the best results and the most profit. Brooklyn-born Dick Kane, eponymous founder of the US agency Marden Kane summed it up nicely: "If you screw your staff, your suppliers or your customers, sooner or later they will screw you".

By the end of 2004 it was generally agreed that the downturn in promotional marketing that marked the millennium was over. The ISP came up with some statistical evidence that indicated business was looking up. Its key indicators, such as membership, education and the legal advice service were generally showing reasonable, if not dramatic, increases. Things were tight but they were improving. There were a number of top-level changes at the highest levels of the ISP. Randle Stonier handed over to the new chairman Peter Kerr and some heavy hitting promoters joined the board of directors, including Tim Green from Coca-Cola, Jerry Higgins from Weetabix, and Unilever Bestfoods' Diane Rowe.

Recruitment, turnover and profits were on the increase for the agencies and marketing spend seemed to be on a similar upward climb. Everyone was excited about new media with text messaging leading the way. Good old prize draws, instant wins, coupons, sampling and the other standards were still the basis of the business. Cause related marketing was popular and growth areas were finance, leisure and good old FMCG.

Two thirds of agencies had been adding graduates to their staff, an increase on the previous year when it was 49 per cent. They identified finding and keeping quality staff as their top problem and oddly 28 per cent were still worried about European legislation on promotions, although this proposal was stalled for the foreseeable future.

THERE'S MONEY IN MOTIVATION
Another aspect of promotional marketing that had been around for a long time became prominent under another name in the first few years of the 21st century. Previously known as sales force or staff incentives, it was now upgraded to motivation with associated specialist agencies. A survey showed that almost half of these claimed to do the full SP gamut and it is interesting to compare them with conventional SP agencies. It should be noted that RSCG Skybridge, which had previously been second for profit and third for turnover, declined to take part in the 2003 survey. Motivation agencies were expecting growth in next few years although profits had been flat across the sector. Mind you, they had been making some very good money.

The majority of their work came from either sales, marketing or HR departments. At this time the dreaded procurement department had only got their teeth into seven per cent of the business. When asked where they thought future business was likely to come from, top of the list was the public sector, owing no doubt to Mr Brown's very generous funding and the enormous growth in public sector staff. The top three were Maritz Europe Grass Roots and P&MM (now Motivcom).

In August 2004 Motivcom, with a turnover of £36.5million, went public at a float valuation of £13million. It was one of the few marketing service businesses to float since the Eighties and by the middle of 2007 it had a market valuation of £38million. There is a declaration of vested interest to be made here, as co-author Colin Lloyd is the non-executive Chairman of Motivcom.

Technology was on the march. By the middle of 2004 it was estimated that there were 32 million mobile phones in use in the UK. At that time the under tens were the fastest-growing sector of mobile phone ownership and the numbers were rising exponentially. Companies supplying the electronic requirements for SMS promotions such as Flytxt and MindMatics were booming and claiming 600 per cent or more increases in turnover, admittedly from a low base.

Another example of the popular 'Change the name, do the same, but charge more' technique turned up in 2004 when handling houses were suddenly reinvented as response management agencies or RMAs. They had moved firmly into the electronic age, dealing with digital response (web, SMS, e-mails etc) as well as regular stuff such as opening envelopes, mailing prizes, and collecting names and addresses (sorry, data capture).

UP, DOWN AND OUT

A high profile name from the industry moved on in 2004 when promotional marketing agency Black Cat, which had been purchased by JWT, was merged into RMG Connect. Black Cat had been founded in 1991 by ex KLP MD Stephen Callender, together with Diana Tombs and Charles Lauder, and after the merger all three departed for pastures new. Also departing at the end of 2004 were some other previously high profile agencies which had financial problems and folded. Mercier Grey was wound up and 50 jobs went with it. This is remarkable because it was declaring a £6million gross profit on a turnover of £11.4million in 2004. Where did all the money go?

Brian Gibb's Promotional Risk Management (PRM) went into administration at the end of 2004. It seems that they had failed to manage their own risks. Another failure was a company with the unusual name of Mr Smith. It must have been one of the shortest lived on record as it went into receivership, having lasted just one month after being reborn out of Interfocus.

While on the subject of names, a new agency popped up at the end of 2004 headed by Steev (sic) Glover called Biglove. It also had an interesting approach as it said it was "a company, a concept and an ideal" before modestly claiming it would develop programmes that would improve sales, increase profitability and drive awareness and market share. Its capabilities included promotions, incentive and motivation programmes, creative design, print production, web design, customer relationship management, radio advertising, web advertising plus database building and management.

At the end of 2004 Reed Exhibitions cancelled the 2005 Incentive World show, due to be held at Earls Court in February 2005. This followed the launch in October 2004 of the Total Motivation Show at Olympia which had lower numbers but seemed to attract the right sort of customers. The cancelled show would have been the 10th anniversary of Incentive World, launched by 'Mr Exhibitions' Ian Allchild. He had sold the show to Reed in 2000 and it moved from Wembley to Earls Court. In 2001 it had around 500 exhibitors and more than 7,000 visitors but the numbers had gone down steadily since then. Ian had continued to run the show until a new director was appointed in 2002 followed by two more since that year. Despite attempts to revive the show with heavy marketing and linking it with the International Direct Marketing Fair, the show continued to fade and Reed decided to concentrate its efforts on the National Incentive Show (NIS) at the NEC in September.

The BPMA was an associate partner for Incentive World and their chairman at the time, who by a strange coincidence was Ian Allchild, was quoted as saying that it fully supported the decision and would continue to work with Reed on the NIS. However, you can't keep a good showman down and before you could say "shell scheme", Ian and a new partner, Simon Tilley, had launched the Promotional Marketing Show. Ian resigned from the BPMA to avoid any potential conflict of interest. The new show attracted some 2,000 visitors to the Barbican maze in March 2006. There are probably a few more still looking for the exhibition hall. With 168 exhibitors, it was a launching pad for the 2007 show which took place in March of that year and moved to Olympia, where the visitor count moved up by 7.5 per cent.

HOW WERE WE DOING?
This chapter closes with a comparison of the five years between 1999 and 2004. The business was holding its own at a time when the country was gradually recovering from a tough few years. In these five years the top 10 agencies were producing about the same gross profit and employing about the same number of people. Not much progress, but they were making a decent living. Looking at the recruitment pages in the trade magazines of the time, salaries on offer in 2005 were much the same as those five years earlier. Graduate trainees earned from £12,000 to £17,000; account executives, from £15,000 to £19,000; account managers, from £18,000 to £28,000; account directors, from £28,000 to £40,000 plus, and board directors, £50,000 and upwards.

The figures below are gross profit.

AGENCY	98-9 (£m)		Staff	AGENCY	02-03 (£m)	Staff
1	Carlson	£23.3	540	Proximity	£22.1	240
2	Tequila UK	£16.5	210	Carlson	£21.7	291
3	Joshua	£14.3	n/a	Marketing Store	£14.1	196
4	IMP Group	£13.7	180	Joshua	£13.9	210
5	Mosaic	£13.6	160	Arc Worldwide	£13.3	133
6	H & M	£13.1	233	Tequila	£11.2	130
7	Clarke Hooper	£12	172	Triangle	£11.1	129
8	KLP Euro	£11.2	189	Haygarth	£10.9	136
10	Marketing Store	£10.5	196	Geoff Howe	£10.7	104
11	Skybridge	£9.8	n/a	KLP Euro	£10.2	94
12	Haygarth	£7.3	104	Dynamo	£9.9	120
13	Dynamo	£6.1	95	Logistix	£7	62
14	Perspectives	£5.2	70	TRO	£6.9	95
15	Black Cat	£4.7	65	Billington Cartmell	£6	61

In the 1998-99 tables there are some missing names who decided they did not want to be considered Sales Promotion agencies. Now it was all about interactive communications, direct marketing and anything else that you could get someone to pay you to do. A typical example was Claydon Heeley, which dropped out of the tables after some soul searching. They had souls? They had started a very successful DM subsidiary called Jones Mason Barton Antenen as a joint venture with BPP DDB and then merged with its own subsidiary as Claydon Heeley Jones Mason. It's not clear what happened to Barton and Antenen, but the new stationery order must have been substantial.

Also missing from the tables is The Sales Machine, now TSM. They are now in the business of integrated customer relationship marketing, and in this rarefied atmosphere 'sales' is a four-letter word. Also missing was Manifesto. The latter included a real SP pioneer, Chris Killingbeck (the K in FKB), who has also moved upwards and onwards to pastures new. It's all interactive media and DM these days, nothing to do with the boring old business of promoting sales.

There had also been numerous takeovers, mergers and such, so that many well-known names had rolled into bigger companies, very often adverting agencies, which knew where the money was going. One of the best known was WPP-owned Promotional Campaigns which had slipped down to 19th the previous year and had been rolled into Dialogue Marketing Partnership, another recent WPP purchase. Proximity (owned by Omnicom, founded in 1991), Logistix (owned by Emak Worldwide, founded 1989), Arc Worldwide (owned by Publicis, founded 1989) and TRO (privately owned, founded in 1982) did not appear in the top 40 Agencies in the 1998-99 Tables.

The only privately owned agencies in the 30 listed here were Iris, Triangle, Haygarth, Geoff Howe, Dynamo, and Black Cat. In 1999 Holmes & Marchant was the last of a disappearing breed - the publicly quoted agency. It was soon to be mopped up by Huntsworth, which closed most of the Sales Promotion companies in the group and, as we have seen, sold the others to Media Square, who they possibly saw coming as they got a cool £60million and landed Media Square with a lot of problems, judging by the results. It also sold H&M on and in 2007 it was concentrating on design in beautiful downtown Marlow. In the fast moving world of agencies this may seem like so much ancient history but it does show how the industry was evolving in the new century.

CHAPTER 16

Coupons

Coupons in the 19th century
FSIs - boom and bust
Targeting takes over and DM flourishes
Goodbye door to door
Misredemption, and more misredemption
The internet voucher boom
Then – a result!
Fakes and forgeries

Apart from straight price reductions, coupons and vouchers have been by far the most common promotional technique over the centuries - we have traced them back to at least 1850. There is a slight problem in identifying which is which. When is a coupon not a coupon but a voucher, and vice versa? The dictionary has a long definition for 'coupon' but the theme that runs throughout is that they are 'detachable'. They can entitle the holder to a discount, a free gift, be exchanged for goods (usually by collecting them) and one or two other things unconnected to Sales Promotion such as rationing or interest payments.

Vouchers can also have a number of meanings including serving as evidence for some transaction, such as a receipt, offered instead of cash (specifically designated as a gift voucher) and several legal meanings outside our remit. For the purposes of this chapter we will define the coupon at something exchangeable for a discount and a voucher as a gift voucher which is a substitute for a cash payment. Here goes with the history of both.

You will find the earliest reference we have come across in Chapter One. In 1850, Benjamin Talbot Babbitt of Bab-O Cleaner cut his soap into convenient sizes at the factory and wrapped them neatly in paper. When this proved much less popular then he expected, he simply turned the wrapping paper into a coupon and offered to redeem 25 of them for a coloured lithograph print. Asa Chandler, the man who bought Coca-Cola, was handwriting coupons around 1900 which must have been worse than writing lines as a school punishment.

By 1914 Quaker was using coupons, but these were proof of purchase for SLPs and became known by the glorified name of the 'modified premium system', and were given a boost by the big new medium of radio. Driven by advertising and the depression quite a number of offers redeemed more than 500,000 units and some reached one million. Remember, these are paid for by the consumer along with some proof of purchase so had a tiny budget, if they had one at all. It is possible that they made a useful profit. Procter & Gamble got into below-the-line activity just before 1900 with offers such as watch chain charms in return for soap wrappers, and CW Post had one cent money off next purchase coupons on Grape Nuts boxes.

Over the years coupons have proliferated by the billion, particularly in the US where they play a very big part in housewives' shopping habits. The figures below relate to 1988, when the population of the US was about five times that of the UK.

Coupon comparison	USA	UK
Issued	221.7 billion	4.8 million
Redeemed	70.5 billion	3.11 million
Regular users	77%	51%
Av. number redeemed	8	2.25
Av. saving each visit	$3.75	50p
Likely to use for 1st time buy	50%	58%

One other interesting fact from research carried out at the time in both the US and the UK, is that 90 per cent of American customers are convinced that the coupons are checked when used and that they would be refused if the product was not bought. In the UK, the opposite is probably true, unless of course the coupon is issued by the store where the customer is attempting to redeem, when they are normally checked.

The issues of misredemption and malredemption could fill a chapter. We have mentioned it before and will so again. To make the difference clear, misredemption usually refers to coupons being redeemed when the brand has not been purchased, while malredemption is some kind of cheating, usually by a retailer or a forger and is quite rare. Misredemption has been going on for a long time and at long last in 2007 efforts were being made to reduce it. Malredemption leapt into prominence in the 2008-09 credit crash having been reasonably dormant for a quarter of a century.

DISTRIBUTION METHODS

Coupons of all sorts grew steadily over the years and the distribution systems became standardised. Door-to-door, and newspapers and magazines handled the bulk of the traffic but in 1989 things were about to change. The launch of The Coupon Book, Britain's first Free Standing Insert (FSI), copied the major coupon distribution method in the US. It was triggered when Graham Morse, previously managing director of Masterguide, left the company and got together with his old partner and co-author, Ken Spedding. They decided that the time was right for a British FSI, because coupons were growing fast and FSIs had been proved to be the most cost effective method of distributing them. Research with clients got a good response.

Their timing looked spot on because, as is usual in hard times, coupons were booming, reaching a peak in 1991. In hindsight, they should have started five years earlier but still, armed with their research, they went to Reed Regional Newspapers with the plan. Reed had a very efficient distribution system for free newspapers with national coverage. They could offer a 10,000,000 circulation and worked within TV regions. Reed liked the idea so much that they suggested a joint venture with the two founders signed up for a three year contract to run the operation.

At first thing went well. A regional test was a success and The Coupon Book went national to the full 10,000,000 circulation, and by the third issue was showing a handsome profit. It proved that it was the most cost effective method of coupon distribution apart from on-pack. This apparent gold mine soon attracted competitors. By late 1992 two more were on the stocks. A consortium of Mirror Group, The Telegraph and The Express was planning to launch Brand Movers with a 9.5 million circulation and News International was planning to use its Sunday newspapers to distribute Shoppers Friend. Both competitors were two years behind Reed and their timing was abysmal, as the figures below will indicate.

YEAR	COUPONS (millions)	REDEEMED (millions)
1984	2,591	274
1985	2,631	263
1986	4,432	343
1987	4,695	411
1988	3,934	290
1989	4,865	311
1990	5,074	376
1991	8,109	451
1992	5,402	365

Coupons had hit a brick wall. Sainsbury and Tesco had announced that they would accept coupons personalised to the other retailer so you could walk into Tesco with a bunch of Sainsbury's coupons and redeem them, possibly without even buying the product. Redemption rates soared, but sales didn't because this was open house for misredemption. The supermarkets advertised the fact that you could pretty much ignore what it said on the coupon apart from the value.

What was self evident was that the rate of redemption had increased by more than 20 per cent in 12 months. Manufacturers understandably took one look at the figures, compared them to sales and stopped the mass distribution of coupons. The FSI concept had worked up to this point. Compared to conventional newspapers and magazines, they were extremely cost effective. In 1991 for instance, 30 per cent of all coupons went out in the press, but only 12 per cent of those redeemed came from that source. From nothing in 1989, The Coupon Book had been responsible for distributing three per cent of all coupons and four per cent of all redeemed. In 1990 it distributed four per cent and redeemed six per cent, but in 1992 they had almost vanished, distributing just one per cent and redeeming two per cent. FSIs were dead in the water and Ken and Graham had to find other jobs.

CASHING IN ON COUPONS

A major research project in 1990 which covered aspects of Sales Promotion activity also had a good look at misredemption. It came to the firm conclusion that it was widespread across all the socio-economic groups with at least half the people admitting to misredeeming. They were firmly of the opinion that the supermarkets were the guilty party, not the customer. Another odd justification put forward was that for every person using a coupon without buying the brand, someone else was buying the product without a coupon, and they felt this was a satisfactory state of affairs. We can't quite get to grips with the logic of this.

Even more entertaining was the discovery that a few members of the focus groups did not know how easy it was to misredeem coupons. Having heard from others in the group how simple and profitable it was, they decided that they were missing out. Only a tiny number of ladies in the survey felt that it was cheating. This coupon survey also discovered that canny shoppers handed in coupons after everything was put through the checkout, working on the premise that the checkout girls were not going to search through bags of shopping. The research even scored the various retailers on the likelihood of being the store of choice for misredemption. Tesco came top of the 'most likely' list with 26 per cent, closely followed by Sainsbury on 23 per cent. The 'least likely' at eight per cent was Waitrose. Waitrose customers must have felt that they did not need the money that badly. Well, have you seen their car parks?

MISREDEMPTION QUANTIFIED

In 1992 the ISP Coupon Review Committee produced a report. It estimated that 27 per cent of coupons were misredeemed at a cost to the manufacturers of around £30million. Incentive Today contacted three major retailers for comment. Press communications at Asda was "constantly unavailable". Her opposite number at Sainsbury responded with the not terribly helpful quote: "We don't want to make any statement that will be printed", and Tesco stonewalled with a straight "no comment".

Also in 1992 Tesco insisted that coupons would have to be barcoded if they were to be redeemed in its stores. It also issued an edict that on pack coupons would no longer be 'on pack' but 'in pack', to avoid barcode confusion. Tesco had a problem, but someone else would have to carry the cost and complication of solving it. Nothing new there. It also stated that it was tackling the question of misredemption, but as usual from a one-sided viewpoint. Its software would validate the chain's own vouchers and reject any which were presented without the appropriate purchase but, surprise, surprise, this would not apply to manufacturers' coupons.

The downward trend in couponing continued for several years. It only began to rise again in 1990, at which point it had climbed back to the 1986 level of 4.4 billion. The major movements were away from manufacturer-funded coupons and a massive increase in retailer funded, up by a staggering 60 per cent in 1995 and accounting for 36 per cent of coupons in the UK. In the early Nineties they represented just seven per cent of coupons. Direct marketing was claiming more and more of the distribution side of the business, responsible for almost 30 per cent of coupons, a trend that has continued.

COUPONS RULE OK IN THE USA
Coupons' Indian summer was further threatened in 1996 when Procter & Gamble in the US announced that it was testing the elimination of coupons. It ran the test in various large cities in New York State and claimed to be replacing coupons with everyday low pricing, or EDLP. Coupons are an enormous business in the US with almost 292 billion coupons distributed in 1997, of which two per cent were redeemed. A year later P&G was forced into an embarrassing about face due to consumer pressure. As is often the case in America, the consumer pressure involved lawyers and a pretty powerful one at that - the New York State Attorney General no less. The inhabitants of the three cities were so incensed that they appeared to be missing out on offers that they stirred up a legal investigation and P&G was forced to issue $4.2million of promotional coupons in newspapers covering the affected areas.

DM TAKES OVER
By the new millennium things had changed in the world of coupons. The numbers had climbed back to the high spot of 1991 but redemptions had not reached the same level until a big jump in 2002. What had changed was the method of distribution. Mass distribution was out, targeting was in. For coupons sent out by DM, upwards of 90 per cent could be redeemed. DM has all but killed door-to-door distribution. In 1987 door-to-door had accounted for 35 per cent of coupons given away. By 2005 it was down to 2.9 per cent. The next largest behind direct marketing were magazines, carrying an average of 12.4 per cent of all coupons over the years 2001-2005.

Door-to-door coupons may have almost vanished from the scene but the technique is still alive and well. It has an interesting history over the past fifty years or so because as Sales Promotion grew in stature, various ancillary businesses grew with it. We are grateful to Graham Dodd for an insider's view of this major distribution technique. He first entered the door-to-door arena in 1970 when he joined Marketforce as an admin assistant. Some 37 years later he can look back and contemplate the many, many changes that have taken place. In the early 70's, Royal Mail D2D and free newspapers did not exist as door drop options and the supplier world was pretty much dominated by Marketforce and Circular Distributors, with Vernons the only other main operator.

In those days teams were the only route to market, via either 'Shareplan', in which several leaflets were delivered at once, or on a solus basis where a client with a bigger budget had their material delivered on its own. In 2007 none of those names are still in existence, although CD has re-branded as TNT Post. Several people played pass-the-parcel with Marketforce with management buy outs, a sale to AC Nielsen, re-branding as MRM Distribution, which was bought by Taylor Nelson Sofres, who then sold it to The Leaflet Company, where the name disappeared.

In the Eighties free newspapers started to mount a serious challenge to the domination of team-based companies, and over a period of time stole considerable market share. This was helped by independent validation, which had come into existence around the same time and demonstrated that free newspapers were a far more reliable route to the correct front doors - or to any front doors for that matter.

AREN'T THOSE MY LEAFLETS?
The team distribution method, which was all there was in the beginning, had a poor reputation for accuracy. There were dreadful stories of large bundles of leaflets found up alleyways, in ditches and once under the garden hedge of the marketing director of the client company. Another classic example of Murphy's Law, also applied when a member of a door-to-door company's distribution staff was out on a field visit with a client who wished to be assured that the quality of the drop was top drawer. The visit had gone really well. They had visited teams working and re-traced their steps to back check areas covered the previous day, with good results. They then stopped for lunch and were sitting in the garden of a lovely country pub with a small river running alongside. The client was just about convinced about the drop, when floating along came hundreds of his leaflets. The mood quickly changed.

Rumour had it that distribution companies would ask the agency for the address of anyone involved in the client's marketing department and a team leader would personally deliver a leaflet to these homes. As if they would do such a thing! High street retailers in particular left the Shareplan option behind as newspapers offered faster, cheaper and more effective distribution, a situation from which the cut price Shareplan market has never really recovered.

IT'S TARGETING TIME

Postal sector ranking was first developed by CACI in 1987, changing the face of targeting for ever. Before that the client was faced with the choice of covering all of a town or city or a level of selectivity based upon the classical demographic groups of ABC1C2DE. The problem was that the selectivity was based a very crude visual selection of property. With the UK universe in those days having around 18 million front doors and literally hundreds of teams throughout the country dropping leaflets, the degree of consistency was variable to say the least.

There was also the problem of matching different clients' requirements for ABC1 coverage against C2DE coverage on the same shared drop, so the medium had to move forward. Postal sector targeting gave the medium that impetus and the ability to select postal sectors with a nominated high density of any given target market revolutionised the medium and introduced many new users. Today there are a range of sophisticated targeting products available to the client marketplace, some driven by census data, others by lifestyle data. Further data sources such as TGI, NRS, and shopping catchment areas, can all be overlaid on to any client's requirements creating sophisticated targeting models. It is also increasingly common for door drop solutions to be provided using any combination of Royal Mail, free newspapers and team systems, with each option providing different strengths. This sort of thing can keep planners out of mischief for days.

Other developments have been sub sector targeting, allowing clients to target smaller units of households - hundreds rather than thousands – and making the value of the targeting infinitely stronger. Test activity for some clients is already showing increased levels of ROI and while not necessarily relevant for all clients, it will play a major role in the future.

The brands using coupons in 2005 may surprise you. They are not, as one might expect, totally dominated by FMCG. Top of the list with 112 million comes beer and wine which increased by 50 per cent in 2006, driven by the drinking surrounding the World Cup. This was followed by bakery at 71 million. Next was household cleaners with 64 million, dairy products at 59 million, and toothpastes and mouthwashes on 52 million. Down in tenth position was tea, coffee and hot drinks.

By 2005 the face value of redeemed coupons was up to £1.06billion and in 2006 this continued to rise to £1.11 billion according to the Valassis Coupon Report. Until recently it was better known as NCH Marketing Services and before that as Nielsen Clearing House. It was established in the UK in 1970 by the American AC Nielsen and has always been the dominant company in the UK for coupon processing and clearing with 85 per cent of the market. In 2003 its Corby headquarters was completely gutted by fire just after it had been taken over by the US-based printing, media, couponing and database software giant Valassis. It stayed in temporary accommodation for two years before opening a brand new purpose-built headquarters on the same site in 2005.

HOW IT LOOKED IN 2007AND 2008

The Valassis 2007 Coupon report, covering January to December 2006 showed that the numbers distributed and redeemed were much the same, but there had been moves in the method of getting coupons to the punters. The rise and rise of DM had been reversed and newspapers, magazines and in store were on the up. Three and half billion coupons were distributed and 3.59 million redeemed. The highest redemption rate was retailer coupons at 24% and over half of all coupons went out by direct mail.

There has been a great deal of excitement about electronic coupons but the impact has been small to date, taking less than one per cent of the market. However, it had grown by 20 per cent, far higher than the five per cent between 2004 and 2005. Direct marketing redemptions continue to rise to 16 per cent of all coupons issued by that method and the 'others', which include electronic, reached 10.6 per cent, up from 2.7 per cent in 2005 but from very small numbers. The average face value of coupons in this category was £2.10, compared to an overall average of just 72p.

When the 2008 report was available in 2009 things had moved on. The so-called credit crunch appeared to be affecting the public's attitude to coupons and vouchers in general. In that year the number of coupons distributed had gone up 29% and the total value redeemed had risen by 20% to almost £500 million. This was driven by a 30% increase in consumers actively seeking offers compared to previous years.

IT'S ON THE INTERNET

This also led to a proliferation of internet sites offering coupons and vouchers are all kinds. Previous growth in coupon usage in hard times shows that it is a natural development. For instance, in the 1991-92 period of falling house prices and other problems there was a 60% increase in coupon distribution and since then the internet revolution and voucher distribution methods have become far more diverse.

Many retailers have begun to circulate viral e-mails with discount vouchers, particularly brands that rely on discretionary spend such as restaurants and clothing stores, but even the mighty Asda set up a permanent voucher page on its website. In the 12 months leading up to February 2009 online searches for discount vouchers grew by 133% and visits to the various, comparatively recently launched, voucher websites rose by 45%. The consumer had really latched onto this. In November 2008 for instance, more than 20,000 variations on the word 'voucher' was searched by Google. A typical site, one of many, is myVoucherCodes.co.uk.

This offers discounts of varying kinds over literally hundreds of different retail and other outlets ranging from 'My Gift from the Gods' aimed at the ladies, to ZYB which is a voucher site within a voucher site linking to another range of potential discounters. Rather than having to print out vouchers from these sites the usual practice is to collect a voucher code and then visit the retailer's own site to make use of it.

Another electronic introduction was rebate toolbars. These are installed by the consumer and automatically search for discounts associated with whichever site the user is on, so they are automatically notified when a deal is available. In addition to all this there are also a number of cash-back sites, a form of affiliate marketing. In this case retailers pay commission for each online sale the sites generate, which in turn is usually passed back to the consumer, aimed at increasing loyalty.

One such site called Quidco launched in 2005. By the beginning of 2009 they had built up relationships with over 1200 online merchants including big names such as Asda, M&S, Tesco and several banks. It gives all commissions back to the consumer but Quidco's income comes from a five pounds annual subscription. Another recent introduction was cash-back for a high street purchase with sites such as the splendidly named Greasypalm.co.uk.

Across the board at this time, when retailers were closing on an almost daily basis, any technique that moved sales was welcomed with open arms. However there is always a trade-off between benefit and cost and price cutting is all very well in the short term but in the long term can destroy a company. Discounting of this type can add real value but they are also rather like a drug. It is easy to become addicted but in the long term they can do serious injury. They cannibalise margins and tend to erode brand equity. This seems a long way from the basic aim of Sales Promotion to add value to a purchase, and it remains to be seen what will happen when the economy moves back into more normal and hopefully more profitable areas.

"WHAT MISREDEMPTION?" – SAINSBURY AND OTHERS

In 2005 a company called First Ondemand linked up with Oracle to produce a system that in theory could have done away with misredemption. The plan was that when coupons were issued, information details would be entered into the system's authentication engine. When the coupon was scanned at the checkout, the online database would automatically validate it. It sounds simple but to no one's surprise, retailers didn't exactly jump for joy. The ISP did not expect the retailers to have anything to do with it as coupons represented easy money for them. It was quoted as saying: "Misredemption of coupons is one example of how the retailer's power has gone too far".

Once again, when canvassed, the retailers were not exactly helpful. Sainsbury commented that it did not believe the company had received any complaints from suppliers. As if they would dare! Tesco maintained its right to silence on the issue. A project manager at Asda admitted that certain brave manufacturers had moaned about misredemption but he did not take it seriously. Asda's view was that price reductions would be more effective than the proposed system. This is not surprising as price cuts are usually more profitable to the retailer as they try to retain the same margins. Asda disagreed about an estimated cost of £1,000 per supermarket to set up the scheme, saying that it would cost £100,000 per outlet, which of course they would require the manufacturers to offset. Despite another advantage of the system being real-time verification for the increasing number of non-cash payments there was no serious progress.

Towards the end of 2006 the ISP went very public with its viewpoint, saying things that no individual manufacturer, not even the likes of Lever, P&G or Heinz would dare say. The then director general Edwin Mutton accused the UK's largest grocers of costing their suppliers up to £60million a year by accepting money off coupons when they had not sold the product. He estimated that around 50 per cent of all coupons were not properly redeemed and that Tesco and the others had a policy of accepting coupons for any product they stocked even if the consumer had not bought it. This was reinforced in 2009 when the ISP published the appropriate section of Tesco's Terms and Conditions for suppliers which were:-
21 - Coupon Handling Procedure
21.1 - The Supplier acknowledges that due to the flow of customers at the point of sale, the Buyer's policy (in accordance with industry practice) is to redeem all coupons presented by customers and not to check non-retailer-specific coupons in supermarkets.
21.2 - The Buyer will redeem all coupons without requiring proof of purchase and will debit the value of the coupon to the Supplier's account.
 Tesco says that it trains its staff that customers must buy the appropriate product to qualify but in real life it doesn't seem to be put into practice. Edwin said that it was unclear whether legally it was fraud, but it almost certainly is. The small print on the back of coupons makes it clear that they are only to be used when the product is bought but, as the consumer has discovered, they are as good as cash and retailers have no compunction in doing just that.

The ISP has in the past involved the Financial Services Authority and also the Office of Fair Trading but this did not produce much progress and so in 2009 they decided to play hard ball for the first time. The situation had become so bad they the whole issue may well end up in court. The ISP said that the supermarkets' attitude was, and we quote, "No different to allowing customers to shoplift". They were taking legal advice as one in 6 of the 450 million money off coupons distributed in the UK during the previous year were redeemed against the wrong product, costing the manufacturers some £50 million. Although a little less than the figures previously quoted, it is not small change and the situation is not helped by websites advising readers that supermarkets will often accept coupons as cash, so spreading the good news, good for the consumer that is.

The legal eagles were being asked if manufacturers could force retailers to only redeem a coupon against the purchase of the named product. Tesco and Co were unlikely to be shaking in their shoes and a spokesman commented that they allow cashiers to accept "single coupons but not multiples" without checking if the item had been purchased as it was not practical to spend time checking. They did not suggest that the consumer could be asked to present the product and the coupon together nor that they should spend money on adapting their tills to match bar codes. They can do this for the coupons they issue but not for anyone else – too expensive! A year later not much had happened but at the end of 2009 something did!

A RESULT!
Much to everyone's surprise, a very short time after these Terms and Conditions were widely circulated, Tesco changed its coupon policy, and announced that it would now only be accepting coupons if the relevant product is in the shopping basket. The Road to Damascus springs to mind but perhaps this was the Road to Cheshunt!

The retailer stated that it was currently instructing checkout staff of the change in its policy. Notices will be posted in stores to inform customers of the new rules. Annie Swift, chief executive of the ISP, says: "Tesco's policy change is great news for brand owners, many of whom have been put off using coupons because of fears over possible misredemption". There are some retailers, however, who are still allowing consumers to redeem coupons for products they haven't bought, and we need to get them to rethink their stance. We think that the ISP can take some credit for this major rethink on the part of Britain's largest retailer. As we go to press Waitrose [thought by the consumers to be the least likely to missredeem] have announced they are following suit so we will have to see if other the other retailers join the good guys.

FAKES AND FORGERIES AND A £157MILLION SCAM
In the past malredemption, that is either illegal or faked coupons, was not considered a serious threat and only a few cases had occurred over the years. However at the beginning of 2009 a number of serious frauds were identified. Thanks to the ease of circulating coupons on the internet together with the high quality of copying devices available, many more vouchers appeared in the system than had initially been planned or in fact actually produced. Newspaper stories suggested that this was becoming so serious that coupons might be scrapped owing to the damage done by these scams.

One area was the way in which coupons can be altered to give a much bigger saving than the original design. Criminals found that they could manipulate the bar codes so that when read, they greatly increase the initial offer. One example was a coupon worth 30p which had the bar code altered to give a discount of around £8. It seems that this cost the issuing company £150,000. Another was a claim for £9,000 for coupons of a face value that had never been issued. Just one of the handling houses who receive coupons from retailers, pay them and reclaim the money from the issuing company, identified 15 cases where stores had tried to claim for more cash then the total value of all the product sold in that outlet.

In some cases staff and customers had been recycling coupons many times over. One company found that a £2 food product voucher e-mailed to a list redeemed many more than the 8000 that had had initially been produced. This cost them £80,000. More than 90 percent were said to be redeemed through one unnamed supermarket chain with 10,000 going through one store. In another case a small start-up company in the food and drink sector was hit by a bill in excess of £40,000 after conventional money off coupons were massively over redeemed.

There has also been a large increase in the number of people selling coupons on eBay. They cover almost every type of money off or discount coupons from all the big name retailers and major brands. They even include sheets of coupons for discounted newspaper subscriptions. The sellers appear to have the ability to acquire large numbers of coupons which they sell at well below the face value which makes them attractive to the shopper. Some claim to make a good living from this practice and efforts are being made to discover where the coupons are sourced, but so far no one has been reported to the police or identified as a fraudster. At the time of writing some efforts are being made to control this business.

However, all this activity in the UK is very small beer compared to a case in the USA where they usually do thing on a bigger scale, which this certainly is. Two managers from International Outsourcing Services, the world's biggest coupon handling house, have admitted that they were involved in a $250million (£157million) coupon fraud. This being the US these two managers having admitted their guilt, presumably agreed a plea bargain and are lined up to testified against another nine of their ex-colleagues, including Thomas 'Chris' Balsiger, formerly the CEO and also Bruce Furr, the former chairman.

The basis of the scam was the acquisition of huge numbers of unredeemed coupons from sources such as Sunday newspapers, which were then presented to the manufacturers as if they had been redeemed by consumers through retailers. Of course this meant that all the cash remained in the hands, or more accurately in the bank accounts, of the handling company. One nice point in the evidence which demonstrates the scale of the fraud is that it involved so many coupons that bundles of uncirculated ones were thrown into a cement mixer to make them look used. Our information does not tell us how long it took for the manufacturers to realise the gap between sales and coupon redemptions, but it finally dawned on them and Balsiger and Co are also being sued by some 20 major companies including Kraft, P&G, PepsiCo and Kellogg. The ISP are keen to point out that such a fraud could not happen in the UK as "the UK coupons handling industry is very different".

CHAPTER 17

Vouchers

Big money big ideas
The £1.6billion business
Red Letter, red face
Paper v plastic
Big advertisers
Swimming with sharks
Cut price travel

Various vouchers have been around for a long time and over the years the best known were probably book or record tokens. Various other organisations got into the business which grew steadily, but it was when companies began to use vouchers as a sales incentive that the business began to be serious.

By 2007 there were well over 200 different vouchers available. Vouchers are a business turning over a serious amount of cash. Looking back to 1998 the sales growth is impressive:

1998	£700million
1999	£798million
2000	£887million
2001	£1.15billion
2002	£1.21billion
2003	£1.36billion
2004	£1.42billion
2005	£1.47billion
2006	£1.6billion
2007	£3.2billion
2008	£3.8billion
2009	£4billion (estimated)

Sales leapt to £3billion in 2007 according to the trade body The Voucher Association. Its members are responsible for around £1.7billion of this sum. The Voucher Association was formed in 1996 as the Voucher Industry Forum where professionals could meet on a regular basis. In 1998 it changed its name to The Voucher Association or VA but this was sometimes confused with that very nice museum in South Ken. So the name changed again in 2009 and became the UK Gift Card and Voucher Association providing the not too catchy acronym, UKGCVA. It spent some time between 1999 and 2003 lobbying the government over tax issues affecting vouchers, such as VAT, NI contributions and suchlike. Despite its efforts the Treasury was unable to resist getting its hands on some additional cash.

However, by 2007 the VA had around 80 members and in 2009 over 90, including just about every major retail group including Tesco, Sainsbury, ASDA, Debenhams, M&S and John Lewis, plus a number of specialist suppliers such as security printers, gift card processors and companies providing magnetic cards. Why, even the big banks were launching gift cards.

EXPERIENCE AN EXPERIENCE

Towards the end of the Eighties, a new aspect of the voucher industry began to grow. Initially 'experiences' were a cottage industry. Various people who had bits of kit or skills in certain areas would occasionally sell it to companies for corporate hospitality or team building but few were set up specifically for this particular market. Possibly one of the first was Mithril Racing, which set up on the famous old Goodwood circuit and had its first race day on 8 May 1984. The brain behind Mithril was a Lever Brothers brand manager, Mike Boyd Mansell who, in his spare time, raced Formula Ford 2000 single seater cars. As a marketing man, it occurred to him that he could turn his hobby into a business. He bought a few superannuated cars, found an office in the old control tower at Goodwood, and went into business. On the grounds that he had given it a good deal of business, Masterguide hosted the very first event and invited a fair number of Lever marketers. In the early days Mithril even allowed guests to drive their own cars around the track, a practice long since banned.

On that first day two senior marketing managers took advantage of this using their company cars. One was a Porsche, the other a Volvo estate, and much to everyone's surprise the Volvo was lapping faster than the Porsche. No one who was there will forget the sight of this massive machine going sideways in the chicane, straighten up and take off past the pits with the engine revs well into the red. line. When it finally pulled into the pits the brakes were red hot. It was only afterwards that the driver admitted that he had at one time been a UK junior kart champion. Fortunately the fleet hire manager was not present that day. They also had a trophy awarded at the end of the day called 'The Mad Dog Award'. This was given to the driver that the staff thought was most likely to have an accident on the way home.

Some 20 plus years later Mithril is still going strong and is still at Goodwood, although its portfolio now includes Ferraris, Lamborghinis, a skid pan, aircraft, classic cars and various other bits of kit in which guests can scare themselves.

RED LETTER DAYS

The lady who turned this cottage industry into a serious business was a 29-year-old accountant called Rachel Elnaugh who, in 1989, recognised that at no one was really marketing these various attractions effectively. She had the simple idea of offering to represent them all, run a marketing campaign and sell vouchers which would be redeemed at the various locations. The concept was brutally simple. Red Letter Days did not own any hardware, locations, operating staff or any of the other set-up costs. All it had to do was to produce a nice brochure, get it into people's hands, take bookings with cash upfront, issue a voucher and pay the operator if and when the voucher was redeemed. Should have been a wonderful cash flow situation.

Experience shows that experience vouchers have the highest 'breakage' rate in the industry. This refers to vouchers that are never used and the higher the cost of the experience, the lower the breakage rate. It also represents a large part of the profit for some voucher suppliers. By contrast, in Canada and some US states, suppliers have to show that they are actively encouraging recipients to use vouchers and any breakage money is either taxed or given to charity. Please don't tell the Treasury.

Twelve years later Red Letter Days was turning over £20million a year but somehow in 2005 managed to go bust. The media went into overdrive because Elnaugh had been featuring in the Dragons Den TV show where budding entrepreneurs pitched their ideas and were generally rubbished by the experts. To add an additional twist, the company was then bought by fellow Dragons, Peter Jones and Theo Paphitis (previously chairman of Millwall – an interesting qualification for his TV role) who proceeded to sack the founder. On the grounds that nothing succeeds like failure, she now appears to be making a good living lecturing all and sundry on how to motivate your staff and be a success in business.

Since those small beginnings, the business has grown enormously with operators such as Virgin and the reborn RLD offering a bewildering selection of experiences. These days you can drive almost anything with an engine and wheels. You can fly in pretty much anything with wings, from a microlight to a second hand Russian supersonic jet fighter or even fly without wings in a 'body flying experience' or by parachuting. You can pretend to be in the SAS and you can be on the water in almost any kind of boat either powered or sailing or underwater with a scuba outfit on your back. You can be pampered in just about every imaginable way. You can enjoy a curry master class, jousting or even organic gardening. There are even scaled-down versions for children.

The first supplier to join up to the Voucher Association in 1999 was Red Letter Days, followed by The Virgin Voucher, Experience More and others. The difference between conventional vouchers and experience vouchers is that the former is effectively a cheque with a cash value to be spent at the nominated outfit. Experience vouchers can usually be exchanged for some kind of experience at no cost to the voucher holder. They make excellent present, although if your children keep buying you more and more dangerous experiences, they may be trying to tell you something.

One aspect of the success of vouchers has been their generous contribution to the Sales Promotion industry in terms of advertising spends. They have been the biggest single source of both press advertising and investment in exhibitions for many years. For instance in March 2005 Sales Promotion magazine ran a complete voucher edition running to 28 pages, with more than 50 per cent of it made up of full-colour advertisements from the various companies. The publisher did it again in September 2005 and increased the size to 36 pages. No other group of companies in the Sales Promotion business can come close to this sort of spend. When did you last see an advertisement for a Sales Promotion agency?

PAPER V PLASTIC
In 2001 the first plastic gift cards arrived in the UK high street courtesy of US companies, closely followed by Debenhams in 2002. They were predicted to storm the market as they had done in the US where, within three years, they had an 80 per cent share and triggered a 300 per cent growth in the market. It seems that British consumers are more traditional and are comfortable with what they know: and what they know is paper. The VA estimates that purchasers of vouchers would go 70:30 for paper but a survey of B2B voucher users split 52:48, just in favour of cards, although it was thought that this was likely to change dramatically but the death of paper coupons appears to be exaggerated. In December 2008, for instance, Sainsbury mailed millions of selected Nectar card holders with a collection of paper coupons. Domestos sent out over 1 million paper coupons and got an impressive redemption rate of over 7.5 per cent.

The gift card and two more recent introductions, the stored value card and the prepaid debit card, are certainly convenient to use and have other advantages such as storage and security. There is one problem about these different types - even the VA does not have a clear definition of the difference between the three and they all do very much the same thing. In marketing terms, 'gift card' sounds better than 'stored value, pre-loaded card' or 'prepaid debit'. One advantage claimed for plastic is that the issuer can see exactly where the money has been spent.

The gift card is simply a piece of plastic with a magnetic strip that can be loaded with a cash value and used to purchase items or services rather like a simplified debit card. The holder can continue to use it until the cash runs out. Unlike a debit card, you cannot go overdrawn.

They also look very pretty and supermarkets and other outlets have set up gift card centres offering a range of cards from different suppliers. They are easy to print and can carry any design without the problems of security print for paper vouchers. This allows new designs and limited editions to be launched very cheaply. Cinemas are linking to blockbuster films in this way.

The US situation was also affected by the relatively small size of the paper voucher market compared to the UK when plastic was introduced. Although plastic vouchers have eroded the paper voucher business in the UK, people retain affection for paper, possibly because they can see the value immediately. Plastic is also a two stage process; firstly getting the money loaded and then being able to spend your reward. It has also been suggested that chip and pin technology has slowed the plastic bandwagon. However, between 2005 and 2006 the number of cards available rose from 15 to 53 and are steadily growing, although a number of voucher companies are struggling to cope with an entirely new system to deal with redemptions.

However, a number of significant players are moving into the gift card market, over and above their present paper voucher business. Chief among these is the voucher that has for years been the default position for any voucher buyer – Marks & Spencer. Plastic was also backed by trendies such as experiential and digital enthusiasts pushing various online options. Despite this, a survey in April 2009 showed that paper still ruled the day, particularly in the corporate market.

There were several reasons for this Luddite approach. Andrew Johnson, head of the recently renamed (again!) UKGCVA, came up with a very practical one: "It's still cheaper to pick up a £5 paper voucher and put it in the post". John Lewis for instance, having introduced online redemption for paper vouchers, thinks that this gives them enough edge to dismiss the plastic option for the foreseeable future. Other reasons for the continuing triumph of paper over plastic include that they are hard to load with value, complicated in accounting for issued card value until they are spent, the difficulty of knowing what value is left on a card and the fact that not all retailers have the systems in place to handle them. So for the time being at least, good old fashioned paper is king.

Plastic is here to stay but only time will tell if it finally supersedes paper. Looking into the future, Andrew Johnson of the VA expects the market for vouchers to keep growing, particularly in the gift card area. He also expects to see a major growth in e-vouchers. These are ideal for online retailers such as Amazon as they avoid security problems. They are not so good for companies that combine bricks and mortar. Receiving an e-voucher does not quite have the same feel as a nicely printed paper version or even a shiny gift card. In addition there is a major security risk as several companies have already discovered.

HAVE VOUCHER, WILL TRAVEL

Over the years a third type of voucher has developed and is now a major feature of Sales Promotion activity. It is not a conventional money off coupon nor a cash value voucher. They usually allow the recipient to enjoy a reward of some kind at a discounted price, but usually without a specific financial value. One of the earliest which was extremely successful throughout the Eighties and Nineties was free hotel accommodation. Like most of these offers, this was based on the fact that hotels, like many other operations, usually in the travel and leisure market, had surplus capacity. If they discounted, customers who were paying full price would not be happy and it would reveal to competitors that they were price cutting.

Most nights, hotels have unoccupied rooms which obviously bring in no revenue. They also have restaurants and bars selling food and beverages which generate revenue with good margins. If someone stays in the hotel and eats in the restaurant the operator makes some money, even if they did not pay for their room. Rather than the hotel advertising the fact, they allow a third party to sell the surplus accommodation on the understanding that the customer would pay an agreed minimum amount for breakfast and dinner in the hotel.

Companies such as Flexibreaks and Reader's Offers signed up hundreds of hotels to this arrangement, put together illustrated booklets showing all the hotels and the fixed cost for each and then sold vouchers to companies as a promotional item. The actual cost to Flexibreaks and Co. for the voucher was very low, just some print, once the initial organisation had been set up and the brochure produced. As an offer it was very attractive as vouchers could be bought in quantity for less than one pound and had a perceived value of a lot more. Over the years these vouchers sold in hundreds of thousands, Flexibreaks set up an operation right across Europe while other companies such as Reader's Offers concentrated on the UK. With the growth of the internet the whole thing could be run on line. This basic technique grew into a major promotional tool. It was so universal that brand managers grew tired of it and it went out of fashion, but it is still popular with the public who buy it on line. As Ian Fryer had said in a previous chapter, staff at the companies get bored with a promotional technique long before the buying public do.

Another form of promotional voucher, which was extremely popular for many years, was usually referred to as a 'holiday voucher'. This offered money off a wide range of package holidays and could vary from as little as £25 up to perhaps £200. Sometimes lower value vouchers could be collected to add up to a maximum sum. The reason for their popularity was that they offered a high perceived value for the consumer at a very low cost to the promoter. Vouchers worth £100 off a package holiday for two people, usually with a minimum spend, would be bought by the promoter from the company handling the deal for as little as a few pence each.

To operate the programme, the company marketing the vouchers needed to own or work closely with a travel agency. This would enable them to get commission of between 10-15 per cent from the tour operator and the discount offered would be roughly the same amount, so they would at worst break even. If they managed to sell insurance, car hire and so on, they could make a profit. The promotions company sold a good few thousand vouchers or even offered a fixed fee for an on pack voucher, knowing that the level of redemption would be extremely low.

This was long before booking on line became possible and popular. The main reason for low redemptions was that booking with a distant travel agency rather than popping into a high street outlet was complicated and fraught with many little inconveniences. You could not study brochures, although you could send off for them. Long chats with a travel advisor ran up your phone bills, and there could be a similar deal available from your local travel agency. All this reduced the redemptions to a single figure percentage and the fee charged to the promoting company was pretty well all profit. All they had to do was print some pretty vouchers. The travel agency would at worst break even and could usually sell some extras such as car hire. In addition they god at new customer who may well come back on an other occasion.

CHAPTER 18

The past few years, 2005-2009

Looking up and down and up
Disappearances
Mobiles, mobiles and more mobiles
New communication, old techniques
What's up Down Under
Sex sells

THE ISP IS 75

This book has concentrated on the early years of the industry, the majority of which took place before most of the people working in Sales Promotion today were born. This chapter looks briefly at what has been happening in the very recent past and also compares it to the more distant times when SP and the authors of this book were considerably younger.

The business seems to have been pretty stable over time and is gradually improving. In May 2007 the regular survey of the marketing industry, The Bellwether Report, came up with the first upturn in below-the-line budgets for two-and-a-half years, and the Chartered Institute of Marketing found something on the same lines. Marketing expenditure was up by 4.6 per cent with the new big thing, internet marketing, up by 7.2 per cent. On the back of this, businesses understandably expect to sell more – between 8.9 per cent and 10 per cent, depending on the products involved.

However, in January 2008 the next Bellwether report had concerns over the fall in budgets in the last quarter of 2007, the steepest in two years. The big cuts were in TV and press advertising and the only rises were in internet advertising, and, good news folks, Sales Promotion. The best the report could say about 2008 was that it was cautiously optimistic. Overall budgets were up but if revenue failed to pick up, budget cuts could be expected.

There had been a good few company failures including at least three high profile agencies, Mercier Grey, Yellow Submarine and Cramm Francis Woolf over the previous12 months and there were some rocks ahead. At the end of 2005 the trade press was reporting a squeeze and the smaller and medium-sized agencies were struggling. Costs were up by around 15 per cent and competition for new business was fierce.

As pointed out in an earlier chapter, salaries and charge out rates had hardly moved in the past few years for these companies although the larger outfits had managed to get their rates up and were getting as much as 40 per cent more than smaller outfits. The minnows had to cut their fees in order to win business. Procurement departments, not known for their understanding of the creative process, were getting in on the act. Some were even demanding details of salaries and multiples. Some attempts were made to retain intellectual property rights but this did not go down well with clients.

The Gambling Bill was just getting going, to finally arrive in September 2007. Meanwhile pressure groups were building up a head of steam on smoking, alcohol, 'junk' food, marketing to children and the bureaucrats of the EU were still trying to come up with something to stop UK Sales Promotion being so much better than the rest of Europe. According to a survey at the beginning of 2005, agencies were not as profitable as they might have been. The report said, and this takes some believing, that there was a lack of action on profitability. Costs were uncontrolled in 35 per cent of agencies polled and 64 per cent did not have a computerised accounting system to manage expenses. New business development, the posh name for sales, was treated as a cost in 43 per cent and 13 per cent had no limits on the cost of pitches. What it all added up to was that creativity was king and that the bean counters did not have much say in how the business was run. This may not be great but is almost certainly better than the other way round.

MULTIPLYING MOBILES

The industry's obsession with mobile phones and the internet continued to grow as the decade went on. By 2005 there were 1.5 billion mobile phone users worldwide, compared to 1.2 billion land lines. However, there were a few voices raised in the trade press suggesting that all was not necessarily well. As long as your target audience was aged between 11 and the mid twenties, SMS worked well. The internet was okay for an older audience, apart from communities, which only seemed to work with people under 40. As almost everyone working in promotions fitted these age criteria, it was natural that they concentrated on what appealed to them. Saga has launched a site for over 55 customers which is proving popular, but there are unlikely to be many mobile phone pictures of OAPs happy slapping or drunkenly taking their clothes off.

Another problem with texting is that it only works if its simple. The great appeal is the low cost. In 2005 the average cost of reaching a potential customer by SMS was 10p and it cost around 4-5p to send a return message. Three separate techniques had emerged. These were Text to Win (an instant win promotion), Text to Collect (a collector scheme) and prize draws, typically a prize every hour or such like. They became first choice for any cool (!) brand and if you did not have an agency with 'digital' in the name, you were so last century. It resembled the Eighties and Nineties rush to add 'Direct' to everything.

A typical communication led major promotion was a Walkers Crisps effort that used just about every electronic method known to man. However, the basic idea was as simple as the 'Win a Car a Day for 100 days' programme run by Heinz more than 25 years earlier. Walkers produced 600 million packs and 9,000 prizes; odds of 6,666:1. However the prizes were themselves relatively cheap, although highly desirable, Apple iPods. It was giving one away every five minutes, 24 hours a day for a month. It used text to win, the internet, dynamic texting, screen savers, interactive e-mails and surprise, surprise, a very old fashioned method of communication called the telephone. In case you have forgotten, this is (or was) a method of actually talking to someone. How last century. Walkers even provided website bar charts showing the best and worst times to try for a prize, set out in five-minute slots.

Although on the surface a fairly straightforward instant win promotion, this was one of the earliest text to win programmes and well timed, particularly if you are aimed at 12-year-old tweenagers who had just got their mobile phone at Christmas and could not really afford to do much other than send text messages without blowing their monthly allowance. It did serious damage to chocolate sales at Christmas as instead of buying sweets, the kids were spending their pocket money on top up cards for their new phones. In the next few years just about everybody over the age of five got a mobile phone providing a steady stream of new customers for this type of promotion.

Walkers choice of prize was intended to attract a 'grown-up' audience, although it seems to us that not many people over 30 go around with a constant supply of music in their ear, but a lot of them eat crisps. Could it be that the agency and marketing people involved were in the age group that does just that? Also, didn't a lot of people have iPods already?

Anyway, looking back to the Stone Age, where to enter a competition you had to buy the product and supply proof of purchase by collecting labels, finding an envelope and a stamp and sending them off to a handling house, followed by an fairly long wait to see if you have won, compared to a quick look at the code on the pack and a rapid text, you can see what has changed. The communication technique, that is, not the offer. Despite such a complicated historic method of entering, Heinz still got almost five million entries. IPods were not around then but cars are still at the top of almost everyone's wish list today.

Another fairly typical promotion of the time was run by Golden Wonder on Wheat Crunchies. This had what seemed at first glance a generous prize fund of 25 VW Beetle Convertibles, a pretty cool car in some circles. Cars v iPods – no contest. All (all?) you had to do was guess and text an eight digit code using the numbers 0 to 8. If your selection matched one of the preselected numbers you won a prize. Go figure as the Americans say. You can tell the chances of winning from the fact that PIMS-SCA, the fixed fee insurance company, carried the risk on 24 out of 25 prizes and they are whiz kids when it comes to working out the odds. PIMS and Golden Wonder were so sure that the only real risk was that no one would win, that if this had happened, every entrant would go into a free draw for one of the cars. The offer was poor, if you worked out the odds, but it was using SMS, so it had to be good.

RINGING THE CHANGES

There was a steady stream of new applications at this time, including coupons sent to your phone. One product was called m-bar-go (say it to get the idea) and another, Wireless Brand Channel required a machine to print out a bar code when it scanned the phone's screen. Someone else added hyper tags to digital posters. Point your phone at this and you were bombarded with mobile content. WAP had arrived and was going to be the biggest thing since whatever was the biggest thing before bread was sliced.

Billons of pounds were spent without much return for years. And then there were ring tones! Large fortunes were made in a very short time by selling people dreadful tunes that played when your phone rang. Giving them away was a useful and low cost promotion at the time. Apart from shifting some product, they played a useful part in retaining the sanity of a large number of adults. Anything was better than Crazy Frog.

The growth of interactive TV, thanks to satellite and digital, also opened up a new technique. IPS (interactive programme services) or red button click had been around for years but in 2005 Ofcom changed the rules and allowed click through from sponsors' idents. They got 35 seconds of air time in a 30 minute programme and the red button could be on the screen for all of this time. This was important because consumers did not consider this to be a low cunning approach to selling them something, like the ads, but part of the programme and so more trustworthy. Are consumers that naive? After the phone-in scandals who trusted a TV company?

The 2005 ISP Promotional Marketing Awards (that year's title) turned up as usual around May. The set up was pretty much the same as it had been for some years. Half a dozen awards adjudication panel members, 20 odd panel chairmen and 90 plus judges. A good sign was that entries had increased by 50 per cent on the previous year. There were 28 categories, plus the relatively new Service Partner awards, the Special Awards, the Roll of Honour (which was in fact the people who won last year) and a nice page of Highly Commended campaigns, so that everybody got a mention somewhere, if at all possible.

A REAL SMOOTHIE

The big winner won Gold in the Beverages category plus the Grand Prix. The brand was Innocent, the right-on smoothie. It was in fact a CRM campaign with the money raised going to Age Concern and Extra Care. However it was a CRM with a difference. It came up with possibly one of the most original ideas seen for years, called 'Project Supergran'. The brilliantly wacky idea was to keep bottles of product warm in the fridge over the Christmas period by giving each one a little woolly hat. Keeping things warm in the fridge seems to qualify as not just wacky but seriously crazy, but it worked! Having decided that the idea was not quite as crazy as it sounded, most people would have sourced in the Far East but the really, really clever twist was that Innocent asked consumers to hand-knit the hats and mail them in. They would then be sold at Innocent outlets and for every hat sold it would donate 50p to the charities.

It tied up with a chain of 40 premium cafes, EAT, which agreed to put hats on bottles, distribute postcards with knitting instructions and contribute half of the 50p donation. The initial target was 20,000 hats to raise the £10,000 target and the apparently weird idea delivered excellent PR coverage, but was the 10,000 target wishful thinking? Not at all, in fact Innocent got 24,200 woolly hats, a year on year growth of 50 per cent and a charity donation of £12,200. The bad news for the agency business was that the company came up with it in-house. This was probably because even the most creative agency would have thought twice before presenting such an obviously stupid scheme.

You may remember that the 2004 Awards included a number of campaigns with risqué connotations. Perhaps spurred on by this success, Penguin Books and agency Angel dug up some research that said women were more attracted to men who read books. The 'Good Booking' campaign was publicised in store and on a lads' magazine type website. Malibu's agency Triangle had the same line of thought, linking with student unions to run 73 'Seriously Easy Party with Shaggy' nights. Shaggy was a cartoon character with an afro, but you knew that didn't you.

There was not much ambiguity in the promotional material for Dove Firming. Picking up on the above-the-line coverage, the promotional material featured a group of various sized ladies in their underwear, being quite physically friendly. The basis for this was a nationwide search for a group of 'Firm Friends' to star in the next Dove poster campaign. Entrants had to submit a team photograph and the campaign by Triangle claimed a remarkable 700 per cent sales uplift during the promotional period plus, we suspect, some harmless entertainment for the judges.

WHAT A DRAG

Another award winner (Silver in Event Marketing) was a campaign for Domestos by iD Live Brand Experience. The brand had launched a Pink Power variant and the agency supplied what are now known as brand ambassadors dressed in bright pink sequinned outfits and sporting striking blonde wigs. They were called, in case you missed the point, Domestos Drag Queens. Their job was to tour supermarkets with 7 foot tall pink bottles of Domestos and chat up the customers.   How did they get around the ban on allowing sexual orientation to affect anyone's chance of employment?

Finally on this subject, a pub chain called Screamer Pubs had a promotion from Gloria Mundi called Real Men. This was a collector scheme for Action Man type models of 'real' men and the slogans were fairly heavy on the double meanings. They were "real men always use protection"; "real men are coming"; "real men have impressive equipment", and "real men: good with their hands".

ROAD SHOWS, OR FIELD MARKETING OR IS IT EXPERIENTIAL?

The year 2006 saw, among other things, a new ISP logo, incorporating the words "when promoting sales is your business". In keeping with the current trends there is not a capital letter to be seen. There was also a link between the ISP and Sales Promotion magazine which turned into a full blown ownership the following year. This was the year when experiential marketing came of age with multi-million-pound budgets up for grabs. A survey claimed that it was responsible for one third of all marketing budgets, which seems doubtful, but there is a lot of it around so we thought it would be useful to see how it is defined and how it differs, if at all, from road shows and field marketing, which may seem to the less hip among our readers to be much the same thing.

Although everyone appears to consider experiential marketing the new 'Big Thing', field marketing has a pedigree and seems to cover much the same areas. So which is the top dog? The DMA and The Field Marketing Council said:

"Field marketing is the provision of highly skilled and trained people to conduct brand-building strategic (long-term) or tactical (short-term) exercises on behalf of clients. Staff are employed by the field marketing company, which in turn is outsourced by the client to complete specific goals and targets. Field marketing delivers results and ensures brand development in terms of accountability, visibility, availability and sales."

They went on to say: "The range of field marketing services offered includes: Auditing, Sampling/demonstrating, Merchandising, Sales Roadshows/events/experiential marketing, Mystery shopping, Data & IT and Support services.   Experiential marketing is a live and interactive marketing discipline which builds positive emotional sensory engagement between a brand and its consumers."

An emotional sensory engagement sounds very sexy, doesn't it? Now before you think 'free samples' or 'man dressed as a chicken', think again because here is another quote. "Experiential marketing encompasses destination events, guerrilla marketing, exhibitions, roadshows, ambient and in store, among other activities. It provides a platform to increase brand advocacy and consumer call to action."

SO NOW YOU KNOW. OR NOT?

As an after thought, do you know what guerrilla marketing is? Just for the few readers who are not completely up to date with such a term, it dates back to 1984 and was the title of a book about what was considered to be at that time an unconventional maverick 'weapon'. Here are a few quotes from various self styled experts in the business. "It started out as being quite edgy and used by left field brands". "It has been transformed from the back of the van style of yesterday." "Site opportunities that appear on the surface to be guerrilla marketing but are actually fully costed authorised forums."

Without the jargon it means gate crashing some big event sponsored at vast expensive by someone else (think the Olympics or Soccer World Cup) and getting some sort of advertising message across, hopefully legally but if not, keeping it in place long enough to get noticed before being forcibly removed. The removing might be a good opportunity for some more exposure, in the same way that banned advertising gets free publicity in the media with a story about the banning showing the offending ad to a wider audience than if it had been left alone by the ASA or whoever took offence.

By 2009 Field Marketing seem to be getting a new lease of life, spurred on by the rise in convenience stores. This was compounded by the supermarkets who, never ones to miss a trick and chance to make a profit, expanded into this area with brands such as Tesco Express and Sainsbury's Local. The overall numbers had grown by 6% in the last year so the general perception that the local shop was as dead as a dodo was dead wrong. There are 50,000 of these smaller shops and 23,100 are still independent. The Symbols such as Spar and Londis run 14,300, another 8,600 are on garage forecourts, the Co-op has 2,400 and Tesco and other big boys have 1,600, so the corner shop is alive and reasonably well, despite rumours of its demise.

Between them they have 20 per cent of the food and grocery market worth around £29billion a year so the manufacturers somehow had to deal with them but without the vast sales forces of yesterday. They realised that going out of stock was very bad news as shoppers switched to another brand and might well stay with it.

What to do? The answer was a tribe of field marketers who would visit the shops and make sure they were well stocked with the client's brands as well as making sure they were making good use of any promotional activity. Unlike the major supermarkets that were heavily controlled by head office the local stores are quite happy to talk to a human being and can be influenced by these contacts. All good news for the companies providing this service.

THE TV GAME SCAMS

Trust in TV companies got a knock in 2007 when there was a considerable scandal over the multitude of phone in competitions running on television. Entries were made on premium lines and many millions of pounds were earned by the TV companies. In many cases, entrants were still telephoning and contributing long after the prize winners had been chosen and even the BBC's whiter than white Blue Peter programme was found guilty of simply picking a winner from some visitors to the studio because their computer system had crashed.

It is interesting to note that in Australia the law limits the length of time that a premium line call can run to 42 seconds, and there is a set price of A$0.55, or approximately 25p. With practice, advertisers can get the basic information such as a phone number or an address in 25 seconds, leaving 10 to 15 seconds for a question. It is legal and effective for data collection.

TRY IT. YOU'LL LIKE IT!

Another survey around the same time came up with the glad news that Sales Promotion actually works. Not only that, but it worked better than advertising when it comes to persuading consumers to try new products. More than 50 per cent of shoppers were persuaded by below-the-line promotions compared to 31 per cent driven by advertising. It also found that the universally popular BOGOF worked as well as TV advertising at 25 per cent, and next came overall price reductions, three for two offers and word-of-mouth recommendations.

Things varied between types of product with BOGOFs working best on non-perishables such as toiletries, soft drinks and cooking sauces. Less good news was that only 14 per cent of consumers said that they frequently carried on purchasing a new product after a promotion, while 36 per cent said they rarely or never did so. What a promiscuous (fickle) lot!

There was a new kid on the Awards block in 2007. These were the Impact Awards and were set up by Promotions & Incentives and Marketing magazines, both owned by Haymarket, which had recently parted company from the ISP Awards after many years of working with the daddy of them all. The twist here was that all the judges were major clients. They rounded up seven unfortunates, from BSkyB, P&G, Honda, Britvic, Telegraph Group, Woolworths and Kellogg UK – an impressive line up with a great deal of spending power. The awards (14 in all with no second or third prizes) were very different in terms of categories.

Every one was something or other "….of the Year". There were Agencies of the Year in Sales Promotion, Direct Marketing, Digital, Experiential, In-store Marketing, Integrated and Motivation. Then we had "Campaigns of the Year" covering Consumers, Trade, Integrated and Motivation, followed by The Agency of the Year which turned out to be The Marketing Store. There was a Campaign of the Year (the famous Eurostar Da Vinci Code effort) and the Marketer of the Year, someone called David Walker of Kellogg UK. Strange, someone with the same name and working for the same company was a judge!

YOU'RE NICKED!

One really remarkable event took place towards the end of 2007. The big retailers, who were busily taking over the planet and who had survived unscathed from several government investigations into their activities, particularly their dealings with their suppliers, finally got clobbered. What got them into trouble was a bad case of price fixing on milk, butter and cheese. The Office of Fair Trading, after a long investigation found that Asda, Tesco, Sainsbury and Safeway (now owned by Morrisons) had conspired, along with five dairy processing companies, to fix prices. The OFT had been tipped off when a processing company 'fessed up' and did a plea bargain, becoming immune to prosecution.

The OFT handed out fines of at least £116million. Sainsbury, for instance, received a bill for £26 million. Fines would have been higher if most of the companies when faced by overwhelming evidence, including damning e-mails, had not pleaded guilty. Now you might consider that the retailers were planning to make a few more million out of this racket, but of course not – how could you think such a thing? All they were doing, according to Sainsbury's CEO Justin King, was "trying to help the British dairy farmers" and Asda claimed that, in its usual altruistic way, it was also trying to "provide more money for dairy farmers". All three of the remaining dairy farmers that retailers had not managed to make bankrupt told the media that they had not got any more money. Where could it have gone?

The trade publications had seen a number of changes over the past year or so. The ISP had acquired Sales Promotion and the BMPA now published a glossy called Promotions Buyer which incorporated Incentive and Motivation which used to be Incentive Today. Meanwhile, Haymarket's Promotions & Incentives incorporated Incentive Business but published its last printed version in January 2009 when it went digital. We hope you are keeping up.

So now there were only two print magazines competing for the advertiser's cash and the reader's attention. As Promotions Buyer concentrated on the widget - sorry, promotional merchandise business - which is where most of the advertising spend comes from, this left Sales Promotion as the only serious home for advertisers who wanted printed as opposed to digital ads. In the spring of 2009 Sales Promotion was keeping a steady 30+ pages, much the same as before the credit crunch, and Promotions Buyer was a bit bigger at around 50 pages. Their members tend to do more advertising while ISP members do very little.

It might be interesting to see what the March 2009 issue of Promotions Buyer contained. Despite the constant effort to find really original items of promotional merchandise, the old favourites still lead the way. Branded clothing has more than 10 ads or reviews, followed by soft toys and particularly teddy bears or the like. Then come five pen companies, some of whom must have sold an awful lot of cheap ballpoint pens to a number of charities, if our mail is anything to go by. What can be classed as novelties came next with four ads and here there was some creativity, trying to find something useful to carry a brand name. There was the same coverage for wallets, purses and diaries and the really new area in the last few years, electronic gadgets, memory sticks and the rest notched up least six advertisements and some editorial coverage. This is probably the only type of merchandise that would not have been on offer 40 years ago in the era of the infamous 'black bag' salesman.

As a comparison we decided to look at the April 2009 issue of the other print magazine available, Sales Promotion. It ran to a reasonable 34 pages plus a four-page cover. Of these, 19 were advertising that included four pages from a company called Capital Incentives and Motivation, supporting a long feature on what appears to be the current buzzword 'engagement'. They must be in the 'engagement' business. Also spotted were number of other current buzzwords such as guerilla sampling, shopper marketing, brand activation, online coalition and the SOHO market which stands for Small Office Home Office, not what you thought!

References to online activity and websites popped up everywhere and Chris Bestley, who runs education at the ISP, was warning all concerned that the ASA were about to start clobbering digital activity that broke a new and strict set of rules. There was a good reason for this as within a year complaints about promotions with a digital element had increased by 750 per cent. This was blamed on either ignorance of Sales Promotion rules by the digital experts or maybe they considered that they were outside the law. More on this later.

Possibly the most surprising feature, seeing how the experiential gang had been sweeping all before them in the past few years, was a two-page feature on something called 'roadshows'. We thought that these things along with field marketing and such had been consigned to the dustbin by title inflation and replaced by the more impressive sounding and probably more expensive, experiential marketing. Another revival was the reference to a few 'integrated' agencies. This had been very fashionable about 20 years before but had been overtaken by 'media neutral' for a time but seems to have made a comeback. If all this retro stuff continues we might go back one more step to 'one stop shops', circa the 70's or the 'whole egg' as Y&R used to call it.

LET'S SAVE THE PLANET!

Climate change in all its ramifications was very big news at this time, with trade press editorials urging companies to run green promotions. Readers may remember that back in 1989 there were a number of such promotions, including some giving large sums of money to the Woodland Trust. Let's hope that all the trees that were paid for are now strong and healthy. The urge to climb aboard the green bandwagon produced a magazine feature on green pens of all things. This did not refer to the colour of the ink but to the use of recycled material or alternatively so called 'eco-friendly' pens made from such things as sustainable European timber. This does not seem to require a lot of timber, sustainable or not. You would expect to get a lot of wooden pens from one fairly small tree, but if you see a bandwagon, why not jump on it.

Users would also be pleased to know that one company was using inks that are free from xylene and toluene, not to mention heavy toxic metals. Another manufacturer claimed that its pens had a low carbon footprint because they were made in Germany. According to the authors, the question most frequently asked by potential customers was just what pen makers and their suppliers were doing to offset their own carbon footprints. Surely they can't be serious? One might have thought that the most frequently asked question would be "How much?"

At the end of 2007 there was a conference called 'Profiting from Green Policies' where research showed deep cynicism among consumers about the motivation of companies waving green flags, and that the said customers thought there was a lack of commitment to environmentally friendly practices. Hopefully, these cynical customers then went home and changed their light bulbs.

The humble plastic carrier bag was also under the spotlight of the Waste and Resources Action Programme with the nice acronym of WRAP. It even persuaded London councils to dream up a bill that would outlaw the free distribution of plastic carrier bags in the capital. The chief executive of the Association of Convenience Stores noted that if retailers didn't have to hand plastic bags out for free, they could make savings. Amazing!

Tesco latched on to this idea and tested charging 5p for each bag, although with its usual generosity it said that the money raised from these sales would be invested back into local environmental regeneration projects. It then tried a carrot instead of a stick and handed out Clubcard points for recycling. Sainsbury did its bit by selling a reusable carrier bag designed by Anya Hindmarch and shifted 20,000 of them, which produced useful income, not to mention acres of media coverage. Another 'Where have we seen that before?' moment looked back at the Eighties when Threshers asked customers to pay a few pence for each bag and donated all the income to Radio Lollipop, which operated in children's hospitals.

When announcing the categories for the 2008 ISP Awards the Institute went all ethical. Most of the categories were much the same as or variations on the previous years but two new and very politically correct introductions were "The use of Sales Promotion techniques to foster and communicate social responsibility" and another category for campaigns that encourage a healthy lifestyle.

LET'S TRY AND MAKE SOME MONEY

Another move from real life to the virtual life via your computer was going strong around this time with sites such as Facebook and MySpace and the success of 'Twittering'. They were all trying to come up with new ways of relieving customers of some money and getting some income apart from advertising. They tried all sorts of things, for instance Facebook invented a virtual gift service. You could pay one dollar to send animated icons of novelty items such as cakes, teddy bears or bottles of beer and unbelievably, it quickly managed to sell 24 million.

Promoters were quick to catch on to this with Wal-Mart making 300,000 sponsored ghost icons available for Facebook which could be obtained by visiting the Wal-Mart online shop. Unilever's US deodorant brand Axe managed to move 250,000 virtual gifts as part of a promotion. Sites were being bought and sold for vast sums, totally unrelated to the profits earned, which was beginning to look a bit like the infamous dot.com boom of a few years earlier.

There are however a few small clouds on the horizon and these are not exactly virtual. The problem is the increased commercialisation of social networks and particularly the use companies are allowed to make of personal information appearing in these sites. Not everyone is enthusiastic about the idea of being hit with an advertisement for a product which some comment on your site suggests might be of interest to you. If too much of this goes on then there may well be a backlash against the various sites and, who knows, people might actually go back to meeting each other in three dimensions.

INTERLUDE FIVE - IT SEEMED LIKE A GOOD IDEA AT THE TIME

WHO CHECKED THE COPY?

Beating the odds

How many redemptions?

That wasn't quite what we had in mind

Sunglass saga

In 2007, Harrah's Joliet Casino near Chicago had a small printing error on coupons it mailed to its customer list. It could have cost them £2.9million. The mailing to loyalty cardholders included a coupon that members could redeem at the casino. Only 15 or so coupons were supposed to be worth £260, but a printing error resulted in 11,000 coupons worth that amount. The coupons were bar coded, but most codes didn't match the $525 printed on the coupon's face. Casino staff turned away a number of cardholders because of this. The regulator quickly investigated, then ordered the casino to honour all the coupons and is advising consumers to go to the casino whether they've still got the coupon or not. It also advised people to go in with proof of identify as the casino knew who they were. When the odds are in your favour you can afford to appear generous.

Don't expect the spell check to save you. A very subtle copy error appeared on a voucher for a free channel crossing. It was meant to say that "only five foot passengers", that is people who would be travelling on foot, could take up the offer. What it actually said was that "only five-foot passengers" could travel, which produced a spate of phone calls, asking why children under that height couldn't travel. This supports the authors' hard learned lessons that most copy mistakes are in the headline - which nobody seems to check.

Very minor errors can be potentially very expensive. Take the example of an American Express promotion in 2006. This was fairly typical of a period when almost every card issuer was offering an Interest Free Transfer'. The idea was that you transferred the amount owed on one of your cards to a new one, and did not have to pay interest on that amount for some fixed period. As competition increased, the period of interest free moved steadily upwards from three months to a year or even longer. So-called 'rate tarts' simply left the card untouched for the free period and then transferred the whole amount to another new card. The card companies got wise to this after a while and introduced a transfer fee, perhaps two or three per cent, with a minimum and maximum figure, but for multi-thousand pound debts, it was still a very good deal if your money was earning six per cent in a savings account.

Anyway, Amex set up just such an offer intending to give an interest free period of six months with a transfer fee of two per cent. Good, but nothing out of the ordinary. Much to Amex's surprise, it was swamped with applications partly, it thought, because of a fairly short deadline. However, everyone was transferring larger and larger amounts, up to their credit limit, and trying to get this increased. Then some bright spark reread the copy. The wording said that the interest free period was for "the lifetime of the loan", in fact for ever, or at least for the lifetime of the card holder. Of course it should have been for the six-month period as planned. The offer was shut down in a flash and applicants told the unfortunate truth. However, they did get the two per cent fee repaid. When you think that Amex has 72 million card holders worldwide, this could have made Hoover look like pocket money.

TOYING WITH DISCOUNTS

The digital age opens up the opportunity for a whole range of new disasters. Hamleys, the upmarket toyshop in London's Regent Street, had such a glitch during Christmas 2006. The company had produced three discount codes, each worth 20 per cent on a range of products with the idea that only one code would be applicable to one purchase. However some bright lad found that all three could be used together giving a 60 per cent discount.

Sainsbury also had a discount scheme that went rather further than it intended. It was possible to get 60 per cent off wine and beer and an online site called hotdeals.com soon broadcast the information far and wide. Sainsbury was inundated with orders.

Both of these companies shut down the unintentional offer as soon as possible but Threshers, which had a similar problem of unintended consequences, decided to turn a potential disaster into a minor triumph. An online discount voucher gave 40 per cent off and was intended for staff, their friends and families. It turned out these staff, friends and families had lots of other friends and families and a veritable blizzard of vouchers hit the internet in a matter of hours. Threshers allowed it to run and saw a 60 per cent uplift in sales, often from people who had never visited before.

While on the subject of trouble with numbers, in the early Eighties, Daz ran an on-pack Bingo game. Different packs had different numbers printed on them, which were stuck on a collector card. The idea was to inject a bit of interest and also to make the budget go further by making it harder for the consumers to get the numbers required. The consumers were smarter than that, and soon discovered that they could rummage around the shelves and collect the packs carrying the numbers they needed. Redemptions had the potential to skyrocket. Immediate action was called for and P&G launched a product recall programme. It even had employees purchasing Daz at the retail price to get the packs off the shelves.

A SEXUAL ERROR

It is also a good idea to make sure photographs, if there are any, match the copy. One unfortunate example related to a competition in which the consumer was invited to 'Win a Race Horse'. The horse in question was referred to in the copy as a "fast filly", however the photograph showed a different horse, which was obviously a well-endowed stallion.

Gerber baby food showed a photograph of a baby on its jar. In parts of Africa with low literacy levels, the contents of the jar were shown on the label!). However, when it started exporting to parts of Africa, with a lower level of literacy, it had not realised that most companies showed a photograph of the product on the outside of the pack to the benefit of those who did not have a very high standard of reading. Consequently, some consumers thought it was a fertility drug or, better still, an aphrodisiac. That must have helped sales.

Not only do the words and the pictures need checking carefully, so do numbers. A major petrol company ran a loyalty card offer, which it sent to 250,000 cardholders. In order to take up the offer of hotel accommodation it was necessary to call a hotel company for details and to make a booking. However, rather than printing a call centre number, it printed the office number, resulting in blocked lines and chaos. It took five days to link up the extra lines, but probably less to line up the culprit.

Mike Slipper, who is currently part of the ISP Legal Advisory Service set up, started working for Unilever in 1959 and spent 42 years doing various jobs, all connected with sales and marketing. He therefore knows where a lot of the bodies are buried and recalls when a tiny numerical mistake required two lorries to shift a large number of coupons that included a closing date in the previous year. Luckily the company also owned a paper mill at that time that was happy to dispose of the coupons.

On the question of numbers, a lack of mathematical skill can be dangerous, as in the case of a supermarket that used an interesting device for a competition. Punters were asked to make as many words as possible from a short sentence – naturally a paean of praise about the retailer. The idea was that, while studying the sentence, consumers would absorb its message. The ten words provided entrants with around 70 letters, including all the most widely used in English. They had not worked out that there were around half a million possible permutations. Heaven help the poor judges.

LANGUAGE, LANGUAGE
Translations are another minefield. For instance, it seemed like a good idea for the Nova car to retain its name in Spain, until it was realised that it read as "It doesn't go". A manufacturer of vacuum cleaners used the expression in a Scandinavian language that in English translated as "Nothing Sucks Like an Electrolux". An American company sold chickens with the slogan "It takes a strong man to make a tender chicken", which in Spanish became "It takes an aroused man to make chicken affectionate". Finally, a major beer brand had the slogan "Turn it loose" which, also in Spanish, turned itself into "Suffer from diarrhoea".

A really expensive copy error was an Argos online offer of £300 TV sets. This was phenomenally effective as it omitted both zeros. Even more expensive, because the promotion could not be recalled quickly enough, was a free sunglasses offer on Newcastle Brown Ale. The promotion went very well, and if it had not been a fixed fee arrangement with the sunglasses supplier, there could well have been an over redemption problem. However, the sunglasses were described as 'Wayfarer' which is a trademark for an expensive Bausch and Lomb design. The glasses on offer were a look-alike design from the Far East and cost around 40p.

Bausch and Lomb threatened an injunction and the client withdrew the promotion, but only after 40,000 enthusiastic customers had sent in their proof of purchase. A decision was taken not to buy the genuine item as £1.6million was a little outside the budget. What the brewer did was ship everyone a case containing 12 bottles of the product as this was equivalent to the amount that had to be bought to obtain the sunglasses. The cost of transport was huge and it often required up to three visits to a house to find someone in. Pouring the beer through the letterbox was not an option. The original budget was £50,000; the final bill, for which the brewer sued the agency, was almost £500,000. Luckily the agency was insured, but the next year's premium must have stung.

CHAPTER 19 -

Views from two bridges

SP's MP
The battle for Europe
Mutton takes up the ISP baton
The challenge ahead

We interviewed two people with very interesting views on the Sales Promotion industry. The first has a view of the industry from Westminster Bridge as a MP, and the second is the view from the bridge of the industry itself, that is as seen by the now retired director general of the ISP. First, let's examine the view from Westminster.

In 1987 an ex-Metropolitan policeman turned insurance broker stood for the Yorkshire constituency of Ryedale and won the seat for the Conservatives. He was John Greenway and he has become very much connected to Sales Promotion for more than 20 years. In his election campaign he had been advised by Ian Martin, a constituent involved in the Sales Promotion industry and public relations, and when he was returned to parliament, John was asked to return the compliment. He was introduced to the business via Ian Allchild,

In the spring of 1988 they promoted the idea of National Motivation Week and John persuaded more than 100 MPs to sign an early day motion, a sort of political banner waving, that said that motivation was a 'good thing'. They also came up with an award for Motivator of the Year and with an eye on potential PR coverage handed it out to Sir Richard Branson. To really make sure it garnered column inches they arranged for the award to be presented by Jeffrey Archer. Serious name dropping.

John followed his first parliamentary effort by arranging for a number of MPs to visit the Sales Promotion exhibition of the year, whatever it was called at the time, and this has continued up to the present day. However he did have one or two occasional problems when visiting MPs somehow got the impression that anything on the stands was available as a sample to take away. The stand holders did not quite see things in the same way and there was occasional friction. Apparently crystal glass was particularly popular amongst our legislators and probably among their wives. At this stage a formal agreement between the MP, Langford's Exhibitions, the BPMA and the ISP produced an annual retainer which, welcome as it was at that time, has not increased from that day. John is quite happy with this situation as he feels that it cements the relationship and neither side can feel that they are being taken advantage of. Since that time John has been the official parliamentary adviser to the BPMA and the ISP. The tradition has also been carried on by the various organisers of Sales Promotion exhibitions.

Another good reason for having an MP on board was the ongoing potential problem of the European Union or Common Market, as it used to be known, which threatened to harmonise Sales Promotion practice across Europe. As its idea of harmonisation was to reduce everything to the lowest common denominator, i.e. Germany where promotions were practically impossible to run within the law, no one in Britain was in favour of the idea. As a parliamentarian John Greenway was very involved in the various discussions held at that time. He recalls that there were two strategies. One was that the UK should keep its head down; as if it appeared above the parapet someone might want to do something about the laissez faire approach here. The other side of the coin, which in fact proved to be far more sensible, was that the UK should try and influence the lawmakers by showing how self-regulated business, as run in the UK, could be extended to Europe to the advantage of the European consumers. The Sales Promotion industry put its hands in its pocket and funded a professional lobbyist in Brussels who pushed the case.

SEEING OFF THE EUROCRATS
This approach was taken and has proved successful. By 2007 the challenges of such harmonisation had disappeared over the horizon, much to everyone's relief. However, John's view is that there has been some positive harmonisation in that the iron grip of Napoleonic Law across Europe, which we referred to in a previous chapter, has been relaxed a little and that there has been a movement towards the less hidebound UK version. This has proved particularly popular with the big international promoters who like to run schemes across many countries and do not want to have to make major changes for each in order keep within the strict rules. There was in fact a recommendation and a Draft Directive in Brussels which would have had this effect. Unfortunately this was partially hijacked by the powerful anti-advertising consumer lobby, so did not quite live up to the high hopes of those who had worked so hard to achieve it.

The consumer lobby and the director general of consumer affairs in Brussels tended towards the anti-Sales Promotion thinking that had been prevalent across Europe. Their view was that consumers were so stupid they would buy things that were either not good value or which they did not really need because they would be 'bribed' by a promotion. Fortunately the British government has more regard for the intelligence of our citizens. As John Greenway puts it, "We had won the argument". The argument, which he has put across to his colleagues and contacts in Europe, is that the consumer actually benefits from promotions. He found that one of the most telling arguments was frequent flyer miles, a promotion which was benefiting just about everyone he spoke to.

Despite this victory in what might be termed a battle, the overall war with the various interests that are trying to restrict commercial activity in various ways is still continuing, and they appear to be winning. Apart from the banning of all tobacco advertising and the smoking ban which certainly have some arguments in their favour, there are various pressure groups arguing over which foods can and cannot be advertised before the nine o'clock watershed, or at all. They have their own definition of junk food, which they want to force on the rest of us. At the same time companies are being told what they have to print on their packaging and what sort of packaging they should use. The first is to fight obesity and the second to save the planet.

As an aside on the anti-obesity war, this is based on a one-size fits all formula relating height to weight but completely ignores build. If you apply this formula to, for instance, the England Rugby XV, who probably do not have a spare ounce of fat on their bodies, they are almost to a man either overweight or obese. Perhaps a campaigner should personally point this out to a couple of 6'6", 18-stone second front row forwards and see how they react.

LAST ORDERS?

John fears that the long-term objective of many campaigners is to do to alcohol what they did to tobacco. Binge drinking has become an excuse for potentially draconian regulations and consumers are even being told how much they should drink at home, let alone at 2 a.m. in the high street. As usual the first and almost only ideas are to increase taxes, ban advertising and force the prices up by increasing the taxation element. The last is particularly popular with politicians. John sees a potential problem in the European Parliament where, as he says, they do not have much to do. The Parliament now has acquired some clout as it can introduce and alter legislation. Should something unpleasant happen in the advertising and promotional world, it could well introduce some ill-thought-out, knee-jerk regulations.

After his long association with the industry, he feels that he has a fair understanding of how it works, why people are doing what they are doing and is able to pass it on to his fellow MPs. He sees the business as a village where everyone knows everyone although there are new faces appearing regularly and in his opinion they all seemed to be fitting in very well.

He considers that the industry has a very bright future, particularly when money becomes tight. Sales Promotion always seems to blossom in a recession. From his seat in the House, he notes that the government is leaning more and more towards promotional activities, witness the 2004 ISP Grand Prix for "The Sexual Lottery", a campaign to reduce sexually transmitted diseases, which also won international acclaim. As the chairman of the Responsibility in Gambling Trust, he wishes he had the budget to do something similar on gambling awareness. John is convinced that his involvement with Sales Promotion over the years has enabled him to keep in touch with what is happening in the real world, rather more so than some of his colleagues. Finally, he points out that although we don't have the best soccer team in the world, the British Sales Promotion industry is the most sophisticated and well developed in Europe, and can compete on even terms with anywhere else in the world.

MUTTON'S THE MAN

Now we move on to the man who has been at the helm of the ISP as Director General since 2002 and retired from the full-time job at the end of 2007, although he will continue in a consultancy roll. Edwin Mutton probably has one of the best all-round views of what has been happening in the industry over the past few years. He became involved in Sales Promotion in 1980 when he joined Kimberly-Clark, having previously been a civil servant and then had his own business where, without realising it, he ran a good deal of promotional marketing activity. He says that he made all the mistakes in the book and that this is in many ways the best way to learn and to avoid them in future.

As Kimberly-Clark's trade promotions manager in the Eighties, it was possible to negotiate deals with individual stores and with a much larger number of store chains. He also had to work with a sales force of about 100, something else that has changed radically. His boss was Brian Mitchell, one of that band of Sales Promotion managers that did so much to build the industry but who have now practically disappeared. Brian taught him all that he knew and allowed him to make mistakes, which he then had to put right.

Brian Mitchell was considered to be an excellent practitioner in on pack promotions and the company ran a number of very successful offers on Kleenex Tissues and their other brands (this was before Kimberly-Clark took over Andrex). He has fond memories of one particular promotion carried across all their brands with the overall strap line of "Soft and Strong". The charity promotion was raising funds for the RNLI and offered a model Lledo lifeboat (it's first ever model without wheels) in exchange for a one pound donation to the charity. The specially commissioned illustration, of which Edwin is particularly proud, showed a beefy lifeboat man lifting a small girl clutching a teddy bear from the cockpit of a sinking yacht. It was the company's first promotion across all brands and was extremely successful.

When the company acquired Andrex, it started a long line of successful offers and, unlike many other brands, did not feel that it had to do something new on every occasion. Apart from the endless variations on the Andrex puppy, they also ran several variations of the hay fever kit on tissue brands. Both of these have collected armfuls of ISP awards. The story behind the initial hay fever kit is interesting. It was started by an approach from a drug company which wanted Andrex to offer a free sample of its new drug designed to relieve hay fever symptoms. Worried about the backlash should the drug produce any side-effects, Kimberly-

Clark decided against the idea, but it suggested to them that hay fever was an area it could target, improving sales in the summer. The idea was extended into winter survival kits and various other combinations, with all the items supplied free of charge by third parties.

THE ISP CALLS

When in 2002 Edwin decided to move on from his time at Kimberly-Clark, he was offered a short-term job for six months or so to try and sort out the various problems at the ISP. He describes the situation when he arrived as "pretty parlous". The finances, not for the first time, were in a critical position and the then secretary general, who had held the job for many years through thick and thin, had been badly affected by the pressure of running what was effectively a one-woman band, so much so that her health had suffered. Edwin found he had to visit every aspect of the organisation, covering not only finance but all the internal procedures of the ISP, right down to staff holidays. It was, he said, an "ad hoc mess" and it was a question of starting at the bottom and reorganising just about everything in a professional manner. With no extra money or staff available, board demands for overheads to be cut on a regular basis and nothing like the income required to run the operation to the standard the members would expect, it took from 2001 to 2005/6 to get the accounts into the black. It took another year or two put some money into the coffers.

The struggle for financial security was made worse by the inability to speculate to accumulate and at the same time try to improve the services and acquire new members without spending additional cash. Fortunately Edwin found himself working with two extremely good chairmen. The first was Randle Stonier, the only chairman to do two stints, four years in total. He devoted a vast amount of time and energy to the Institute, not to mention taking out costs by using his own company's resources. He was followed by Peter Kerr, who also devoted a tremendous amount of time to the job despite being involved in a management buyout of his company.

Edwin says that they were two very different types of chairman and of course came from very different sides of the industry, Randle from the agency business and Peter from what used to be called a handling house but is now probably something involving the word logistics. Neither took a penny in expenses, although he knew for a fact that in both cases they had to spend several thousand pounds a year. The Institute owes a great deal of gratitude to both.

Another change that greatly affected the way the Institute was run was the chairman's insistence that board members became responsible for various aspects of the organisation and did more than just turn up for board meetings. This has developed to a point where, at the end of 2007, the director general is standing down and the Institute can afford a team of professionals to run the office under the guidance of the chairman but without a full-time DG.

At the end of 2008 Annie Swift was appointed as CEO and is moving things on with an exciting agenda. The chairman has becomes what might be termed non-executive and the staff have enough time to do the various things that would have been desirable in the past but could not happen because of either a shortage of cash or a shortage of bodies. Previously there was a DG plus administrators, but now there are specialists, each dealing with their part of the Institute's affairs.

FUTURE CHALLENGES

Asked how he saw the next two or three years of change and of development in the Sales Promotion industry, Edwin Mutton's view was that, along with the rest of the world, the industry is becoming more and more dominated by electronics. Looking back on 18 years of ISP awards, he sees a tendency for the method of communication to become more important than the message. Although the entries are more professional than in the past, there is a great deal of 'me too' activity and each year it is much easier to find the one or two outstanding promotions that are head and shoulders above the rest. Some 10 to 15 years ago there were probably four or five really exciting promotions, any one of which could have ended up as a Grand Prix but nowadays there is usually only one that is outstanding.

An example, he says, is the Eurostar promotion that went on from winning the 2007 ISP Grand Prix to being acclaimed as the best in the world and pointed out that it used a whole range of different channels. It could really claim to be a totally integrated promotion as every part of it supported the rest of the programme. Many of its competitors had one whizz-bang idea and everything else was just bolted on because they were expected to be there but added very little to the overall idea or the programme's effectiveness.

Edwin also thinks that the industry is becoming much more proactive, whereas in the past a promotion was just an add on, subordinated to above the line activity. With the growth of experiential marketing and the ability to accurately target consumers, promotions are standing on their own feet and leading the selling drive. On the other hand, along with the increased professionalism of the business, has come a considerably less colourful bunch of characters. There are no longer any big names and personalities around, very few people stand out and those that do are almost without exception, as Edwin puts it, 'old farts'.

Another change is the fragmentation of the industry where, on the one hand, several of the bigger agencies are getting together and combining their activities while, on the other, start-ups continue to emerge. This may be considerably harder than it was 30 years or so ago but it is still possible to set up on a shoestring with a couple of clients who are prepared to move with you. Edwin is convinced that there are plenty of opportunities for young people with the right qualifications to move into Sales Promotion, or promotional marketing, but he feels that it is less exciting than it was.

Although there is still plenty of creativity around, there are also plenty of brand managers who feel they can do what in the past an agency may have done, and of course there is the iron hand of procurement which is as far removed from the concept of excitement as it is possible to get. A relatively recent introduction to the ISP awards is the consumer panel where customers are asked what they think of promotions. This does not always agree with the professional view and on occasion has scratched its collective head and asked "What was that all about?" Sounds like the reaction to much TV advertising.

THE SMALL PRINT

One interesting aspect of the Institute's work is that it is the recipient of the majority of consumer complaints about promotions. The vast majority are about non-arrival of prizes and of these a large number relate to internet activity. Since the massive media coverage of various TV premium line rip-offs, it seems that the consumer is more prepared to complain if they feel cheated. The point Edwin makes is that creativity is all very well but the ability to fulfil is as important. A legally tight promotion can be let down by scrappy prize distribution.

The ISP is prepared to do rather more than rap the knuckles of the defaulting promoter. If it is not going to do anything about the missing prize, the consumer is actively encouraged to take the promoting company to the small claims court, something that is relatively simple, inexpensive and usually results in a judgement in the consumer's favour. Not getting the prize or perhaps finding yourself in a three-star hotel when the copy said five-star, is a simple breach of contract and the courts have no difficulty in seeing it that way. One example was a promotion by a magazine (publishers are some of the worst offenders) where the prize was a garden makeover. The makeover company went bust and the promoter said "Oh sorry, we can't provide the prize". With the ISP's prompting, the case went to the small claims court which found the promoter was liable and it had to meet its obligation. This is not the sort of practical thing that the ASA does. However, over the years the relationship between the ASA and the ISP has improved considerably, and the ISP is considered an important part of consumer protection.

Another area of co-operation that has changed over the years is the relationship between the ISP and the Advertising Association. Although the ISP had been a member of the AA for a number of years, it had been very much the junior partner because most of the issues were much bigger than it was. Edwin gives the example of the ban on tobacco advertising. It affected everyone and the Sales Promotion aspect was just a small part of the overall problem. The turning point was when the EU decided to have a look at Sales Promotion activity with a view to harmonising it. The AA realised and admitted that it knew nothing about Sales Promotion but the ISP was working hard to prevent the changes with lobbyists in Brussels, frequent meetings with all concerned, discussions around the embassies and an MP who was also fighting its corner. It won that one.

Then came the Gambling Act where again the people working below-the- line had a much better knowledge of many aspects of how it would affect sales and marketing, together with a sponsored MP who was chairman of the appropriate committee. All this raised the profile of the Institute in the AA which, until then, had been dominated by ISBA and the IPA. However, in the current situation with pressure groups fighting for more and more control over advertising, particularly food advertising, the ISP may once again find its profile reduced as the problems are far greater than just promotional activity. Despite this, the current chairman and board will continue to make the ISP's voice heard. Above the line advertising is currently static while below the line business is growing steadily and in cash terms is just as important, although not as visible to pressure groups or legislators.

COMPERS – WIN, WIN AND WIN!
Another group which also had a good relationship with the ISP are those enthusiasts known as 'Compers', who you may remember are consumers who take a great interest in promotional activity, take part in it on a regular basis and are also extremely good at winning.
 An interesting new development between the Oxfordshire Press and the ISP is 'Winners Gallery', a website which hopefully will list all the winners of every known competition. In time this may produce an income stream from advertising on the site. It may also overcome one of the great bugbears of the industry - the unavailability of winners' lists despite this being an important part of the code. The ISP has made a practice of asking for these anonymously, but about 40 per cent of lists do not turn up. Edwin calls the 25,000 or so serious compers the eyes and ears of the Institute as they provide a steady stream of leaflets, entry forms and complaints, which the ISP can check.

IF YOU EVER THINK ABOUT ENTERING A COMPETITION HERE ARE A FEW USEFUL TIPS FROM THE EXPERTS AMONG THE "COMPERS"
1. Find out what promotions are running by subscribing to a comping publication and/or entry form supply service.

2. Interact with other compers – e.g. by joining a comping club – to gain inspiration and locate sought-after entry forms.

3. Obtain entry forms before starting to draft tie-breaking sentences; stores often quickly run out of forms.

4. Buy products with on-pack promotions as quickly as possible, before they disappear from the shelves.

5. Obtain (and later enclose) the right proof of purchase (POP).

6. If a till receipt is to be provided, try to use one which also covers the purchase of other items, to disguise the fact that you are a comper!

7. Read the terms and conditions / rules very carefully, especially eligibility, closing dates and any requirement to use black ink.

8. Enter exactly in the prescribed way – e.g. for entry by text, only include your name and address if this is a requirement.

9. For the completion of tie-breaker sentences, don't exceed the word limit, and remember that contractions (e.g. I'd) are likely to be treated as two words.

10. Think of the tie-breaker sentence as if it was an advertisement slogan. Imagine it appearing on a billboard. Would you read it twice?

11. It is important to follow on from a tie-breaker lead-in in a way that completes a sentence.

12. For tie-breakers, the use of rhyming couplets (i.e. two lines of verse) will often increase your chances of success.

13. For tie-breakers, ensure that the words you use are spelt correctly – use a dictionary!

14. For a tie-breaker competition, if possible, delay posting your entry for at least a day. If it then still sounds good, send it off; otherwise, refine it.

15. Make sure that your writing, on entry forms and postcards, is clear. Use block capitals.

16. For picture postcard entries, write your name and address at a right-angle to the destination address, to reduce the risk of the card being delivered back to you by Royal Mail.

17. Avoid using staples to attach till receipts to entry forms; if the receipts are torn off, your entry may become damaged.

18. If there is a choice of putting your entry form in a box, in-store, or sending it in the post, do the latter; boxes in stores sometimes do not get emptied in time.

19. Post paper-based entries in plenty of time. Remember that envelopes to freepost addresses are treated as second class mail.

20. If you win a prize, particularly a valuable one, write to the promoters to thank them. This encourages them to spend their marketing budget in a similar way in the future.

Our thanks to Dallas Willcox of the South East Essex Compers' Group for this contribution.

The change in the law allowing promoters to ask for proof of purchase for instant win promotions or free prize draws will reduce the number of complaints. The new rules which do away with the plain paper entry route, as long as the price is not increased during the promotional period, work fine on normal FMCG products.

Finally, we asked Edwin about the low point and high point of his time in the DG's chair. The low point was the day that he had done his six months temporary stint and was told by the board that he had done such a good job that they were not going to look for a replacement and he was stuck with it! He also names two high spots. One being the day that the ISP accounts went into the black and the second being the Awards night when a large number of people came up to him and said that under his leadership they had seen great changes in the ISP and that these changes had all been for the better. We agree.

As he looks round the industry just before he leaves the bridge he is very optimistic about its future. Promotional marketing is not just on pack offers and BOGOFs he says. It is about taking the creative message and using all the multiplicity of channels to get it into the market. The ISP's new strap line sums it up: "when promoting sales is your business". It is not just about being in Sales Promotion, it is all about promoting sales in myriad ways. A lot of very expensive above the line advertisements, particularly on TV, seem to be a long way from this objective.

CHAPTER 20

Where do we go from here?

What does the future hold for promotional marketing?
John Hooper feels confident
John Williams identifies a vicious spiral
Bob Bayley is downbeat
Tim Arnold is controversial
Dinner guests discuss
A teacher talks
We hear from the CEO and the Chairman

If you have managed to reach this far in our book you will realise that Sales Promotion, in its many forms and with several names, has been around for a long time and affects just about everybody in some way or other. Like many other facets of life, it has developed extremely rapidly during the last hundred years and has probably accelerated even faster in the last 40 with the development of the highly professional agencies and the introduction of a wide range of communication methods. In fact the people who founded and built the agencies, plus the various service companies, can claim to have invented an industry. We asked a number of very experienced promoters and practitioners, both individually and in a discussion group, where they thought the industry is going in the next few years. First as individuals, this is what they had to say:-

JOHN HOOPER OF CLARKE HOOPER AND MORE RECENTLY DIRECTOR GENERAL OF THE ISBA

Until comparatively recently the business was comparatively simple! You thought of a great idea, put it on the pack, the supermarkets stocked it and you were famous. It was easy. But now, media holds the key. To succeed you need a very clear understanding of the channels of communication. The approach to the consumer has to be far more sophisticated and cognisant of the permission society. We have moved away from the caveman society where you could hit the consumer over the head with a large lump of wood. Now we have to cajole, caress, collar, seek permission, understand the persona and know the best way to reach that particular consumer. But, we still need the great creative idea behind the promotion although the way in which we reach the consumer is now critical.

I don't think creativity has gone away but it is not as noticeable as it was. When I was active in the industry, Sales Promotion was first and foremost in a grocery store. Now it is everywhere. You cannot move for Sales Promotion, but it is not as intense as it was in the major categories of the supermarkets. SP is now a huge and vital part of the marketing palette. It has increased in influence because we have a generation that has grown up surrounded by Sales Promotion. It is part of the way of life; it is the way we do things.

It is at this moment an immensely compelling and interesting industry. I just wish I had greater confidence that those who are running it have an understanding of the huge legacy that has been handed to them. I think that we have the right to demand of them the same help for the people of the future that we gave them and which enabled them to get where they are now. To be successful, you can only think about being better then you were the year before and investing in the people. It is not about building up a business for three years and then selling it on. This approach will ultimately destroy the business.

JOHN WILLIAMS, PREVIOUSLY MANAGING DIRECTOR OF TIM ARNOLD ASSOCIATES, FOUNDER OF MARKETING PERSPECTIVES WHICH BECAME PART OF WPP

Where is the industry going? Well, one of the problems today it that it is much harder to make money because everything we touch is being "nickeled and dimed". Procurement is cutting the price of everything but in many ways we have only ourselves to blame. Historically, we have almost given away for free our most valuable asset and marked up things that really we should not have done. This has caused clients over 30 years to undervalue the ideas, the creativity, and they then realised that the areas where we were adding value and of course a profit could be brought a lot cheaper.

What I hope will happen is that the part of the business that is currently being treated as a commodity will rise up and be recognised as having real value for which people will pay real money - the ideas. If this comes about the agency of the future need no longer carry the various executional departments. Clients can execute but they cannot generate ideas. So the agency of the future may well consist of a group of smart, very bright people whose job is to solve problems and come up with ideas and be paid a lot of money for doing so. If there is a lot of money to be made the business will attract smart, intelligent people into it. The best people will go where the money is to be made and if the brands, that is the clients, refuse to pay good money for good ideas the best people will not be attracted to the business and the quality of the ideas will be less, so the brands will suffer. This would produce a vicious circle spiralling downwards into mediocrity.

BOB BAYLEY, UNIGATE, CADBURYS, MARDEN KANE, THE SALES MACHINE, OPTION ONE, ETC.

Having spent some time thinking long and hard about the future of Sales Promotions my first reply is "What Sales Promotions?" Where are you seeing promotions these days? There are promotions out there but they are far less visible than they used to be. If asked to name my favourite promotion of the moment I would be hard pushed to think of one. FMCG has almost disappeared from the promotional scene, possibly the hugest change at the last few years. My rather pessimistic view was that Sales Promotion agencies as such may cease to exist. The business had gone in a full circle and now resembles the early days around 1970 when I joined the business and it was considered a little bit tacky and rather second rate, although the money was good.

I do not think anyone today in their right mind would join a Sales Promotion agency. The rapid and exciting growth through the 60's, 70's and 80's and possibly just into the 90's was due not to the cleverness and brilliant creative thinking of the agencies but to the fact that they had fantastic, brave, bold and ambitious clients. But not today! The typical client is incredibly cautious, wildly risk averse, and completely driven by costs. The bean counters are in charge. In FMCG there are trade marketing managers with hardly any true marketing people left in that side of the business, with the possible exception of giant brands such as Coca-Cola and the like. Everyone is completely beholden to the retail trade.

My view is that SP changed every five to 10 years. In the 70's and early 80's major promotions were run successfully but had a very low visibility as they were mainly on pack. The only people who saw them had either considered buying the pack or actually bought the product. The link with direct marketing in the 80's was a turning point. DM was considered respectable and it gave Sales Promotion a new acceptability. It became much more mainstream and much less tacky. The next major change of view came about in the late 80's and early 90's when advertising became widely available and the power of direct marketing added a phone number, a website or e-mail address to every advertisement. Promotions became more visible and more successful but the depression that struck in the 90's with downsizing, reduced budgets, sky high interest rates and the rest gradually brought about the current situation about which I despair. I am a great believer in supply and demand and at the moment I consider that there is a lack of client demand for great Sales Promotion. No demand equals no supply!

TIM ARNOLD, SERIAL ENTREPRENEUR AND NOW A MARKETING DIRECTOR AND WRITER OF "THE MARKETING DIRECTORS HANDBOOK"
Where do I think Sales Promotion is going? Despite it being yesterday's name, I prefer to call it Marketing Communications although I have to admit that I had always thought of it as Promotional Marketing, the current favourite. Looking at advertising and Sales Promotion, the ying and yang of marketing, there are those who want to do things for immediate effect and those who look at things in a strategical sense. Sales Promotion could be thought of as tactical marketing.

I consider that the greatest changes in the last few years have been in the methods of communicating promotions, many of which are referred to as that other popular piece of jargon 'Media neutral'. I think that they are becoming "Media Dominant". Typical of this is the obsession with "Text to Win" which controls the creativity because the SMS texting cannot be anything but a string of words. Somehow they have to be linked to the brand image, not easy to do in the circumstances.

I have also come up with a new piece of jargon which I call 'Channel Discrete'. In other words it is first decided that there is to be an SMS promotion or an in store promotion rather than starting with a major overall theme. I feel that instead of deciding what the overall theme or message is in order to reach the objectives, the first thought is "Which channel should we choose and now let's decide what the message is going go to be". The more channels there are, the correct tactical approach becomes even more important, but within the framework of the brand environment.

I am critical of the Tesco Club Card. Having produced the electronic miracle which tells the retailer just about everything they need to know about their customers apart from their shoe size, what do they do with it? They use that good old blunt instrument, a manufacturer's coupon. I feel that this is part of the typical major retailer's view of marketing which could be summed up as 'This is what we want to do, who is going to pay for it, it won't be us!' I think that, compared to the time when the Sales Promotion industry started to grow into a real business, there is less entrepreneurial sprit around, apart possibly from the dot-com people in garages, and this is part of the whole risk averse sprit of the day.

Finance, or lack of it, has much to do with this. Banks are not keen on start up businesses. The previous generation knew that their properties were a fall back situation or could use them, and the steady growth in their value, to either fund the business or bale them out if it went wrong. Very few people in their twenties of even thirties have this comfort because very few of them can afford to buy a property, and if they do they have an enormous mortgage and very little equity in the building. Not to mention the student loan and various credit card debts.

NOW, A GROUP DISCUSSION

In 2008 we assembled a wide cross section of very experienced senior people in the industry around a dinner table and took them through a series of subjects – we think what they had to say is interesting even controversial, but you can read on and see for yourself, and also see how right they were a year or so later when the final chapters were added.

IN ADDITION TO THE TWO AUTHORS THE CONTRIBUTORS WERE:

Louise Wall

Previously MD of a number of major agencies, Clarke Hooper, Option One, Triangle and EHS, and now running her own training and recruitment company, the Off the Wall Consultancy One of the most successful ladies in the business.

Ed Downey

Came to UK from Ireland in mid 80's and worked at Marketing Solutions in it's heyday as a Managing Consultant, then joined Momentum (part of AMV Group). Became Vice Chairman and in 2000 broke away to start up Steam UK Ltd where he is MD and joint owner. A relatively young contributor to our group.

Graham Kemp

Chairman of RPM and former founder and Global CEO of The Marketing Store and past Chairman of the MCCA. He has worked at a top level in the USA so can bring international experience to the party.

Geoff Howe

Chairman of Geoff Howe Group. His name has been over the door of one of the longest lasting, stable and successful agencies.

Andrew Marsden

Formerly marketing director of Britvic, responsible for Tango and Pepsi for 10 years and past chairman of the Marketing Society. Andrew is a very experienced client.

DO WE MATTER?

The dinner guests could look back on some centuries of involvement in promotional marketing (added together of course, not individually!), so they were asked if promotional marketing would be as important in the next decade as it has been for the last 30 years or so.
 The general consensus of opinion was that it would continue to play a crucial part in the marketing mix. One reason for this is that the fragmentation of media away from the domination of television allows promoters to accurately target their audience and tailor make promotions that will specifically appeal to them.

As we shall see in a later paragraph, promotions can also be used to differentiate competing brands and speak to a consumer directly rather than through the retailer. The power of direct marketing is also closely linked to promotional marketing, as almost every direct mail piece and the majority of online websites have some kind of incentive attached to them. All variations on the various promotional techniques adapted to the form of communication.

Promotions can also offer a less expensive alternative to the ubiquitous BOGOF and enable manufacturers to shift their products at a price that offers them a decent margin rather than simply getting into a price war with all its serious and long-term drawbacks.

BUDGET? WHAT BUDGET

They were also asked whether expenditure would rise or fall in line with other marketing techniques. The opinion of the contributors is that it probably would, but that the way in which the money is spent has been changing, mainly because internet communication, growing daily, is relatively inexpensive compared to other media. This means that, for the same budget, the reward offered to the consumer can be a larger proportion of the budget so that consequently a lower budget may still be equally effective. Someone remarked that Sales Promotion agencies rarely got their hands on the media spend, so as far as they were concerned this could be an advantage. Unfortunately it was suggested that what usually happens is that the budget is reduced and the chunk that goes through the hands of the SP agency stays much the same. Added to this of course is the problem of the procurement people squeezing every last drop out of the available funds. More on this later.

COURAGEOUS? YOU MUST BE JOKING

We asked the group if brands will be as courageous testing new formats and ideas. For instance, will we see anything as groundbreaking as Shell 'Make Money' or the Heinz 'Car a Day' promotions? The immediate reaction was that it is quite unlikely, though each of the guests admitted that they occasionally saw a promotion and were impressed by the fact that the promoter had the balls to run it. The motto that seems to be hanging in neon letters over most brand managers desk is 'Don't Screw Up'.

However as the client representative at the table explained, in his first brand managership back in, would you believe,1978 he was given a job description. It said all the things he was responsible for which he thought were great, but the final line read "To have overall responsibility for the management of the brand". When he asked his boss exactly what that meant he was told that the brand had been there before he arrived and he had to make bloody sure the brand was still there when he left.

This was considered an excellent motto for all managers, particularly today when brands are so valuable, forming a very major part of the assets of a company although they are of course intangible.   Chairmen are terrified of being asked by some teenager scribbler why they were doing this or that to their brand that might damage it. This means that the pressure on brand managers to perform is immense which militates against them doing anything that could be considered in any way risky.

The only really dramatic action in recent times that the group could identify was the Carphone Warehouse Talk Talk's offer of a free laptop when you signed up for their broadband etc. This, it was agreed, showed that someone, somewhere in the industry said "Let's do something really different!" as opposed to "Let's do what we did last time but just give it a new twist" or even "Let's do what everyone else is doing but try and make it look different" which seems to apply to the vast majority of current promotional activity.

There were some brands of course where doing something outrageous was exactly what the brand was about, Tango being possibly the best-known example. Here, doing something boring and ordinary would be more damaging to the brand than doing something different and hopefully exciting. Occasionally agencies or brand managers might consider taking a risk because if it came off, they could very well move on to a bigger and better job. But these days the pressures within the companies are such that this is never really likely to happen. To summarise therefore, the idea that a brand manager can look at a proposal and say "Yes" is a fiction. Decisions of that sort are taken much higher up in the company by some extremely tough people and their view is that failure is not an option. Something that pretty well excludes risk taking of any kind.

THE "TESCO EFFECT"
Asked about the role of retailers, the group thought that the ability to talk directly to your customers by means of the various electronic communication systems, does mean that manufacturers can communicate over the heads of the retailers, but to go behind their backs would be an extremely dangerous thing to do. As an example, they suggested that for a wine importer to set up an online coupon deal exclusively with Threshers, although 25% of their business went through Tesco, would be close to commercial suicide even though it could be done easily, cheaply and effectively with an electronic coupon. That said however, this ability to deal directly with your customer does help to restore the balance between manufacturer and retailer.

The retail trade, and here we are talking about grocery retailers who are the most profitable in the world, are never going to give up their pricing policies but Sales Promotions transmitted directly to a brand's customers are a very valuable part of the marketing armoury and will continue to be so. The vexed question of the misredemption of coupons came up, with the general agreement that the retailers would do absolutely nothing about it unless it was either in their financial interest (unlikely) or they were forced to. The most likely - but not very likely - way for this to happen would be that somebody in Brussels decided it was 'A bad thing' and decided to make it illegal. No one was holding their breath.

WHERE, IF ANYWHERE, HAVE THE PERSONALITIES GONE?

The guests were asked to consider whether or not the business still has the sort of personalities that were prominent in the past. Arguably, some of them were sitting round the table although several of those present admitted that they were unlikely to get a job if they were being interviewed today. The general feeling was that promotional marketing is much more professional, controlled and organised. New businesses are harder to start and new business is harder to get because of the general aversion to risk. Brand managers are not keen on giving money to people they do not know and who have no track record.

However there are still some entrepreneurs out there, but they may be a new breed of creatives driving the business forward rather than the previous generation of founding fathers. Someone pointed out that very few companies these days have anyone's name over the door, unlike the high days of the 80's when all of the publicly quoted agencies were known by their founders names, albeit abbreviated to initials.

A way of comparing the situation in the industry now (almost at the end of the first decade of the 21st century) with the early 1970s when agencies were just beginning to make themselves felt, is to look at the number of people involved. The feeling in the group was that at that time there were probably as many people working full-time in the industry as there are now passing the ISP diploma each year - somewhere around 150. These days, with these sorts of numbers, it is much harder for an individual to be noticeable.

Another possible reason for the lack of high profile personalities is that the requirement these days is for everyone to be a specialist. You have the strategists on one side and the operators on the other. The most noticeable people in Sales Promotion and those who helped to build it so effectively were generalists who could and did turn their hand to practically anything. They had no qualifications because no qualifications existed; they just made it up as they went along. These days everyone has to be pigeonholed. Despite all this, it was agreed that there were personalities in the business who no doubt would be more visible as time goes on because, as one person said, every generation needs its superstars.

IS THE MOBILE THE MESSAGE?

The group then discussed the way that promotions are becoming integrated with the product and in particular mobile phones. There was a feeling that technology was advancing faster than the consumer could cope, leading to considerable confusion and making it difficult to compare competing products and suppliers. The general consensus here was that, as far as mobile phones were concerned, the vast majority of promotions related directly to the equipment and its use. It was all about the number of free texts, off peak calls etc. plus the powerful loyalty programme which provided replacement phones on a regular basis for anyone who had a contract.

Across the whole electronic communication arena it seemed that there was very little in the way of conventional promotional marketing, apart from the occasional dramatic effort such as giving free laptops - admittedly very basic ones - to people signing up for broadband supply. Generally it is all about prices, in particular stepping up the quality of the gear and offering more for the same price. There are a few examples of basic and well tried techniques such as cash backs

Another example is the competition between energy suppliers. Where again all the promotional activity appears to be linked to the cost to the consumer and the company's efforts concentrate on either persuading the consumer to save by paying by direct debit or buying both gas and electricity from the same supplierThe main promotional activity in this area appears to be featuring on the various comparison websites.

HOW GREEN IS OUR VALLEY?

Next, the subject of environmental concerns. "Is this just a passing fad?" was the question and the answer was a very definite NO! Governments on a worldwide basis are committed to trying to do something about climate change which meant that the tipping point had been reached and everyone would have to go with the flow. However, one guest put it "The business is littered with smartarsed, non-scientific, really bad claims used as marketing tools". There is going to be a major clampdown on this. Claims will have to be scientifically verified and relate to such things as the whole life cycle of the product.

How will promoters be able to take advantage of this whole environmental movement? It was generally agreed that at the moment there was immense confusion, particularly about the product life cycle. An example given was the current enthusiasm for so-called hybrid vehicles using a mixture of petrol and electric power. As a marketing tool, this so-called environmentally friendly vehicle appeared to offer numerous advantages to a purchase, not to mention the planet. However it was not only extremely inefficient on main roads or motorways, but at the end of its life will provide a serious problem because of the difficulty in disposing of the batteries.

It was agreed that this whole subject is so immensely complex and that no ordinary consumer can really grasp exactly what is involved. This allows an unscrupulous marketing man to take advantage of this confusion and sell a product that, on its face value, is environmentally friendly but once the whole construction and disposal of the product is taken into account, may well be anything but. A typical example was the energy saving light bulbs that everyone is going to have to use. These contain mercury, something extremely difficult to dispose of and highly toxic, far more dangerous in the long run than the existing bulbs which are being phased out. Worse still, many people find that the light they give is not that good.

In summary therefore, there is no doubt that environmental concerns will play a major part in promotional activity. Companies have to provide details of their 'environmental policy' as part of a presentation and the 'every little helps' in terms of 'doing your bit to save the planet' has really caught on. Commercially, it is not all always easy to see how such concerns can be used and it is noticeable that they are of particular interest to women and younger people, so if these are the target for brands, they should certainly look at the possibility of linking to environmental activities.

HELP! IT'S PROCUREMENT

They then moved on to the dreaded Procurement! The group discussed what effect the intervention of procurement departments have on the creativity of promotional marketing and in turn its effectiveness. The scenario put forward was a number of agencies pitching for the business and the decision has to be taken between the final two. At this point the procurement department becomes involved. Agency A has the more original and highly creative ideas but agency B put forward a programme that appears to be more 'efficient'. The inference of the procurement means that agency B gets the business.

It was agreed that this does happen but that if the marketing people are worth their salt they should not allow it to do so. It's often a question of a power struggle in the company. In the short term giving too much power to procurement can be dangerous as talented people will take their talents were they are rewarded. There are plenty of bright, intelligent hard-working people out there who can put together very effective promotions if they are allowed. In the long term it is hoped that procurement departments will become more professional but at the moment agencies are under extreme pressure.

There was some discussion over the question of integration, where a client chooses an agency that is part of a network such as the massive WPP. They can then be persuaded to use the various other companies in the network for PR, handling or whatever and they would get what amounts to a network discount. In other words they will pay a lower fee for the other activities than if they were buying this elsewhere. This has great appeal to procurement departments, perhaps not so much to the marketing people who might prefer to choose their own suppliers in the different areas. However with the number of amalgamations, takeovers etc. going on at the moment is likely to crop up more and more often in the future.

WOULD YOU DO IT AGAIN?

Finally we asked everyone around the table whether, given the choice, they would follow the same career in promotional marketing. The answer was a unanimous YES. They may well have done a few things differently but taken all-round, they feel that they are very fortunate to have been working in an industry at time when it was so dynamic. They also felt that they had been very fortunate in working with people who they variously described as bright, intelligent, opinionated, difficult, creative, stroppy and entertaining. No one had ever been bored although they had been wildly frustrated at times. Without exception they felt that they had been very privileged to work in the business when they did and they hope that the new people coming into it will stay with it and enjoy it as much as they themselves did. It helped of course that they had made a decent living for themselves and often for a few other people too!

LEARNING FROM THE TEACHER
Next we talked to the man who really has his finger on the pulse on the human aspect of the industry, the new recruits who will be taking it forward for the next 20 years or so. This is Chris Bestley, who has been the Director of Education for the Institute of Sales Promotion since 2000. He is well qualified for this job having spent over 30 years working in promotional marketing, making good use of his zoology degree which helped him to deal with some of the animals he met. He worked for some of the biggest names in the industry as it grew in the 70's and 80's, who have cropped up frequently in previous chapters. These were Promotional Campaigns, IMP and for 13 years at Tim Arnold and Associates, seven of which saw him as MD. Having got tired of working for other people, he has been running his own consultancy for the last 15 years and still does so alongside his work at the ISP.

As we mentioned, back in the Chapter about the revival of the business after the 2nd Word War, Education has been something of a growth industry in the business over the last few years and Chris has been an important part of this. In the last 10 to 15 years, promotional marketing has become more and more professional, and more and more professional qualifications are required. This was also driven by the rapid development in channels of communication and the exploding digital age.

As our previous interviewees commented, there are not really any pure Sales Promotion agencies these days. If you're working in an agency you need to know a bit about direct marketing, in fact possibly a lot about direct marketing. In addition, you have to be quite good at motivation, quite good at in-store marketing, quite good experiential, you have to know a fair bit about the various digital channels, building websites etc., a bit about advertising and a working knowledge of marketing generally. Oh, and you also may have to do some actual Sales Promotion but you will not be doing it on a day in day out basis. The staff in an agency has to spread itself quite thinly across a whole range of disciplines and they are becoming generalists rather than specialists.

As we have heard, the excitement today seems to relate more to the channel of communication, finding new ways of reaching customers and also new ways of communicating with the company. The actual promotion is almost a bolt on goodie to the actual promotional offer. This means that there seems to be more emphasis on the various other aspects of promotional marketing and less on the content, and Chris agreed that, as far as the consumer is concerned, it is the content that interests them, not to the means of communication. The courses therefore are designed to teach a wide range of skills as well as a solid basis in planning,,running and evaluating the actual promotions. In the past this was the whole of the Diploma and Certificate courses but these have been expanded and new programmes added.

The basic Diploma was created by Alan Toop and Christian Petersen and launched in the early Eighties. As mentioned in an earlier chapter, there were now two Diplomas, one in Promotional & Interactive Marketing (the original Diploma) and another in Motivation (started in 2005) together with Certificates in three areas - Promotional & Interactive Marketing (set up in 2001) together with the recently discovered joys of Experiential Marketing and the even cooler Digital Promotions. (Both these latter launched in 2009). There are also intensive one day courses covering Measuring Promotional Effectiveness, Strategic Thinking, Promotional Marketing for Brand Managers and Creativity That Sells. Anyone interested can find dates and details of all these courses on the ISP website www.isp.org.uk.

FIXED FEES
Chris also commented on the growth of 'fixed fee' promotions which are those where the agency comes up with the creative idea then hands over the whole operational aspect of it to a fixed fee company who quote a price that is just that, a fixed fee covering all the costs and eliminating any risk of the client going over budget. The agency simply handed over the whole promotional budget, apart from any creative fee, to the fixed fee company. In other words there is absolutely no risk to the client that the promotion will go over budget whether it is the supply of merchandise or the redemption of 50p coupons. The fixed fee company takes the risk that the cost will be lower than the fee charged as so provide them with a profit.

Of course, if it comes in well below budget the fixed fee company still get paid the full amount. If this is the case, the client will have paid over the odds for the programme, but in today's risk averse climate this has a serious appeal.

He said that for anyone who has spent their career in the business, this takes a little getting used to as in effect the fixed fee company is doing what the agency used to do with specialist buyers and other expertise. They not only dreamed up the promotional idea but also put together the whole scheme and operated it. Originally the fixed fee started out as an insurance policy that simply covered the redemption or other costs that could not be controlled, and the company providing insurance did just that.

Typically, the most popular promotions to insure were large-scale coupon drops where over redemption could amount to quite large sums of money. The usual system was for the insurance company to look at their previous experience of this type of offer and decide on the likely redemption level, which they would propose to the client. Based on that figure, they would then agree to two break points. The client would be responsible for all redemptions up to the first break point that was usually around the maximum the client expected to get and was happy to pay for. The insurance company would pay out for any above that figure, up to a second break point that was generally the highest redemption that insurers thought possible. If the redemptions went above that figure, the cost was back with the client.

CHANGES
We asked Chris how the educational aspect of the ISP was doing these days (late 2009). He said that it has been affected to some extent by the current financial downturn as companies are thinking twice about paying for education, but in fact the number of people taking the diploma, the backbone of the programme, has stayed very steady for the past seven years. He believes these courses are direct barometers of the industry's level of recruitment of new graduates.

The weekend residential courses for beginners, previously called Brighouse after the original location (but later moved to the southeast) have now finished owing to a major drop in demand. The agencies said that they work their people so hard these days that they cannot expect them to work at a weekend. It would appear that some people are taking the fashionable work/life balance debate seriously and of course save themselves money. However with a whole stream of new courses now operating, there are many more opportunities and hopefully these will gradually build as they become part of the mainstream education for people in the industry. Although the government seemed very keen on training it has proved impossible to obtain any government grants for the Institute's activities.

However with many decades of history it is pretty sure that education will continue to play a major part in the Sales Promotion industry, providing better and better training and therefore better and better operatives to fit a highly professional business which requires a great deal of expertise in a very large number of areas. Across the board, promotional marketing is involved in just about every method of communication and every type of sales activity and will almost certainly continue to be so into the foreseeable future.

FINALLY, THE CHAIRMAN AND THE CEO
About a year after this dinner, we were able to interview two other prominent people in the world of Sales Promotion, or promotional marketing, whichever you prefer. These were Clive Mishon the present Chairman of the Institute of Sales Promotion and Annie Swift, the first

ever CEO of the ISP. Her key role is to ensure that the ISP accurately reflects the needs of its members and of the industry at large. She is also responsible for launching new initiatives, and in May 2009 introduced the ISP Seal, a consumer-facing accreditation scheme designed to promote responsible marketing among brand owners and to provide reassurance to consumers. Her view is particularly interesting because she has no pre-conceived ideas about the ISP and the industry as a whole.

Prior to joining the ISP, Annie spent 25 years working in the media across a range of marketing-related publications and websites. After six years at Haymarket Publishing Annie joined Centaur Media plc in 1988. Five years later she became a board director and took over as Publisher of Marketing Week. Her next move was as Publishing Director of Centaur's Marketing and New Media division and then to her present job.

Clive has been Chairman of the ISP since 2007 and spent 25 years in the marketing service sector, having acquired Marketing Drive from DMB&B in 1987. In 1998 they were acquired by True North Communications where Marketing Drive Worldwide became the global brand for what is referred to as non-traditional advertising services within the group.

From 1998 to 2000 he was chairman of the Sales Promotion Consultants Association which turned itself into the Marketing Communications Consultants Association and Clive became the first Lifetime Vice President of the MCCA in 2001. He has also been involved with the Code of Advertising Practice and became a fellow of the ISP in 2002.

In order to see how their views either agreed or disagreed with those expressed a year earlier, which was before the credit crunch crunched, we used some of the same questions and discussed the same points with our two interviewees.

DO WE MATTER?

Clive was certain that promotional marketing matters more than ever because of the need to achieve one-to-one communication. It is not in his view a discipline; it is a matter of content. It is not a media channel, and in what is now a narrowcast world, not a broadcast world, the chances are that with more direct media, it is very likely that the content will be promotional marketing. In these situations the content is likely to be the most effective method of persuading consumers to change their behaviour by giving them a tangible or even intangible reward. He felt that now the problem was what to call ourselves.

Both he and Annie agreed that what the industry does is promote sales and that is still the most accurate description, but unfortunately it seems to have acquired a hangover from the early days of plastic daffodils and the like which is why promotional marketing has become popular as a title for below the line activity. Having quite recently become involved in the industry, Annie had found to her surprise that some people actually seemed tired of the title and wanted to call it anything but Sales Promotion. However, the Institute has stuck with it, despite numerous discussions, and even added the tagline 'when promoting sales is your business' to the new logo which appeared a relatively short time ago.

The way in which the SPCA changed Sales Promotion for marketing communications is a good example of this attitude. Clive took over the chair in the middle of a debate about the name. The first thing he did was to concentrate on more important matters such as getting the content and perception of the organisation right so that a possible move away from Sales Promotion would be credible. As soon as he finished his two year stint his successor promptly changed the name. However, nowadays most of the agencies are not just Sales Promotion agencies as they are not dedicated to just that aspect of the business. They are more likely to identify themselves by their channel of communication. The problem is to educate companies to the fact that they are actually doing Sales Promotion and so embrace the codes that apply.

Although on the surface there seems to be more excitement about the method of communication in the digital age, both Annie and Clive felt that the many new channels of communication simply opened up more opportunities for promotional activity as the important thing to the consumer was the content, not the method of delivering the message. They felt that mobiles in particular are offering numerous new and exciting opportunities and would carry a large slice of the promotional marketing spend in the next few years, but there was still a great need for creativity in terms of the offer with so many channels competing for the consumer's attention. The need for one-to-one contact has driven the growth in experiential marketing which allows face-to-face, rather than digital communication, and which featured heavily in the 2008 ISP award entries.

This raised the age-old topic of defining what is Sales Promotion. In the past a number of ISP award entries have been disqualified because it was considered that they did not actually include a promotion or a 'demonstrable benefit' and this had often applied to experiential activity. However, this year the rule that an entry had to include a demonstrable benefit was modified by the words 'need not be tangible'. An example of this, which also applied to a number of charity promotions in the past, was the successful prostate cancer promotion where the reward to the consumer was the fact that they had given money to the charity. They enjoyed a feelgood factor having done so but this was difficult to define as tangible, but the extended definition made it an acceptable entry.

BUDGET? WHAT BUDGET?

This discussion took place in the depths of the dreaded credit crunch but the annual Bellwether Report, which looked at the movements of spend across the marketing spectrum, suggested that Sales Promotion was doing rather better than the other areas, or possibly that it was not doing as badly. Clive had a problem with the Bellwether definition of Sales Promotion. It covered all the more obvious activity such as competitions, special offers etc., but completely ignored the enormous amount of direct marketing which almost always included a promotional offer of some kind.

Annie and Clive would very much like to know the value of the Sales Promotion but the problem, which has cropped up many times over the last 40 or so years, is that no one can agree as to what should and should not be included under the heading of Sales Promotion. Because of this the Bellwether Report was rather misleading but Annie, who had been speaking to a wide range of people in the industry, felt that there was a general air of optimism which hardly applied to the majority of businesses at that time. If history is to repeat itself, and it appeared to be doing so, Sales Promotion, along with direct marketing, would ride out the recession rather better than other areas.

At times like this it was easier to find money for activities with measurable results and clients were desperately trying to get 'more bangs for their bucks'. In the various downturns, going back to the three-day week in the 70's, Sales Promotion practitioners have generally emerged in a pretty good state of health and the clients have learned to appreciate that promotions can be effective, particularly cost-effective.

COURAGEOUS? YOU MUST BE JOKING

The question was, will brands be as courageous in testing new formats and ideas? Will there be groundbreaking promotions such as Shell's 'Make Money' and Heinz 'Car a Day', both of which were the forerunners of a myriad of similar offers over the years? Based on his own experience and in particular the entries for the 2008 Awards, Clive felt that this was unlikely. The client's drive for risk avoidance has led to a box ticking mentality which never quite gets to the box marked creativity. This was not to say that promotions were not effective, but he did not see anything that would make the pulse race. Effectively the motto was 'safety first'. Neither of our interviewees could name a current promotion that they thought would spawn a number of new and different programmes in the coming years.

THE "TESCO EFFECT"

What, we asked, is the role of retailers in the present climate? Answer – the same as it has been for years. They have massive power over their suppliers as each of them buys a very large proportion of a manufacturer's output. Cross them and you hear the dreaded word "delisting". In almost every way they call the tune.

WHERE, IF ANYWHERE, HAVE ALL THE PERSONALITIES GONE?

Annie felt that across the whole area of marketing, including advertising, there was a dearth of personalities, compared to the names over the doors in the past. Advertising agencies these days seem to be run by accountants. This does not apply to the same extent in Sales Promotion where companies are smaller and run by people who know what they are doing.

She did agree that there no longer seemed to be any high profile people with their names over the door or if not called something like Clarke Hooper, Holmes and Marchent, FKB or a KLP, were at least run by people whose names were known and recognisable throughout the industry, Triangle's Kevin Twittey for instance. They were entrepreneurs and there are still entrepreneurs around but nowadays they are unable to develop the high profile that was possible in the past. They are just not allowed to, as the company or the brand, not the individual, is the thing that matters.

Figures have been published showing that there are around 14,000 marketing services companies but less than 5 per cent employ 15 or more people, so there are a vast number of 1 to 3 man (and of course woman) businesses, none of whom are likely to produce a high profile personality at this stage. In the present climate Clive felt that the squeeze on margins would mean that a large numbers of smaller companies would simply disappear and of course many of the other companies were actually part of a larger group although they appeared to be operating independently. He did not see a great deal of consolidation in the future and thought that the idea that big is beautiful is less popular. The idea that you could start a business, build it up and sell it in a few years time for life changing money is pretty much a non-starter these days and Clive thought that there were no more than 20 out of the 14,000 businesses that could sell for serious money.

Clive's comment was that companies had become much more corporate and were a corporate brand rather than a personal brand. With the various mergers, name changes and general reshuffling, the individuals no longer had the same high profile and could move on without any apparent change in the company as far as the outside world was concerned. The people at the top were now mainly administrators whereas in the previous generation the people at the top were practitioners who not only knew what they were doing but were doing it on a day-to-day basis. He felt that having successful people he could look up to as role models was a great help. The day he did not want to sit in his boss's chair was the day that he would have been in the wrong business.

HOW GREEN IS OUR VALLEY?

Like our previous group, our two interviewees were firmly of the opinion that green credentials were an important part of any company's profile. Many of the Institute's members were making some play of this though they may not be, in Annie's phrase, "marketing the hell out of it". Brand owners expected it and it was necessary to be seen to be green whether or not you actually believed in it. It really was just another part of a company's credentials. It might not be quite as high profile as it had been during the current recession as saving the company in the short term was more important than saving the planet in the long term. But, it is not going away.

HELP! IT'S PROCUREMENT!

Procurement departments have been referred to by our previous panel as the 'dreaded procurement' but these interviewees did not necessarily agree that they were altogether a bad thing, although there are some who were not very good at what they did. Clive said that in his opinion procurement were there for the right reason. Looking at what might be considered sensible margins, he thought that 10 years ago agencies were making unreasonable margins but that a good procurement department would not only try to avoid the supplier making too much money but they were also anxious to make sure they did not make a loss. They were not in the business of putting good suppliers out of business.

Departments that might be referred to as 'dreaded' would simply say that they did not care what it was, it just had to be 35 per cent cheaper than it was last time, regardless of the cost structure. The good departments viewed business as a partnership and expected agencies to organise their companies in an effective and efficient manner in order to provide the service the client required at a price that suited both sides, rather than rub along in an inefficient way being kept afloat by inflated margins. They were not necessarily the people squeezing creativity out of promotional activity but working with the marketing people to produce good promotions at an economic price.

WOULD YOU DO IT AGAIN?

Clive: "Knowing I don't have to, yes I would". However, he would not necessarily encourage other people to do it at this time. He thought he had been fortunate to be there at the right time, and timing was everything. He recently met an old workmate who said that they had been there in a 'champagne' time. They drove nice cars, took clients to nice restaurants for nice lunches which usually included wine, worked hard and long but played hard and long. Nowadays, however, he felt that the clients had more of a champagne lifestyle. As a personal example, 25 years ago, in 1984 he was an account manager in an agency earning around £25,000 a year. At the end of that year he received a bonus of £4,000 which he put down as a deposit on a £42,000 mansion flat in the Fulham Road. Today someone doing the same job would be earning around £35,000 a year. Today that flat would cost somewhere in the region of £250-£300,000. This is why, if he were starting again today, he would probably look elsewhere. Finally we asked Annie "Are you glad you joined?" Her one word answer was "Yes".

THE ISP IN THE FUTURE

The Chief Executive and the Chairman were asked how they saw the ISP developing in the next few years. They thought that by far the most important development was the introduction of the Seal of Approval accreditation scheme because this moves them into a much larger area, working with both the brands and the public. Annie said that it is the biggest thing the Institute has done in the last 12 months but expects there to be bigger things in the next 12, which she was not prepared to name at this point.

They hope to move the Institute towards the American model where the client takes more responsibility for their promotions and their aim is to stay one step ahead of their agency. They think it is important to keep up with the law but they expect their agency to provide the creative input. The various services provided by the ISP, such as legal and education, would play a part in this. At the moment they think the Institute has too high a proportion of agency members and this initiative is intended to reach out to the brand owners, in a way that has not been possible to date, and increase the number of promoters on board. By April 2009 two major promoters, Kellogg and Coca-Cola, had joined and since then a number of others have followed suit.

The feeling was that the increased use of the Seal would be for online promotions which had had the highest rate of complaints in the past year, up 750 per cent on the previous year. To a great extent this was because of the anarchic nature of the internet, where companies either did not know there were any rules, did not think the rules applied to them, or worse, still did not care about any rules. It was not until they got into trouble that they realised they had made a mistake. Annie mentioned visiting a so-called digital agency who, when asked about the CAP (Code of Advertising Practice), just thought it was something you wore.

Though the Seal would appear on packs, point of sale and in direct marketing, they did not expect it to have massive visual prominence in these areas but that it would be publicised in a number of ways by various third parties with whom the ISP is currently working. It was in everyone's interest to push the Seal and to draw the attention of the consumer to it, wherever it appeared.

In total therefore, they thought that the industry was in pretty good shape, was moving forward and had a bigger and bigger role to play for both its members and the consumer. The summer of 2009 saw the first use of the new accreditation on a crisps promotion for Tyrrells with the rather off beat headline 'Win a Tractor'. Just in case your garden was a little too small for a Massey–Ferguson 5455 to cut your lawn and plough the flower beds, the winner could pick up £25,000 in cash. Runners-up prizes were also in a rural theme with 1,000 pairs of Aigle wellies of unspecified colour to be won.

CHAPTER 21

In conclusion – the authors view

Since the sixties we two authors have had an insider's view of how a powerful but uncoordinated marketing tool coalesced into a very big, professional business. Although most of the basic building blocks have been around for centuries, only since the 1960s have the agencies grown into the force they are today, controlling, on the behalf of clients, sums of money that rival those spent on advertising, although in a more fragmented way. At the end of 2009 a research project found that in the 2007/8 financial year, branded goods manufacturers spent £26.5bilion compared to the £18.6bilion spent above the line, a figure supplied by the Advertising Association.

In the time we have worked in Sales Promotion we have seen this activity in all its forms pervade the marketing process, influencing brand propositions and touching almost every citizen in the UK dozens of times a year. Brands have been invigorated and often re-invigorated. Helped by the growing skills of the various agencies, the nation's retailers have become masters in the use of Sales Promotion techniques to build traffic and their share of the consumer's purse. Sales forces and employees have been motivated to perform at ever higher levels and the public have taken to the offers being made to them in their billions of opportunities.

It is held that 95 per cent of direct marketing activity carries a promotional message and that will not change in the future. The DM sector will, at long last, realise that there is more to Sales Promotion than a prize draw.

There will be no let up whilst the regulations for SP remain as they are. There would be a public outcry if 'offers' were stopped by the bureaucrats. People of all social backgrounds and ages like offers and promotions. Research time and time again supports this. Maybe it is part of the British spirit of WIFM when we part with our hard earned money?

Sales Promotion will, in the future, adapt to social changes as it has always done, and use all available media channels and technology to put the right offer to the right consumer at the right time in their chosen channel of communication, with the consumer as gatekeeper for the channel.

WE KNOW WHERE YOU LIVE - AND A LOT MORE
The major retailers will use more and more sophisticated targeting techniques and technology

channels to influence shoppers. The power that Tesco has achieved with its Club Card is a unique blend of information gathering, targeting and Sales Promotion. Some 30 years since Green Shield Stamps dominated the market, now electronically based loyalty schemes have an equally firm grip. Unlike the little sticky stamps, these programmes (and remember these include frequent flyer programmes, one of the biggest, if not the biggest promotion of this type in the world) know all about you.

The companies supplying their customers with their brand of card know who are you, where you shop or travel, what you buy and when you buy it. Off the back of this data, companies will make offers to their customers that will not only be more relevant and precisely targeted, but will also help the design of new products and services, as NPD become less risky. The brands that feed off this data will create new responses and efficiencies as never before. Shopper marketing, although difficult to define, will become the new paradigm for what before was a mixture of trade and consumer marketing.

The financial services sector will be back with a vengeance when they have finished licking their recent wounds. Twenty five years ago promotions were an anathema to this sector; now they are fundamental. No mobile phone company would survive without a plethora of sometimes very confusing propositions to consumers.

The very survival of our National Newspapers has been all too dependent on promotions in their papers and the use of freebies such as CD's in their millions. It will be interesting to see if paid for content on line will take off. Perhaps Sales Promotion can help it. We predict that Sales Promotion in all its facets will play a bigger part in sector after sector, particularly in the economic climate that we face for the next few years.

THE MEDIUM AND THE MESSAGE
Technology will come into its own. Penetration of social networks will grow and grow. The viral effect of offers that are cool going global is something that we have yet to experience and this will challenge the world's marketing laws. How do the codes and laws apply in an instant global promotion environment? Next generation of super fast broadband will be ubiquitous and will open up creativity in a blend of commercial television and Sales Promotion. Perhaps the creatives in SP will finally hold a Golden Palm in Cannes.

The iPhone has shown the way with mobiles and a staggering 2 billion apps have been downloaded already. Walkers Crisps achieved 1 million text messages with their Do us a Flavour promotion. The promotional use of SMS is still in its infancy, which is strange in that it is the most universal of all technologies and is not restricted by formats. The killer app is still yet to be found but it will be. Bar code coupon technology looks as though it has finally been cracked which will open up endless opportunities.

Proximity marketing will grow and annoy in equal measure. Blue Zones at Victoria Station in London offering clips from Lost and retailers' coupons flashed to your mobile as you pass give an insight into what might be ahead.

In a recent speech the CEO of Skype predicted that in five years 50 per cent of traffic through Skype would be video in its many forms. The cost, efficiency and creativity stretch that this open up is phenomenal.

There is no doubt that the bounds of creativity we once knew will be relegated to the history in this book. However, as the various experts we have interviewed have pointed out, as Sales Promotion embraces its future it has to ensure that the medium does not become the message. At the end of the day a clear proposition, augmenting its carrier brand, delivered in a creative, trusted and value-enhancing way to sell something is what it has always been and always will be - the way to make a sale and build a brand.

END PIECE

In writing this book we, the authors, have enjoyed a fascinating journey, finding out many things we did not know about the industry that employed us for many years. Although more money is spent in this area than in conventional advertising it has a low profile with the consumer. We hope that this book will have lifted the lid on the business.

It is also poignant that as this book goes to press the Institute of Sales Promotion has changed its name to the Institute of Promotional Marketing as the industry enters the second decade of this century. With the changes that lie ahead perhaps this name change will mark a new era for what is undoubtedly one of the most important forces in marketing.

Sales Promotion was first recorded in the bible and over millennia developed into one of the most powerful tools available to the world's companies. It can make the marketing difference between success and failure. It can build or damage massive brands. It can reward, motive, amuse and create panic attacks. Careers and money can be made and lost and reputations enhanced or destroyed. Of its many redeeming features, the overriding one has been the exhilaration of creative entrepreneurialism. For the authors, who have been around for a little too long, if we started again we would do pretty much what we did before and would not have missed it for the world.

WE HAVE THE TECHNOLOGY...

...and we would like to hear from you. We realise that, like the authors, a printed book is rather so 20th Century and we also realise that the modern world is becoming increasingly electronic and digital. To demonstrate that we are trying to keep up with the Facebook, Twitter and Blogging generation we have opened a website www.beyondredemption.biz .

This will give you a chance to say what you think about this book, what you think about the sales promotion (aka promotional marketing) industry and anything else that you think might be of interest to the sort of people who read this sort of book.

Tell us what went well, or even what did not go well, for both the education and amusement of other readers. Strangely enough we have found it easier to persuade people to tell us about disasters than about triumphs and these have proved very popular with our readers, so please keep the stories coming. We will understand if you wish to remain anonymous and we will probably resist the temptation to blackmail you, although if we don't sell enough books......!

We hope that with your help our website will become a forum for intelligent discussion of what is happening, what might happen and what you would like to happen in this fascinating and rapidly changing business. It might even be entertaining. So bookmark us now!

www.beyondredemption.biz

INDEX